Advances in African Economic, Social and Political Development

Series Editors

Diery Seck, CREPOL—Center for Research on Political Economy, Dakar, Senegal
Juliet U. Elu, Morehouse College, Atlanta, GA, USA
Yaw Nyarko, New York University, New York, NY, USA

Africa is emerging as a rapidly growing region, still facing major challenges, but with a potential for significant progress—a transformation that necessitates vigorous efforts in research and policy thinking. This book series focuses on three intricately related key aspects of modern-day Africa: economic, social and political development. Making use of recent theoretical and empirical advances, the series aims to provide fresh answers to Africa's development challenges. All the socio-political dimensions of today's Africa are incorporated as they unfold and new policy options are presented. The series aims to provide a broad and interactive forum of science at work for policymaking and to bring together African and international researchers and experts. The series welcomes monographs and contributed volumes for an academic and professional audience, as well as tightly edited conference proceedings. Relevant topics include, but are not limited to, economic policy and trade, regional integration, labor market policies, demographic development, social issues, political economy and political systems, and environmental and energy issues.

More information about this series at http://www.springer.com/series/11885

Everisto Benyera
Editor

Reimagining Justice, Human Rights and Leadership in Africa

Challenging Discourse and Searching for Alternative Paths

Editor
Everisto Benyera
Department of Political Sciences
University of South Africa
Pretoria, Gauteng, South Africa

ISSN 2198-7262   ISSN 2198-7270   (electronic)
Advances in African Economic, Social and Political Development
ISBN 978-3-030-25142-0   ISBN 978-3-030-25143-7   (eBook)
https://doi.org/10.1007/978-3-030-25143-7

© Springer Nature Switzerland AG 2020
This work is subject to copyright. All rights are reserved by the Publisher, whether the whole or part of the material is concerned, specifically the rights of translation, reprinting, reuse of illustrations, recitation, broadcasting, reproduction on microfilms or in any other physical way, and transmission or information storage and retrieval, electronic adaptation, computer software, or by similar or dissimilar methodology now known or hereafter developed.
The use of general descriptive names, registered names, trademarks, service marks, etc. in this publication does not imply, even in the absence of a specific statement, that such names are exempt from the relevant protective laws and regulations and therefore free for general use.
The publisher, the authors and the editors are safe to assume that the advice and information in this book are believed to be true and accurate at the date of publication. Neither the publisher nor the authors or the editors give a warranty, expressed or implied, with respect to the material contained herein or for any errors or omissions that may have been made. The publisher remains neutral with regard to jurisdictional claims in published maps and institutional affiliations.

This Springer imprint is published by the registered company Springer Nature Switzerland AG
The registered company address is: Gewerbestrasse 11, 6330 Cham, Switzerland

To the Daughters and Sons of the great continent of Africa and its ecologies that had to endure the odious struggles against poor leadership, injustices and various abuses of state power. It is dedicated to those that continue to search and fight for an Africa rooted in endogenous forms of understanding justice, political leadership as well as development. It seeks to bring close focus into the state project in Africa for purposes of breaking with Eurocentric notions of state power in order to bring in the marginalized indigenous understandings of power, human rights and justice. This work urges Africans to imagine a decolonized human-centric African where Africa's development takes on new Afrocentric discourses that are anchored in Africa's people and liberatory paradigms. This book is for those who strive for African's self-determination, autonomous development and equality, just and noble governance, leadership and fairness in seeking and applying human rights.

This book also goes out to our families. They supported us in this ongoing decolonial journey of discovery, fraught with lugubrious contradictions and inconsistencies, and help us navigate our way through this treacherous terrain of life. Without you, the journey will be all the more difficult, perhaps impossible. Thank You!

Everisto Benyera
Romain Francis
Ahmed Haroon Jazbhay

Pretoria, South Africa
June 2019

Contents

Part I Conceptualizing Justice, Human Rights and Leadership in Africa

1 Challenging Discourse and Searching for Alternative Paths: Justice, Human Rights and Leadership in Africa 3
Everisto Benyera, Romain Francis and Ahmed Haroon Jazbhay

2 The Colonial State is the Problem in Africa 21
Everisto Benyera

Part II Justice

3 The Tyranny of the Coloniality of Nature and the Elusive Question of Justice 39
Romain Francis

4 Don't Develop Us Without Us! Inclusion of Indigenous Ethnic Minorities in Sustainable Development Goals in Africa 59
Paul Mulindwa

Part III Human Rights

5 Theorising the Direct Effect Doctrine of International Law in Human Rights Enforcement 77
Torque Mude

6 Getting Beyond the Somalia Syndrome? Revisiting the United States' Intervention in Liberia 15 Years Later 103
Raymond Kwun Sun Lau

7 NATO's 2011 Invasion of Libya: Colonialism Repackaged? 123
Chidochashe Nyere

Part IV Leadership

8 **When Mandela Meets Rousseau: An Exploration of South Africa's Civil Religion** 159
   Ahmed Haroon Jazbhay

9 **Pharaoh Let My Children Go: Meditations on Blackness Under Democratized Whiteness** 179
   Hlulani Mdingi

Editor and Contributors

About the Editor

Everisto Benyera is Associate Professor of African Politics in the Department of Political Sciences at the University of South Africa, Pretoria, South Africa. He is a decolonial reader and holds an M.Sc. in International Relations from the University of Zimbabwe and a Ph.D. in African Politics from the same university. He researches on transitology and transitional justice focusing on indigenous, traditional and non-state reconciliation, peacebuilding and healing mechanisms. He is the editor of the journal *Politeia, Journal of Political Sciences and Public Administration and Management*, and his publications are accessible via: https://orcid.org/0000-0002-2706-9097 and https://independent.academia.edu/EveristoBenyera

Contributors

Everisto Benyera Department of Political Sciences, University of South Africa, Pretoria, South Africa

Romain Francis Department of Political Sciences, University of South Africa, Pretoria, South Africa

Ahmed Haroon Jazbhay Department of Political Sciences, University of South Africa, Pretoria, South Africa

Raymond Kwun Sun Lau Department of History, Hong Kong Baptist University, Kowloon Tong, Kowloon, Hong Kong

Hlulani Mdingi Department of Philosophy Practical and Systematic Theology, University of South Africa, Pretoria, South Africa

Torque Mude Department of Politics and Public Management, Midlands State University, Zvishavane, Zimbabwe

Paul Mulindwa Department of Politics and International Relations, SARChI: African Diplomacy and Foreign Policy, University of Johannesburg, Johannesburg, South Africa

Chidochashe Nyere Department of Political Science, Faculty of Humanities, University of Pretoria, Pretoria, South Africa

Part I
Conceptualizing Justice, Human Rights and Leadership in Africa

Chapter 1
Challenging Discourse and Searching for Alternative Paths: Justice, Human Rights and Leadership in Africa

Everisto Benyera, Romain Francis and Ahmed Haroon Jazbhay

Abstract This is the introductory chapter of the book: *Justice, Human Rights and Civil Religion in Africa: Challenging Discourse and Searching for Alternative Paths.* The chapter is divided into three sections on justice, leadership and human rights. It locates the various failed attempts in Africa to develop, democratise and instil virtues of a just state and society, promote benevolent leadership and advance political and economic rights and freedoms in the resilience of the colonial state. The resilience of the colonial state requires a 'new' imagination from Africa itself as opposed to Africa relying on external 'help'. The central argument of the chapter is that the colonial state continues to operate in Africa under various guises such as international law, humanitarian interventions, multilateralism, aid and the threat or actual use of force, economic or military. The chapter distinguishes good from just leadership. Good leadership points outs malpractices while just leadership points out and acts against identified malpractices. The alternative path for Africa out of the colonial state is to demand its right to rights as a *sine qua non* for a just society.

Keywords Leadership · Africa · Just leadership · Decoloniality · Epistemic break · Justice

Introduction

This book is a response to the fundamental question: how do you achieve transformation in Africa developmentally, socially and politically in a way which subscribes to a set of certain normative values. Our argument is that material transformation is unachievable at any level, whether institutional, economical or sociological if you do not have a local value base. Africa is the theatre for the world's most heinous atrocities such as the genocides in Rwanda and Zimbabwe, the persistent massacres in Somalia, the countless deaths in the failed state of Libya and the Democratic

E. Benyera (✉) · R. Francis · A. H. Jazbhay
Department of Political Sciences, University of South Africa, Office 24, 7th Floor
Theo van Wijk Building, UNISA Main Campus, Pretoria 0003, South Africa
e-mail: benyee1@unisa.ac.za

© Springer Nature Switzerland AG 2020
E. Benyera (ed.), *Reimagining Justice, Human Rights and Leadership in Africa*,
Advances in African Economic, Social and Political Development,
https://doi.org/10.1007/978-3-030-25143-7_1

Republic of the Congo's stagnated transition. African leaders are also the International Criminal Court's main customers (Benyera 2018). Issues of human rights are still unresolved despite the end of official colonialism and apartheid. Contestations over the rights to land, economic freedom and epistemic justice are ongoing with no end in sight. African leaders generally suffer from the third-term incumbency with Paul Kagame of Rwanda, Pierre Nkurunziza of Burundi, Paul Biya of Cameroon and until recently Robert Mugabe of Zimbabwe and Jose Eduardo dos Santos of Angola overstaying in power. In (post) colonial Africa, injustice, bad leadership and human rights abuses have become the norm with communities developing various coping mechanisms, while stakeholders offer explanations for the persistence of this nightmare. The recent outflux of Africans into Europe as refugees as a result of the combination of war, human rights abuses, economic hardships, famine and war is evidence that Africans are still some of the world's unfree people.

Existing justice, human rights and political leadership models in Africa, viewed as unitising or galvanising forces for the formulation of an African value base are predominantly perceived and conceptualised from a Euro-North American-centric perspective. In essence, African needs and how these needs must be organised, be they leadership needs, justice needs or human rights needs must not only be conceptualised from an African perspective but also by Africans themselves.

Discourses in human rights, leadership and transitional justice have more often being appropriated and instead of working in favour of Africans, have produced the opposite effect. This is why in our view, human rights and leadership issues remain problematic in Africa and why transitional justice has not worked for victims. Hence the movement from transitional to transformative justice.

We allege that these three discourses (leadership, justice and human rights) among others have been misappropriated and misrepresented to serve specific agendas that are not necessarily African agendas. These agendas undermine issues of human rights, justice and leadership under the guise of taking those issues forward.

In order for justice to function effectively in Africa, and around the world, there is a need for a localised understanding of rights, which encompass an authentic human dimension. A unitary intervention is therefore necessary for any attempt to understand and a true conception of what constitutes right. This intervention must occur through the role of ideology. This is where the chapter on civil religion in South Africa is an important intervention. This chapter helps us with a conception of political leadership which is situated in the local and informed by local principles. The chapter argues for a conception of leadership which is endemic to Africa. As such, Africa needs to build a consensus around justice, human rights and leadership actualised through good people-centred leadership and again the conception of good leadership must be localised. Given this, it will find easy application as local resonance will be almost guaranteed.

Normative change lies at the heart of every transformation. The challenges facing Africa is that the normative base which underlines and informs societal transformation has been hijacked, misrepresented and misappropriated by the specific interests that are non-African and imperial in nature. A good example of the notion which has been the misrepresented and misappropriated is that of transitional justice. Transitional justice has predominantly been conceptualised and funded from the

North but implemented predominantly in the South. While at face value there is no problem with this development, the inherent challenge is the nature of the human rights, which are then transposed onto Africa by these donors and funders in the conceptualisation of transitional justice. When hijacked this way, transitional justice becomes another form of coloniality (Madlingozi 2010, 2015). The challenges facing Africa is that that the normative base which underlines and informs societal transformation has been hijacked, misrepresented and misappropriated by specific interests that are non-African and imperial in nature (Benyera 2018, p. 22; Maldonado-Torres 2018).

This book conceptualises issues of political leadership, notions of (in)justice and other related problematics. The main premise is to offer an alternative perspective and response to the question: why is it necessary to have an alternative path to justice, human rights and leadership in Africa. The motivation for this endeavour is the failure of the *status quo* to hold. The *status quo* in human rights, justice and leadership in Africa does not represent and or articulate the true interests of Africans. These were hijacked by various interests such as colonialism and imperialism for their ulterior motives. They misrepresent and distort Africans' lived experiences and realities, consequently compromising the needs of Africans in terms of the three aspects that we are concerned with here.

Why Look Inward for Solutions to Human Rights Abuses, Bad Leadership and Injustices in Africa?

This misrepresentation and distortion of justice, human rights and leadership in Africa have the effect of perpetuating suffering, injustice and human rights abuses. Essentially, those that are believed to be offering political leadership are in effect working in cohorts and conniving with looters, colonisers and imperialists to perpetuate the subjugation, marginalisation of Africa and its people which results in what Aime Cesaire (Cesaire 1955) and Fanon (1952) termed the thingification of Africans (Cesaire 1955, p. 21). The victims of these injustices are mistaken in their belief that their problems are being solved, when in fact it is being perpetuated. Besides this misrepresentation, there is also the problem of dependency on the part of the African victims of poor leadership, human rights abuses and various injustices as they are dependent on an otherwise uncaring set of elites.

Justice and human rights are never generic and universal, rather they are embedded phenomena. Consequently, the notion of universal human rights is a misrepresentation. What can be common across geographies, civilisations and times are the logics that underpin, inform and nature the various aspects. This results in epistemic dependency (Fernandes 2018; Velleman 2016) which Africans need to break away from and instead push for the establishment of epistemic autonomy (Nhemachena et al. 2016; Suarez-Krabbe 2012). The solution to epistemic dependency in terms of a normative standpoint and value sets should be self-determined and self-defined. The solution is already present in Africa, and it is in the form of traditional knowledge and value systems (Benyera 2014b, 2015; Karambakuwa and Mangwende 2010; Mawere 2010; Ngara et al. 2013). Hence, Africa need not look elsewhere for responses on how to solve poor leadership styles, gross violations of human rights and other forms of injustices. The task therefore is to identify what these traditional African knowledge and value systems are.

A key element of this endeavour is *situatedness*. The significance of *situatedness* is emphasised as a cardinal ingredient in articulating an inward-looking search for an alternative path to justice, human rights and leadership. What do we imply when we say *situatedness* of human rights? We are alluding here to the fact that human rights must be perceived and constructed from local principles and value sets. It becomes almost automatic for human rights to resonate with the local and its lived experiences. The opposite is true of leadership and notions of justice, which, in our view, was constructed elsewhere and then bombed into African, and other communities as was the case in Libya under Muammar Gaddafi, Iraq under Saddam Hussein and Syria under Bashar al-Assad.

Why are we looking inward for solutions to human rights abuses and injustices in Africa? It is because of three reasons. First, human rights can never be universal. What is universal are the logics that inform human rights. For Africa, these logics include the sanctity of human life and the inter-connectedness of humanity. The logics that inform human rights have existed before colonialism; they existed across geographies and civilisations only for them to be replaced by Euro-North American-centric so-called universal human rights. The invention of a notion of universal human rights was rightly characterised as human rights colonialism (Nhemachena et al. 2018, pp. 74–75). Justice and human rights are never generic and universal as they are situated and embedded phenomena. The notion of universal human rights is a misrepresentation and in fact speaks to the colonisation of human rights (Nhemachena et al. 2018). There are universal principles, logics and values that are common across civilisations such as the sanctity of human life (Nhemachena et al. 2018, p. 75) or coloniality of human rights (Maldonado-Torres 2018).

These principles are almost natural and the issue at hand is the manner in which we should address the finer points of divergence of our principles. This is where Walter Mignolo's notion of border gnosis, also known as border thinking, becomes efficacious (Mignolo 2000). By analysing this notion from the bottom-up, it does not imply that we are negating the universal (Mignolo 2000). What we are doing is to look for the finer points of convergence between the universal and the local which gives preference to the local. We are looking for those principles, norms and values, which allows local suffering to articulate their own suffering in their own language. We are advocating for a degree of autonomy which does not negate alternatives. Border thinking teaches us that not everything that is universal or presented as universal is bad for the local (Baez and Soto-Lafontaine 2015; Ghiso and Campano 2013; Mignolo 2000). The local must interact with the universal, but must be able to do so in a manner that allows it to put itself first. This distinguishes the current project from post-colonial scholarship which essentially argues that there is nothing for the local to benefit from the universal. It has to be reiterated that the principles underpinning life in Africa must be self-defined, privileging the local while borrowing the good from elsewhere.

The idiom, *do not throw the baby with the bath water*, is what this book advocates for. In the process of privileging local value sets, we must not be blinded and oblivious to the deficiencies inherent in the local. In other words, the local is not perfect; however, it is better than the universal. In order to improve human rights, justice and have better leadership in Africa, there is a need to identify and address the shortcomings inherent in the local religious, economic, political and social aspects of life and then address their shortcomings. The shortcomings can be addressed either by organically grown solutions or by borrowing from elsewhere.

This book does not advocate for a fundamentalist or essentialist understanding of the local because it acknowledges that there are other principles and value sets. The local is simply saying, *listen to me, privilege my voice and hear me out*. This is what we term localised thinking without dismissing the universal. The main challenge with the universal is the methods and the approaches that are used to attain human rights, avoid injustice and inform leadership. The challenges of the universal will be explained more in the following section.

'All We Demand Are the Right to Rights': Reclaiming Access to Human Rights as the Greatest Right

This statement is traceable to deposed and assassinated Iraqi leader Saddam Hussein who said that *'all we are asking for is nothing other than the right to human rights'*. In Africa, unlike Saddam Hussein who once cooperated with the Americans in destabilising Iran and was thereafter dispensed with, we have Gaddafi who never sold out. Gaddafi was assassinated with the active assistance of the North Atlantic Treaty Organisation (NATO) (Campbell 2013; Gwaambuka 2016; Rotmann et al. 2014) and his biggest crime was to demand and lead Africa's charge towards the economic and epistemic independence. The story of Saddam Hussein is a classic case of how imperialism uses leaders from weak countries to complete imperial injustices, such as killing their own people, and then dispensing these leaders once they have achieved their goals. It is now an uncontested fact of history that Saddam Hussein had no weapons of mass destruction (Latour 2006, p. 68; Mignolo and Walsh 2018, p. 141; Moyo 2017, p. 140) and that he was used by the USA to destabilise Iran (Brown 2010; Buzan 1944, p. 444) after the Islamic revolution in Iran. Saddam Hussein, Muammar Gaddafi and Congolese revolutionary Patrice Lumumba have one thing in common, they rejected imperialist orders and were then dispensed with. In Africa, unlike Saddam Hussein who once cooperated with the American in destabilising Iran and was then dispensed after the American project was over, we have Gaddafi who never sold out. Gaddafi was assassinated with the active assistance of the North Atlantic Treaty Organisation (NATO) and his biggest crime was to not only demand economic freedom for Africa but to lead Africa's economic and epidemic independence (Campbell 2013; Chandler 2004; Morris 2013). The story of Saddam Hussein is a classic case of how imperialism uses leaders from weak countries to complete with imperial injustices such as killing their own people and then dispensing these leaders once the imperialists have achieved their goals. It is now an uncontested fact of history that Saddam Hussein had no weapons of mass destruction and that Saddam Hussein was used by the USA to destabilise Iran after the Iranian revolution (Evans 2013, p. 78; Latour 2006, p. 69; Webel et al. 2015, p. 89). Saddam Hussein, Muammar al Gaddafi and Patrice Lumumba had one thing in common—they rejected imperialist orders and were subsequently dispensed with. From the then Zaire's founding President Patrice Lumumba, we learn that there is a price for good leadership. For African leadership, the current options are either to be compliant and submit to imperial demands or be ostracised, demonised or even to be killed.

What is Africa from an African perspective? We emphasise this Africaness because rights have been conceptualised, formulated and implemented from a Euro-North American perspective then projected globally (by force) as universal human rights. We borrow from Tanzanian Marxist scholar Shivji (2019, pp. 6–7) who conceptualised rights as comprising two rights and four freedoms. He argued there are:

> Two fundamental rights and four fundamental freedoms. The fundamental rights are *right to human existence* to live life with dignity and *right to organise* means that an organised working people are able to defend their interests themselves through their own organisations – whether these are trade unions, workers' associations, working women's organisations, peasant co-operatives or peasant parties. Forms of organisation arise from concrete conditions… Four fundamental freedoms are: *freedom from want, freedom from fear, freedom from violence* (both state and social violence) and *freedom from enforced silence* – in other words, right to speak out [emphasis original]

In agreement with Shivji, this book argues that there are two fundamental rights, which in turn give rise to four freedoms. These six variables are symbiotic and work like a complete electric circuit. If one of them is absent, then the whole system malfunctions. In other words, the collective of their rights and freedoms are functional only in their totality. Therefore, giving African only the rights to sexual freedom is unacceptable and incomplete without other rights such as the right to own and control their land. For Africa, as for Palestine, land ownership and control equal the right to existence. The rights to human existence have not been agitated for in Africa but elsewhere such as in Iraq under Saddam Hussein and Libya under Muammar Gaddafi.

There are a number of key lessons for the local from the way the USA and Saddam Hussein (ab)used each other. From a leadership perspective, the lesson is that local leadership is not immune to international pollution and instrumentalisation. They are also prone to manufactured consent and shear bullying. What Libyan leader Muammar Gaddafi died for is exactly what South African political party, the Economic Freedom Fighters, are agitating for, that is, economic independence.

Another step which Africa is yet to self-introspect is epistemic independence. Epistemic autonomy is efficacious in privileging the local in terms of justice, human rights or leadership. The final destination is therefore an epistemically independent

Africa. The context of Saddam Hussein's demand for the right of Iraqi's to rights was when the Euro-North American hegemony had imposed sanctions on Iraqi. This is a familiar story for many African countries such as Zimbabwe, Libya and Sudan. If human rights are universal, as argued by liberal scholarship, then why is it that economically and militarily powerful countries of the world can withdraw the human rights of other citizens without their consent and using violence of different forms? Such violence includes the weaponisation of the US dollar.

Current African leadership is compromised because it was hijacked by various interests such as capital. This is a leadership which is a product of Euro-North American colonial modernity. This is why current, and most past leadership in Africa, continued using colonial methods after the attainment of political leadership. We return to the case of Zaire's founding leader Patrice Lumumba who was assassinated for spearheading the unification of the Congo. Lumumba wanted the independent Congo to break away from factionalism and ethnicity. He told the colonisers that we want the right to self-determination, not only in political terms, but also in every other aspect of life, including how we rule ourselves. This did not resonate with the colonisers who, as Kwame Nkrumah taught, were in the process of launching the next phase of colonialism—what he termed neocolonialism. The Central Intelligence Association (CIA) of the USA and the Belgians colluded in assassinating Lumumba and they must be rightly blamed for state in which the Congo is in today in terms of it (in)justice, human rights abuses and poor, if not absent leadership (Ndlovu-Gatsheni 2013, p. 29). Lumumba was assassinated because he was about to set, what in the eyes of the colonisers, was bad precedence, i.e. uniting post-colonial states (Jazbhay 2019, p. 40).

The death of Lumumba was therefore a classic Western *modus operandi* of getting rid of alleged communists and their sympathisers (Ndlovu-Gatsheni 2013, pp. 29–30; Shivji 2007, p. 16). Lumumba openly denied that he was a communist or a communist sympathiser, declaring that 'I went to the Soviet Union out of my own volition and on my own accord'. We are emphasising the case of Patrice Lumumba because it was precedence setting assassination such that had his ambition succeeded, it was one bound to set positive precedence in Africa. Most of the current justice, human rights and leadership challenges, which Africa is facing today, could have been addressed had the Congo been allowed independent rule by the colonisers.

Africa must delink from the global politics rhetoric which was once rooted in the East versus the West but which later changed after 9/11 to the War on Terror. Here, the binary is either you are with the Euro-North American world or you are against them (hence with the terrorists or you are one of the terrorists). Nkrumah responded to Africa being forced to join either the East or the West in the now famous words, '*we face neither East nor West, we face forward*'. This political stand can be accredited for the formation of the Non-aligned Movement which sort to accommodate those countries that did not want to side with the Communist or the Capitalist block. This book, therefore, is a contribution to actualising Nkrumah's vision of an Africa which looks neither to China nor to Euro-North America, but one which looks at itself for its development (Nkrumah 1963, 1965). Spoken on 6 March 1957, Nkrumah's words are more relevant now than ever before.

What does this looking forward which Nkrumah advocated for look like? In essence, it is an introspective project, which resonates with the mantra, *African solutions for African problems*. In this process, Africa learns from its pre-colonial, colonial and post-colonial experiences. We have identified dependency as one of the major problems in Africa. In terms of justice, Africa tends to predominantly rely on mechanisms and institutions from elsewhere and expect them to work in Africa. In terms of human rights, the principles that underlie Africa's human rights rely on imposed notions of human rights which necessarily do not resonate with local realities, principles, norms and values. This then results in a misalignment between imposed notions of human rights and what Africa terms human rights from below. Under these circumstances, (in)justices committed in pursuit of human rights are inevitable.

To address Africa's perceived lack of development, Claude Ake argued for what he termed autonomous political development (Ake 1975, 2003) and democratisation of disempowerment (Ake 1975, 2003). This has not been pursued very much in Africa. There are cases of what Claude Ake advocated for in the leadership of Dr. John Magufuli in Tanzania and the current leadership of Ghana under Dr. Nana Addo Kufuor.

Consistent with the theme of the book, we conceptualise and seek justice from within Africa and Africans. The point of departure is that Africa should not seek justice from the same people, mechanisms and institutions that are perpetrating injustices. Why then are we searching for alternative justice for Africa? The existing frameworks of justice constituted by Western legal constitutions and laws based on the Roman Dutch law framework have perpetuated and reproduced injustices. It has been argued that these Westernised forms, notions and institutions of justice actually perpetuate injustice in Africa. The question then is, should Africa continue to rely on them both practically and theoretically? A practical case in point is the continent's reliance on the International Criminal Court to address gross violations of human rights. At a conceptual level, Roman Dutch law continues to be the default legal framework across most of Africa with the exception of few North and West African countries where there are elements of Islamic law. At a theoretical level, conceptions of justice in Africa are still heavily Western-centric with the work of Ronald Dahl and other Western philosophers such as Karl Marx.

African justice must therefore resonate with the material, spiritual and epistemological needs of Africans first and foremost. We allege that Westernised justice, besides being politicised, hijacked and weaponised, has overly become rhetorical and an extension of Euro-North America foreign policies and agendas. The politicisation of International Criminal Court and the injustices of the United Nations Security Council are cases in point of the commission of injustices in the pursuit of justice (see the rhetoric/irony). The barbaric intervention of NATO in Libya and the resultant assassination of General Gaddafi simplify the brazenness and deepened the weaponisation of the United Nations Security Council and NATO against poor defenceless people. When someone such as Gaddafi, Mugabe or Nicolás Maduro or a situation does not fit into the exceptionalism agenda, they are either disciplined, dispensed, or new norms and principles are developed in order to plug this new 'anomaly'.

In this book, we demonstrate how justice was hijacked, both theoretically and practically, by liberals and their Euro-North American backers and sympathisers. A classic example is an exceptionalism in the pursuit of justice. An example of exceptionalism in justice is how the USA and its citizens are out of the jurisdiction of the International Criminal Court, yet the USA uses its power in the United Nations Security Council to refer any person to the International Criminal Court for prosecution. Having the power, will and ability to refer everyone else besides themselves and their allies to a justice system which does not apply to them is the height of exceptionalism. Because the economically and militarily powerful nations own the discourse, they speak on behalf of those they oppress (Spivak 1988, 1999). They own the discourse, hence the rise of the discourse of right. The discourse of right is owned, controlled and adjudicated by the same people. In sports, this is akin to being a player, the referee, the match commissioner and also sponsor of the tournament.

Within the current world order, those who decide what constitutes (in)justice are those who control the rhetoric, institutions and power to formulate and decide what is to be (in)justice. To add to this annormalic complication, the standards keep changing but what remains permanent is the structure of power (Wallerstein 2007, 2011). Institutions that disseminate and adjudicate issues of justice remain heavily theoretically, practically and even financially, Western influenced. The question then is, what have been the ramifications of the above to Africa? Romain Francis responded to this question in his chapter on environmental justice where he argues how existing justice frameworks have perpetuated injustices while attempting to ameliorate issues such as food insecurity.

The Search for Justice in Africa

The search for an alternative path to justice in Africa is necessitated by the irrelevancy and ineffectiveness of current conceptualisations. Current conceptualisations in Africa are irrelevant to the African context and do not resonate with the lived realities of Africans. Termed imported modes of justice (Benyera 2014a), these justice mechanisms, norms, principles, institutions, systems and logics have been hijacked, weaponised, instrumentalised and politicised by the liberal Euro-North American world to perpetuate the subjugation of Africa and Africans. The application of this form of justice in Africa has led to further injustices.

Given the widely publicised and evidently bad leadership styles in Africa such as those characterised by kleptocracy, executive impunity, nepotism and other variants of mismanaging the economy (Benyera 2016, p. 162) which were in turn characterised by William Reno as clandestine economies (Reno 2000), the question we respond to is, is there a model of good leadership in Africa? Theoretically, Rotberg's transformative leadership is an excellent response to the above question (Rotberg 2012). Rotberg developed what he termed the Mandela model of leadership which was moulded around 'consummate inclusionism'. The chapter by Ahmed Jazbhay explores the leadership of Nelson Mandela and positions it as a prototype African—the leadership that Africa is missing. This is transformative leadership, which transforms Africa from a colonial state to a developed state that caters for the needs of its people not only materially, but also epistemologically.

On the Centrality of the Right to Rights as a *Sine Qua Non* for Development and Justice in Africa

Without the right to rights, there can be no genuine development and sustainable justice in Africa. Having the right to rights is a fundamental step because it enables Africans to move away from the realms of subhumans into the realms of humanity. Here, Africans will be free to develop themselves, according to their priorities and not giving into what Dambisa Moyo termed dead aid (Moyo 2009a, b), or to the various enslaving conditions of Western-sponsored development packages. This is reversing the logic which was inaugurated during what Ramon Grosfoguel termed the epistemicide of the long sixteenth century which was headlined by the conquest of Al-Andalucía (Grosfoguel 2013). This is the point of initiation for Euro-North American hegemony. During this period, Caucasians installed themselves as the prototype and 'reference sample' for humans and all others were classified as subhumans (Benyera et al. 2018; Mignolo 2009). Hence, the notion of human rights at present only applies to humans in that sense. According to this logic, not every person is human, other persons can be easily dispensed with (Grosfoguel 2013, 2017; Sithole 2014, p. 89, 2016, p. 36).

From an African perspective, what therefore is the right to rights? Rights in Africa are essentially the right to land. It is land which defines indigeneity and belonging and all other rights are anchored on land. Even the state derives its sovereignty from the land. For without the control of a certain geographically demarcated area in which it exercises the right to the exclusive use of force, the state does not exist. For Mahmood Mamdani, the further one moves away from their locality, the further they move away from their human rights (Mamdani 1996, 2015), hence the African saying, *the king's son is a slave elsewhere*.

This book does not agitate for the demand for human rights because this is an autonomous project, which has nothing to do with the (former) colonisers. The departure point is that, unlike Saddam Hussein who was demanding the rights to rights from the Americans and their allies, we are demanding it from ourselves. By demanding our rights from the (former) colonisers, we will actually be empowering them and indirectly communicating that they possess our human rights and that it is up to them to release of withholding those rights. This formula must be discontinued as it has failed to work. Empowering the (former) colonisers by demanding respect, human rights, development aid, justice *etcetera*, from them, perpetuates both epistemic dependency and epistemic colonisation. It also elevates the (former) colonisers to the pedestals of the patron of human rights, justice, leaders and development. Presently, the USA is busy ordering who should and should not rule Venezuela. Why is it that Malawi or Panama cannot dictate who should lead France, the USA, the United Kingdom or Germany?

By framing the narrative towards getting the right to right as opposed to demanding the rights to rights, Africa is asserting itself as its own centre. This way, Africa is communicating with itself, hence moving away from the master–slave narrative. Africa therefore needs to take ownership of both the project of moving towards having the right to rights, its framing and implementation. By finding from within and not finding from without, Africa is bound to find solutions to justice, human rights and its leadership problems which resonate with the challenges that Africa faces and the principles that underpin life in these communities. This book is therefore a *communique* to Africa which essentially seeks to self-empower the (formally) colonised.

The Euro-North American world is no longer the centre of African struggles. The terms of reference for African self-empowering are no longer located elsewhere. Africa must therefore part ways with notions which interiorise Africa such as the centre–periphery description of the relationship between Africa and the (former) colonisers. Africa must put itself as the centre for Africans in as much as Europe is the centre for Europeans and America is the centre for Americans and China is the centre for the Chinese. The core–periphery binary is no more as Africa is now self-defining and self-centred.

From Good and Bad Leadership Towards Good and Just Leadership in Africa

Given the prevalence of bad leadership, which was compounded by colonialism, Africa needs a moral revolution in order to produce not only good but also just leadership. We depart from the characterisation of leadership, especially public leadership as good or bad to one which is good or just, with just leadership being desired as it produces and results in justice and development. Why a moral revolution? Traditional institutions of the state that are designed for oversight and to mitigate bad decisions or poor judgements by leaders including nepotism, corruption and other pejorative practises, which have become associated with African leadership, have failed to deliver just leadership and development. At best, Africa enjoys good leadership. This book is a point of difference as it argues for just leadership as a prerequisite for justice and development. The distinction between a *good* and a *just* leadership will be attempted next. A good leader calls out maladministration and all other bad vices while a just leader calls out these actions and takes corrective measures even to the detriment of him/herself. Africa had just leaders such as Samora Machel, Julius Nyerere and Kenneth Kaunda who used their countries as a base to act against colonialism and apartheid. Machel was killed by the apartheid regime of South Africa mainly because of these agitations for the end of apartheid (Christie 1988; Machel 1986). Mandela was a good leader, not a just leader. Understandably, the conditions were precarious for him to challenge and uproot the structures of apartheid which today remain firmer and even more lethal than during the days of official apartheid. Hence, in South Africa today, poverty continues to increase, inequality is widening and unemployment is increasing. The structures of apartheid remain largely unchanged.

With mainly bad and good leaders and few just leaders, no matter what systems of governance are put in place, such systems have consistently failed in Africa to deliver a just and developed society. A moral revolution is therefore necessary to address the central issue of an absent, polluted or captured moral agency of African leaders. We define morality simply as a code of conduct that, given specified conditions, would be put forward by all rational persons. Moral agency underpins any successful administration. This moral agency must stem from other imperatives. Firstly, a just leader must have a vision for his society and his people. Secondly, a just leader must be committed to this widely shared vision by *inter alia*, self-sacrifice amid selflessness. Thirdly, s/he must commit and uphold a certain value set consisting of integrity, honesty, truthfulness and trust. These are the key features of a just leader. These attributes sometimes lead to a conundrum where the good leader is expected to act with a firm hand. This can be construed as either dictatorship or authoritarianism. A good leader has to enforce agreements which take her/his people forward and also uphold agreed values such as honesty.

In his thesis on social utility, John Stewart Mills argues that the purpose of a state is to ensure that agreed upon guiding principles are realised in the best interest of society (Mill 1859, 1895). This implies that at times, the good leader has to impose her/his will which may infringe on the freedom of some other individuals, yet observing and upholding these individual freedoms compromise the greater good, which for Mills is the chief law.

This conundrum is prevalent in Africa where a broader developmental agenda is desirable, so is a broader social and political agenda, all aligned towards the realisation of a common developmental goal. Africa's level of development and system of government differ from those in the global West. This means that African leaders lead in the absence of strong institutions, incomplete separation of powers, structural inefficiency. All which is now required are strong leaders capable and willing to fill these gaps by taking decisive actions.

So what constitutes bad leadership? Broadly, a bad leader is someone who takes an oath of office or agrees to occupy an office knowing that they do not intend to uphold that oath of office. This constitutes moral incongruency between moral agency and institutional commitment. The institution compels you to adhere to certain norms and principles of that particular portfolio or office. Another form of bad leadership is agreeing to occupy an office when you know that you possess neither the craft competency nor the craft literacy to deliver on what is required in that position. This form of bad leadership originates from the moment when self-interest prevails over the collective good.

Now to the just leader as opposed to a good leader. We will borrow from Brian Barry in our framing of a just leader. Writing on the issue of morality and the state, Barry asks: what is the difference between a good and a just leader? For Barry, a good leader will call out an injustice, will speak about it but will not act. Calling out injustice appeases the citizens while acting against it will compromise the leaders own interests and therefore a good leader will simply call out bad practises such as corruption, nepotism, state capture etcetera, but will never take decisive action lest s/he compromises her/his own interests. A just leader will call out bad behaviours and maladministration even to the detriment of self. When this analysis of good and just leaders is applied to the South African contest, it can be deducted that President Cyril Ramaphosa is a good but not a just leader. He spoke out against corruption, state capture and other malpractices such as, what is termed 'fruitless and irregular expenditure', yet he never acted out. Similarly, and based on the above framing of good and just leadership, we argue that Nelson Mandela was a good leader and not a just leader. This does not imply that Mandela was a bad leader either. He was a good leader because he called out the apartheid structure. He was not a just leader because he never acted to dismantle the colonial apartheid structures which remained intact and are even firmer today, producing and reproducing more poverty, inequality and unemployment, among other toxins. White liberals like good African leaders because they leave untouched the colonial structures of power, knowledge and being. The colonial apartheid system remains unchanged and continues to function fully as designed, reproducing black subjectivity while maintaining whiteness and white privilege. This is partly why unemployment and poverty continue to rise and inequality continues to widen.

In Africa, we have had good leaders and very few just leaders. Thomas Sankara, Patrice Lumumba, Kwame Nkrumah and Julius Nyerere were just leaders. Just leaders are rarely accorded the chance to lead their people as they are quickly dispensed by the colonial system as aptly demonstrated by the assassination of Sankara and Lumumba.

Conclusion

The Euro-North American world is no longer the centre of African struggles. The terms of reference for the self-empowering of Africa are no longer located elsewhere. Africa must therefore part ways with notions which inferiorise it such as the centre–periphery description of the relationship between Africa and the (former) colonisers (Amin 1976; Deng and Zartman 2011; Frank 1966; Simon 2011). Africa must put itself as the centre for Africans in as much as Europe is the centre for Europeans and America is the centre for Americans and China is the centre for the Chinese. The core–periphery binary is no more as Africa is now self-defining and self-centred.

In order for this to be actualised, Africa needs great leaders(hip). By great leaders, we imply those leaders who put their people first. These leaders are informed by African philosophies such as the isiZulu idiom; *the chief is a chief because of the people*. In conceptualising this subsection, we borrow from what Frantz Fanon's notion of the pitfalls of national consciousness (Fanon 2017) to frame nationalism as a threat to good African-centred leadership. National consciousness has resulted in the current state of affairs in African leadership which is characterised by elite collusion. The solution to the pitfalls of national consciousness in the notion of the nation has been conceptualised in Western terms.

This book has a chapter on the leadership of Nelson Mandela as a prototype African leader. The question responded to in that chapter is, what characteristics did Nelson Mandela possess which made him the global icon that he was. We locate these unique characteristics of Nelson Mandela in his upbringing as a member of the AbaTembu royal family (Mandela 1994). Nelson Mandela learnt the African ways of leadership from his royal upbringing. He then infused these local leadership principles into the modern responsibilities of a statesman. Mandela's leadership style was influenced by his experiences as a young boy sitting at the *lekgotla* which is a traditional gathering where issues are deliberated and debated. As a traditional forum for consultation and dealing with differences, the *lekgotla* is still today used in South Africa (Gready 2010, p. 177). This is the approach which Mandela successively employed over his political career.

The system of leadership worked for him and the people who put him in the position of leadership both in the African National Congress (ANC) and in the South African government because it was an embedded and localised way of leadership which resonated with the people. Mandela spoke of certain traditional values and cultural practices which he learnt as a boy which subsequently influenced his leadership style. We can therefore argue that Nelson Mandela was not a product of Euro-North American modernity colonisation. This is what largely distinguishes his leadership style from that of other African leaders. The argument that we are making here is exactly what Mandela lived as a leader. Therefore, we are not proposing something new which been done. We are actually proposing in introspection of those leadership styles that worked for Africa. We break away from the liberal misrepresentation of Nelson Mandela which conveniently did not emphasise the role played by indigeneity and African traditional value systems in the way he ruled.

References

Ake, C. 1975. A Definition of Political Stability. *Comparative Politics* 7 (2): 271–283.
Ake, C. 2003. *Democracy and Development in Africa*. Ibadan: Spectrum Books Limited.
Amin, S. 1976. *Unequal Development: An Essay on the Social Formations of Peripheral Capitalism*. New York: Monthly Review Press.
Baez, A.C., and M. Soto-Lafontaine. 2015. Sexual Self-determination in Cuba: The Epistemic Decolonial Turn. *Sexualities* 18 (7): 775–797. https://doi.org/10.1177/1363460714544811.
Benyera, E. 2014a. *Debating the Efficacy of Transitional Justice Mechanisms: The Case of National Healing in Zimbabwe, 1980–2011*. Pretoria: The University of South Africa.
Benyera, E. 2014b. Exploring Zimbabwe's Traditional Transitional Justice Mechanisms. *Journal of Social Science* 41 (3): 335–344.
Benyera, E. 2015. Presenting Ngozi as an Important Consideration in Pursuing Transitional Justice for Victims: The Case of Moses Chokuda. *Gender & Behaviour* 13 (2): 6760–6773. Retrieved from http://ezproxy.eafit.edu.co/login?url=http://search.ebscohost.com/login.aspx?direct=true&db=a9h&AN=111670223&lang=es&site=eds-live.

Benyera, E. 2016. On the Question of the Transition: Was Zimbabwe a Transitional State Between 2008 and 2013? *Journal of Human Ecology* 55 (3): 160–172.

Benyera, E. 2018. Is the International Criminal Court Unfairly Targeting Africa? Lessons for Latin America and the Caribbean States. *Politeia* 37 (1): 1–30. http://doi.org/10.25159/0256-8845/2403ISSN.

Benyera, E., O. Mtapuri, and A. Nhemachena. 2018. The Man, Human Rights, Transitional Justice and African Jurisprudence in the Twenty-First Century. *Social and Legal Theory in the Age of Decoloniality: (Re-)Envisioning African Jurisprudence in the 21st Century*, 187–218. Langaa: Bamenda, Cameroon.

Brown, D. 2010. Breaching the Colonial Contract: Anti-Colonialism in the US and Canada. *The International Journal of Illich Studies* 8 (1): 75–79. http://doi.org/10.4198.116.

Buzan, B. 1944. New Patterns of Global Security in the Twenty-First Century. *Source: International Affairs (Royal Institute of International Affairs* 67 (3): 431–451. http://doi.org/10.2307/2621945.

Campbell, H. 2013. *Global NATO and the catastrophic failure in Libya: Lessons for Africa in the Forging of African Unity*. New York: Monthly Review Press.

Cesaire, A. 1955. *Discourse on Colonialism*. New York: Monthly Review Press.

Chandler, D. 2004. The Responsibility to Protect? Imposing the "Liberal Peace". *International Peacekeeping* 11 (1): 59–81. https://doi.org/10.1080/1353331042000228454.

Christie, I. 1988. *Machel of Mozambique*. Harare: Zimbabwe Government Printers.

Deng, F. M., and W. I. Zartman. 2011. Conflict Resolution in Africa. In *The Ancient World-Systems Versus the Modern Capitalist World-System. Review (Fernand Braudel Center)*, ed. Samir Amin, 349–385. Washington DC: Brookings Institution Press.

Evans, G. 2013. The Responsibility to Protect: Rethinking Humanitarian Intervention. *Proceedings of the Annual Meeting (American Society of International Law)* 98 (May): 78–89.

Fanon, F. 1952. *Black Skin White Masks*. London: Pluto Press.

Fanon, F. 2017. Pitfalls of National Consciousness. *New Agenda: South African Journal of Social and Economic Policy* 66: 36–40.

Fernandes, A. 2018. Varieties of Epistemic Freedom. *Australasian Journal of Philosophy* 94 (4): 736–751. https://doi.org/10.1080/00048402.2015.1116015.

Frank, A. G. 1966. *The Development of Underdevelopment*. Boston: MA: New England Free Press.

Ghiso, M. P., and G. Campano. 2013. Coloniality and Education: Negotiating Discourses of Immigration in Schools and Communities Through Border Thinking. *Equity & Excellence in Education*, 46 (2): 252–269. https://doi.org/10.1080/10665684.2013.779160.

Gready, P. 2010. *The Era of Transitional Justice: The Aftermath of the Truth and Reconciliation Commission in South Africa and Beyond*. http://doi.org/10.4324/9780203841938.

Grosfoguel, R. 2013. The Structure of Knowledge in Westernized Universities: Epistemic Racism/Sexism and the Four Genocides/Epistemicides of the Long 16th Century. *Human Architecture* 11 (1): 73–90. https://doi.org/10.1108/17506200710779521.

Grosfoguel, R. 2017. Decolonizing Western Universalisms: Decolonial Pluri-versalism from Aime Cesaire to the Zapatistas. In *Towards a Just Curriculum Theory: The Epistemicide*. https://doi.org/10.4324/9781315146904.

Gwaambuka, T. 2016, April 16. Ten Reasons Libya Under Gaddafi Was a Great Place to Live. *The African Exponent*. Retrieved from https://www.africanexponent.com/post/ten-reasons-libya-under-gaddafi-was-a-great-place-to-live-2746.

Jazbhay, A. H. 2019. African Powerhouses: A Decolonial Critique of Nigeria and South Africa's Perceived Economic and Political Strengths in the Modern World-System. In *Nigeria-South Africa Relations and Regional Hegemonic Competence*, ed. O. Tella, Advances i, 25–42. New York: Springer. https://doi.org/10.1007/978-3-030-00081-3.

Karambakuwa, R.T., and S. Mangwende. 2010. Indigenous Knowledge Systems (IKSS) Potential for Establishing a Moral, Virtuous Society: Lessons from Selected IKSS in Zimbabwe and Mozambique. *Journal of Sustainable Development in Africa* 12 (7): 209–221.

Keet, A. 2014. Epistemic "Othering" and the Decolonisation of Knowledge. *Africa Insight* 44 (1): 23–37.

Latour, B. 2006. *Reassembling the Social an Introduction to Actor-Network-Theory. Politica y Sociedad*, vol. 43. Oxford and New York: Oxford University Press. https://doi.org/10.1163/156913308X336453.

Machel, S. 1986. *A Luta Continua*. Maputo: Afrontamento.

Madlingozi, T. 2007. Post-apartheid South Africa and the Quest for the Elusive "new" South Africa. *Journal of Law and Society* 34 (1): 77–98.

Madlingozi, T. 2010. On Transitional Justice Entrepreneurs and the Production of Victims. *Journal of Human Rights Practice* 2 (2): 208–228.

Madlingozi, T. 2015. Transitional Justice as Epistemicide: On Steve Biko's Pluralist Coexistence 'After' Conflict. In *WiSER Seminar, Wits University, Johannesburg, 27 July 2015*, 1–28. Johannesburg: Unpublished.

Maldonado-Torres, N. 2018, October. On the Coloniality of Human Rights. *Revista Crítica de Ciências Sociais* 114: 117–136. https://doi.org/10.4000/rccs.6793.

Mamdani, M. 1996. *Citizens and Subjects: Contemporary Africa and the Legacy of Late Colonisation*. Princeton: Princeton University Press.

Mamdani, M. 2015. Political Identity, Citizenship and Ethnicity and Post-colonial Africa. In *Keynote Address at the Arusha Conference "New Frontiers of Social Policy"*, 1–18. Arusha.

Mandela, N. 1994. *Long Walk to Freedom: The Autobiography of Nelson Mandela*. Boston: MA: Little, Brown and Company.

Mawere, M. 2010. Zvierwa as African IKS: Epistemological and Ethical Implications of Selected Shona Taboos. *Indilinga African Journal of Indigenous Knowledge Systems* 9 (1): 29–44.

Mignolo, W. 2000. *Local Histories/Global Designs: Coloniality, Subaltern Knowledges, and Border Thinking*. Princeton and Oxford: Princeton University Press.

Mignolo, W. 2009. Who Speaks for the 'Human' in Human Rights? *Hispanic Issues on Line* 5 (1): 7–24.

Mignolo, W.D., and C. Walsh. 2018. *On Decoloniality: Concepts, Analytics, Praxis*. Durham and London: Duke University Press.

Mill, J.S. 1859. *On Liberty by Stuart Mills*. London: Longmans, Green and Company.

Mill, J.S. 1895. *Utilitarianism*. London: Longmans, Green and Company.

Morris, J. 2013. Libya and Syria: R2P and the Spectre of the Swinging Pendulum. *International Affairs* 89 (5): 1265–1283. https://doi.org/10.1111/1468-2346.12071.

Moyo, D. 2009a. *Dead aid: Why Aid is Not Working and How There is a Better Way for Africa*. New York: Farrar, Straus and Giroux. Retrieved from http://cms.medcol.mw/cms_uploaded_resources/4685_4.pdf.

Moyo, D. 2009b. Why Foreign Aid Is Hurting Africa. *Wall Street Journal*, 1–6. http://doi.org/10.4018/IJAVET.2016040102.

Moyo, G. 2017. The Entrapment of Joshua Nkomo Within Global Imperial Snares. In *Joshua Mqabuko Nkomo of Zimbabwe: Politics, Power, and Memory*, ed. S.J. Ndlovu-Gatsheni, 115–147. Cham: Palgrave Macmillan.

Ndlovu-Gatsheni, S. J. 2013. *Coloniality of Power in Postcolonial Africa: Myths of Decolonisation*. Dakar, Senegal: Council for the Development of Social Science Research in Africa. https://doi.org/10.1017/CBO9781107415324.004.

Ngara, R., R. Mangizvo, and R. V. Mangizvi. 2013. Indigenous Knowledge Systems and the Conservation of Natural Resources in the Shangwe Community in Gokwe District, Zimbabwe. *International Journal of Asian Social Science* 3 (1): 20–28. Retrieved from http://www.aessweb.com/pdf-files/20-28.pdf.

Nhemachena, A., N. Mlambo, and M. Kaundjua. 2016. The Notion of the "Field" and the Practices of Researching and Writing Africa: Towards Decolonial Praxis. *Africology: The Journal of Pan African Studies* 9 (7): 15–36.

Nhemachena, A., T.V. Warikandwa, and S.K. Amoo. 2018. Identity, Originality and Hybridity in Jurisprudence and Social Theory: An Introduction. In *Social and Legal Theory in the Age of Decoloniality: (Re-)Envisioning African Jurisprudence in the 21st Century*, ed. A. Nhemachena, T.V. Warikandwa, and S.K. Amoo, 1–72. Bamenda, Cameroon: Langaa.

Nkrumah, K. 1963. *Africa Must Unite*. New York and Washington: Frederick A. Praeger.
Nkrumah, K. 1965. *Neo-Colonialism: The Last Stage of Imperialism*. New York: International Publishers.
Reno, W. 2000. Clandestine Economies, Violence and States in Africa. *Journal of International Affairs* 53 (2): 433–459. https://doi.org/Article.
Rotberg, R. 2012. *Transformative Political Leadership: Making a Difference in the World*. London and Chicago: Chicago University Press.
Rotmann, P., G. Kurtz, and S. Brockmeier. 2014. Major Powers and the Contested Evolution of a Responsibility to Protect. *Conflict, Security & Development* 14 (4): 355–377. https://doi.org/10.1080/14678802.2014.930592.
Shivji, I. 2007. *Silences in NGO Discourse: The Role and Future of NGOs in Africa*. Nairobi and Oxford: Fahamu Books.
Shivji, I. 2019. Social Responsibility of Intellectuals in Building Counter-Hegemonies. *Keynote Address at Launching of African Humanities Programme Books*, 1–7. Dar es Salaam: University of Dar es Salaam.
Simon, W. O. 2011. Centre-Periphery Relationship in the Understanding of Development of Internal Colonies. *International Journal of Economic Development Research and Investment* 2 (1): 147–156. Retrieved from https://www.icidr.org/ijedri_vol2no1_april2011/Centre-periphery Relationship in the Understanding of Development of Internal Colonies.pdf.
Sithole, T. 2014. Violence: The (Un)real, power and excess in Ngũgĩ wa Thiong'o's Wizard of the Crow. *Journal of Literary Studies* 30 (2): 86–103. https://doi.org/10.1080/02564718.2014.919107.
Sithole, T. 2016. The Concept of the Black Subject in Fanon. *Journal of Black Studies* 47 (1): 24–40. https://doi.org/10.1177/0021934715609913.
Spivak, G. C. 1988. Can the Subaltern Speak? In *Marxism and the Interpretation of Culture*, ed. C. Nelson and L. Grossberg, 271–315. Chicago: University of Illinois Press. https://doi.org/10.1590/S0102-44501999000200012.
Spivak, G.C. 1999. *A Critique of Postcolonial Reason: Toward a History of The Vanishing Present*. Cambridge, MA and London: Harvard University Press.
Suarez-Krabbe, J. 2012. "Epistemic Coyotismo" and Transnational Collaboration: Decolonizing the Danish University. *Human Architecture: Journal of the Sociology of Self-Knowledge* 10 (1): 31–44. Retrieved from https://search.proquest.com/docview/920750371/fulltextPDF/E9F0AC4A797349A4PQ/1?accountid=14648.
Velleman, J. D. 2016. Epistemic Freedom. *The Winnower*, 1–17.
Wallerstein, I. 2007. *World Systems Analysis: An Introduction*. Durham and London: Duke University Press.
Wallerstein, I. 2011. *The Modern World-System: Capitalist Agriculture and the Origins of the European World-Economy in the Sixteenth Century*, vol. 1. California: University of California Press.
Webel, C., H. Hintjens, and D. Zarkov. 2015. *Conflict, Peace, Security and Development: Theories and Methodologies*. In ed. C. Webel and J. Galtung. Routledge.

Everisto Benyera is an Associate Professor of African Politics in the Department of Political Sciences at the University of South Africa in Pretoria, South Africa. He is a decolonial reader and holds a M.Sc. in International Relations from the University of Zimbabwe and a Ph.D. in African Politics from the same university. He researches on transitology and transitional justice focusing on indigenous, traditional and non-state reconciliation, peacebuilding and healing mechanisms. He is the editor of the journal *Politeia*, Journal of Political Sciences and Public Administration and Management, and his publications are accessible via: https://orcid.org/0000-0002-2706-9097 and https://independent.academia.edu/EveristoBenyera.

Romain Francis is a Lecturer in the Department of Political Sciences at the University of South Africa (UNISA). He teaches modules at undergraduate and postgraduate levels exploring a range of disciplinary themes including *inter alia* political development, political economy, political theory, philosophy and ideology and contemporary South African political issues. In 2008, he obtained a Masters of Social Sciences Degree (MSocSc) in Political Sciences from the University of KwaZulu-Natal (UKZN). The title of his Master's research was *'The extent of environmental conscientisation and social mobilisation in the context of environmental racism: a case study of the residents of Merebank'*. He is currently registered for and working towards the completion of a PhD at the University of the Witwatersrand (Wits). Evolving from his master's project, his primary research interest falls within the discourse of *Environmental Racism and Environmental Justice*. His passion and interest in the discursive *nexus* between social justice and environmental issues emanate from his positionality of living in a community of colour in South Africa grossly affected by toxic pollution and a deep-seated fascination and love for the natural world. In fact, this experience informed his desire to precipitate meaningful societal or more aptly, ecological change, translating into his early involvement in social activism and community development that has subsequently manifested in his intellectual endeavours. His research assumes a political theory approach interrogating the interrelationship between the following specialised areas within the inherently transdisciplinary subject of environmental racism and justice, namely recognition, justice and ethics. Romain Francis is an advocate of the school of decoloniality, and his research is centred on the philosophical and practical precepts of this intellectual and ethical project.

Dr. Ahmed Haroon Jazbhay has Ph.D. (Political Studies), majoring in Political Theory, from the University of Johannesburg. His Ph.D. thesis was entitled: *Civil Religion in South Africa: Mandela through the lens of Machiavelli and Rousseau*. He is a young developing academic and is currently a Senior Lecturer in Political Sciences at the University of South Africa (UNISA) where he teaches African Political Thought and Political Theory. His research focuses on both mainstream and decolonial political theory and he occasionally delves into issues related to Islamophobia and the Palestinian/Zionist conflict.

Chapter 2
The Colonial State is the Problem in Africa

Everisto Benyera

Abstract The chapter's central argument is that leadership, justice and human rights cannot be discussed in Africa without making reference to the colonial state. This chapter positions bad leadership, lack of human rights and injustice in Africa as desired outcomes of the colonial project. Current (post) colonial states in Africa are argued to be colonial products, structured to sustain colonial power relations long after the end of official colonialism and apartheid. The (post) colonial African state is characterised as a snare wherein African countries are trapped, having been disenfranchised, disorientated and distorted such that it now predominantly serves the needs of those who created it, i.e. global imperialists. The conclusion of the chapter is that Africa must look into itself for redemption. As long as leadership styles, human rights norms and standards and justice models are all modelled around those of the same countries which enslaved, looted and colonised Africa, Africa's subjugation and marginalization will continue. In other words, the colonial state will continue doing what it was created to do: manufacturing, sustaining and adopting colonialism in its various forms.

Keywords Africa · Colonial state · Human rights · Justice · Leadership · Global imperialists

Introduction

One of the foremost questions that deserve interrogation is the debate about the need for African solutions for Africa's peacebuilding mechanisms is to conclusively state whether Africa is a failed continent. The failedness of a state can be ascertained using two frameworks; Rotberg's model (Rotberg 2010a, b, 2012) or Ali Mazrui's framework (Mazrui 1995). Using any of the two, the aim will be to ascertain whether Africa is a failed continent, that is, one where the majority of the member states are

---

E. Benyera (✉)
Department of Political Sciences, University of South Africa, Office 24, 7th Floor
Theo van Wijk Building, UNISA Main Campus, Pretoria 0003, South Africa
e-mail: benyee1@unisa.ac.za

© Springer Nature Switzerland AG 2020
E. Benyera (ed.), *Reimagining Justice, Human Rights and Leadership in Africa*,
Advances in African Economic, Social and Political Development,
https://doi.org/10.1007/978-3-030-25143-7_2

failed states. A failed state will be defined in Mazruic and not Rotberg's terms—a model written predominantly for the US government. For Ali Mazrui, in order for a state to be defined as failed, it would not be able to perform a combination of six core state functions. These six functions of the state are: sovereign control over territory; sovereign control and oversight over national resources; effective and rational revenue extraction from its people, goods and services; capacity to build and maintain national infrastructure; capacity to render social services and finally capacity to govern and maintain law and order (1995: 11). The causal link between failed African states and the three variables being explored in this book is that the sum of poor leadership, abuse of human rights and injustice is a failed state.

These six functions of the state are: (1) sovereign control over territory; (2) sovereign control and oversight over national resources; (3) effective and rational revenue extraction from its people, goods and services; (4) capacity to build and maintain national infrastructure; (5) capacity to render social services and (6) finally, capacity to govern and maintain law and order (1995: 11). This framework is privileged over other orthodox categorisations such as those that use economic, political, social, legal and religious markers as categories for the challenges that face Africa.

For Ali Mazrui, the advantage of using the six markers of a failed state he proposed is that the model has the ability to predict state failure well before it happens. For example, if a state has been captured by corporate capital as is the allegation in South Africa at present (May 1995), or if a state loses the sovereign right to collect taxes from its citizens, it is reliable to employ this model to predict whether the state will fail or not. Once a state fails in one of the six markers, then other continental member states will have the legitimate right to be alarmed as such a state will be on the path to collapse and eventual failure. What Mazrui managed to assert, which is also being amplified here is that once African member states have developed mechanisms to monitor member state status, failed and or collapsed statehood will be averted.

Africa's poor leadership, bad human rights record and injustice are hereby being blamed predominantly on the colonial state. The challenges addressed in this book can be traced back to the colonial state partially because this project is not meant to absolve African dictators and despots off their culpability and complicity in worsening the plight of the people they lead.

Countries in Africa are actually colonial states with more characteristics in common with their colonial cousin states. In other words, Africa is constituted by 54 colonial creations that did not organically emerge. Given this preponderant founding process, it is only natural for current African states to continue along the colonial path which they were meant to follow as set by their Western colonial creators. This was bound to be the trajectory for post-independent Africa in the absence of fundamental structural changes to statecraft.

By largely placing the blame for Africa's triple challenge of poor human rights, bad leadership and injustice, I am not romanticising pre-colonial Africa as having constituted pristine village democracies. These societies had their own challenges and these are well documented by pre-colonial historians (Beach 1998; Mawere 2013; Mudenge 1988; Pikirayi 1999; Vail 1989). The arrival and subsequent imposition of the colonialism and the colonial states worsened Africa's predicament until today. Colonialism was imposed, rationalised, routinised and maintained by violence (Benyera 2017; Mbembe 2000), as such after the official end of colonialism and apartheid, violence remained the tool of preference in settling difference and administering the state.

What the colonial state did to African leadership, justice and human rights institutions, logics, practises, norms and values are immeasurable. Firstly, it demonised them through imposing its own moralities on Africa (Mazrui 1982; Ndlovu-Gatsheni 2015). The colonial state also displaced African value systems and replaced with the ones Africa currently uses. These include the Roman-Dutch law legal framework, and Euro-North American modernity, which fronted capitalism as the only way of organising political and economic life in Africa and elsewhere. Once African value systems (legal, economic, political, religious, moral, etc.) were removed, Africans over generations forgot these systems, logics and values and the colonial order and logic became the default 'operating systems' for Africa.

In terms of leadership, post-independence Africa continued employing and deploying colonial modes of leadership which were alien to Africa. The result was that Africa lost memory of its leadership styles, justice principles, logics and human rights philosophies preferring to continue with colonial logics, institutions and mechanisms. The Westminster type of government, the Roman-Dutch law legal system and the principle of universal human rights are the unquestionable and de facto options globally. Colonialism taught African leaders to neglect the welfare of their citizens and to fear the faceless markets and investors. African leaders no longer consult their constituents. If they do any consultation, it will be to their Western masters, backers, guarantors, benefactors and allies. This explains why unpopular dictators such as Yoweri Museveni continue to rule in Uganda despite his unpopularity among the electorate. When African leaders who are aligned to powerful Western countries exhibit bad leadership, abuse human rights, and rule without justice promoting executives infinity, the West turns a blind eye. This amounts the promotion of bad leadership in Africa such as dictatorship, despotism, and in some cases crimes against humanity by the powerful nations who are also the (former) colonisers.

When it comes to African leaders, they are predominantly colonial products. They were produced by the system which they are meant to lead the fight against. The double tragedy for Africa is that some African leaders who are supposed to be working against the resilience of colonialism are, on the contrary, aiding, abetting and cooperating with the colonial system. South Africa, sitting as a non-permanent member of the United Nations Security Council, voted with the West in favour of Resolution 1973 imposing a no-flight zone over Libya with devastating consequences for Africa. These are still being felt today with the zenith being the assassination of General Muammar Gaddafi. The once prosperous Libya is now a 'class one' failed state, with three separate 'governments' and a haven for terrorist organisations who set up their bases in Libya. South Africa is therefore complicit in bringing Libya down, and in a way promoting injustice, terrorism, despotism and clannism in Libya. By cooperating in the unsitting of an African government and the assassination of a sitting head of an African state, South Africa did not show good leadership, participated in perpetrating injustice and was complicit in human rights abuses not only in Libya but also in the rest of Africa.

Africa needs to revisit its pre-colonial modes of leadership, which were based on inclusivity and popular consultation. There are African phrases that exhibit these institutions and characteristics of people-centred leadership. They include the saying that *a king is a king because of the people*. What this implies is that a king is largely a facilitator of human interactions within a certain jurisdiction. Kings were therefore answerable to the people and not the other way round. In this leadership model, people are not mere recipients of rulership but partners in running the communities they live in. This is contrary to the current forms of leadership in Africa where elected public officials are given high-ranking statuses colloquially referred to as *chief*. How can a servant of the people be their *chief*? This model of leadership is unsustainable and explains the behaviour of *chiefs* and the proliferation of the chief syndrome, where tinpot dictators sprout in every African village (Mpofu 2014: 4). These *chiefs* must be dismounted from the high pedestal of *chief hood* where citizens elevated them. The leadership on Nelson Mandela discussed by Ahmed Jazbhay in Chap. 8 demonstrates what is termed transformative leadership—something Africa is lacking.

For VY Mudimbe, the African problem is that Africa is an invention (Mudimbe 1988, 1991, 1994). Therefore, Africa is an idea with inherent fault lines which then manifests themselves in various ways such as corruption, bad leadership, bad human rights and injustice. Tendayi Sithole appropriately captures a major critique of Mudimbe's thesis by arguing that Mudimbe failed to make a, "distinction between African state and state in Africa in his political thought" (Personal Communication: 14 February 2019).

In terms of justice and human rights, Africa must revisit its logics, which underline the principles and philosophies of justice and human rights. While the philosophies and principles of justice may vary even within Africa, what remains constant are the underlying logics of both justice and human rights (Nhemachena et al. 2018). These logics include the sacredness of certain institutions such as the three realms of human life: the living living, the living dead and the living unborn (Benyera 2016). The term 'living dead' justifiably sounds contradictory. This is due to the challenges of translating an institution which exists in one civilisation into another. In most African civilisations, the medically dead is in fact not dead, but they would have transitioned into another realm of life, from which they perform certain ancestral functions. These are blessing, guiding and punishing the living living and guiding the living unborn.

Heads of African states also attempted to explain the African problem (Gaddafi 1976; Kagame 2014; Mandela 1993, 1994; Museveni 2000; Nkrumah 1965; Nyerere 1968, 2008). Naturally, their analysis was either nationalistic or continental. The logic was that once Africa became a united Africa (militarily, economically and politically), leading a united Africa was assumed easier than one fragmented into 54 parts. For nationalists, the solution for Africa was to consolidate the nation first before uniting the continent. The hand of the (former) colonialists was suspected in manipulating the debate in favour of the nationalists, a project that saw the survival of the colonial state.

The question; what is the African problem has been severally attempted (Cobbe 1983; Derrso 2012; Johnson et al. 1984; van Wyk 2007; Wiredu 1998). Responses identified individual aspects of the African problem such as stunted nation-building (Mbeki 1998; Mlambo 2013; Muzodidya and Ndlovu-Gatsheni 2007; Ndlovu-Gatsheni 2011), ethnicity (Mamdani 2015; Muzodidya and Ndlovu-Gatsheni 2007; Ndlovu-Gatsheni 2010; Nyika 2014; Ranger 1984, 1989; Sithole 1980). Others pointed to corruption (Rotberg 2010b; Saunders 2014; Suberu 2013; Verheul 2013), dependency (Amin 1976; Frank 1966, 1978; Mazrui 1977), nepotism and other various indicators of the African problem. Patronage politics and prebendalism have also been fingered as causes of Africa's triple challenges (Alexander and McGregor 2013; McGregor 2013; Suberu 2013). Others located Africa's challenges in its over-dependence on foreign assistance and investment (Cruz and Schneider 2015; Grimm et al. 2014; Hellsten 2012; Jones and Tarp 2016; Niu 2014; Winters and Martinez 2015), while negating to grow and nature its capabilities, institutions and mechanisms. Yet blamed Africa's problems on the global aid economy (Moyo 2009).

Marxist scholars were convinced that the problem of poor leadership, injustice and human rights in Africa are as a result of capitalism (Gu et al. 2016; Lenin 1963; Lonsdale 2015; Shivji 2009; Southall 2013). For the Marxists, corruption, nepotism, violence, brutality, injustice etcetera can all be explained from a capitalist perspective (Cheng and Zaum 2013; Diaby and Sylwester 2015; Rotberg 2010b; Saunders 2014; Suberu 2013; Verheul 2013). For example, they argue that capitalism uses force, violence and injustice to get maximum profit (Gu et al. 2016; Igreja 2010; Sachikonye 2011).

Then there is what is what is termed state capture and its variant, elite capture as explanations of Africa's injustice, bad leadership and poor human rights record (Grzymala-Busse 2008; Hall and Kepe 2017). For William Reno, the African problem is that of clandestine economies (Reno 2000). Stunted nation-building has also been explored as a causality of injustice, bad leadership and human rights abuses in Africa (Nzongola-Ntalaja 1985; Nzongola-Ntalaja and Olukoshi 2001; Nzongola-Ntalanja 1997; Wamba dia Wamba 1992).

The latest theoretical framework in unpacking the African problem is decoloniality. Decolonial scholars admit that their framework is not new, what is new is the categorisation of the analytical units into three main categories, namely power, being and power. Other analytical units such as nature (Francis, Personal Communication 2 February 2019), markets (Tafira and Ndlovu-Gatsheni 2017) are still nascent and still work in progress.

There are merits in all the diagnoses above; however, their overarching shortcoming is that they did not emphasise the centrality of the colonial state in creating and maintaining the African problem for the benefit of the creators of the colonial state. The African state can therefore be correctly characterised as the fruits of a poisoned tree. The African problem, as will be demonstrated in the following paragraphs, is not an African problem but a colonial problem, precisely the colonial state. The colonial state is guilty of causing many African problems which manifest differently such as poor leadership, dictatorships, despotism, poor human rights and injustice. But first, what is the African problem?

Africa had great pre-colonial civilisations which were obliterated by a combination of Euro-North America modernity, colonialism and imported religions. In these pre-colonial civilisations, there were ways of attaining justice, upholding human rights and modes of leadership. One such civilisation was the now defunct Jenne-jeno whose decline and eventual demise was attributed to Islam. Located in inland Niger Delta region of central Mali, once stood one of Africa's greatest precolonial civilisations in a town known as Jenne-jeno (McIntosh 1995). The decline and eventual collapse of Jenne-jeno occurred between 1200 and 1400 CE and was captured thus:

> This occurs within a century of the traditional date of 1180 C.E. for the conversion of Jenne's king (Koi) Konboro to Islam .... After this point, Jenne-jeno begins a 200-year long period of decline and gradual abandonment, before it becomes a ghost town by 1400. ... Jenne-jeno declined at the expense of Jenne, perhaps related to the ascendancy of the new religion, Islam, over traditional practice. ... Whatever the cause of Jenne-jeno's abandonment, it was part of a larger process whereby most of the settlements occupied around Jenne in 1000 C.E. lay deserted by 1400. What caused such a realignment of the local population? .... Some people likely converted to Islam and moved to Jenne, where wealth and commercial opportunities were increasingly concentrated. (McIntosh Keech and McIntosh 2011)

While there were many factors which caused the decline and eventual demise of Jenne-jeno, the conversion of its inhabitants, especially the elites to Islam, the increase in trade at the new town Jenne and the increasing hostility of the climate which no longer permitted productive crop farming and animal husbandry. The bottom line is that one of Africa's greatest pre-colonial cavillations, Jenne-jeno, fell due to the combination of religion and Euro-North American modernity and commerce. Jenne-jeno, the African state, was killed and in its place Jenne, a colonial creation stands today.

What Is the Problem with African?

The African problem has been well articulated by a number of scholars. It has been variously stated with the dominant paradigm describing the African problem as a series of deficiencies and lacks. These 'lacks' include the lack of history, democracy, human rights, development, history, health and even manners. Decolonial scholars such as Ramon Grosfoguel and Ndlovu-Gatsheni rightly characterised the characterisation of Africa as:

> We went from the sixteenth century characterisation of 'people without writing' to the eighteenth and nineteenth century characterisation of 'people without history,' to the twentieth century characterisation of 'people without development' and more recently, to the early twenty-first century of 'people without democracy'. (Grosfoguel 2007: 214)

One of the foremost questions that deserve interrogation in the debate about the need for African solutions for Africa's triple challenges of leadership, human rights and justice is to conclusively state whether Africa is a failed continent. A failed continent is one where the majority of the member states exhibit Mazrui's characteristics of failed states. According to Mazrui's framework, Africa is not a failed continent. If one is to argue that Africa is a failed continent in terms of human rights abuses, poor leadership and injustice, then the counter-argument is that such a failure is an imported one, engineered and maintained by the (former) colonisers. The recent Arab Springs, the collapse of Libya, the Congo crises, the instability in the Great Lakes region all have marks of the (former) colonisers.

More evidence that the (former) colonisers are responsible for instilling and maintaining colonial states in Africa is the work of the French in their (former) colonies. It is no coincidence that 14 French colonies gained independence in the same year, 1960—a form of fake independence. Fake because the French coerced the 'nationalists' to sign 'independence' agreements wherein they gave up three crucial aspects of their economies. Without control of their currencies, foreign policies, natural resources (Chafer 2002; Eckert 2016; Ogunmola 2009). So problematic was the granting of independence to (former) French colonies that in 1960, the French President Charles de Gaulle almost had to impose independence on a reluctant Gabon—the epitome of an irony. France still controls and causes the problems in its (former) colonies through such institutions and mechanisms such as the French community; the *Communauté financière d'Afrique* (Financial Community of Africa) CFA Franc remains the base currency for Cameroon, Congo, Gabon, and the Central African Republic. On the other related hand, the West African CFA is the base currency for Benin, Burkina Faso, Guinea-Bissau, Ivory Coast, Mali, Niger, Senegal and Togo. Without financial sovereignty, there can be no justice or more so good leadership since the Francophone African leaders are (forcibly) answerable to France.

Stated differently, what was the logic of France demanding compensation from its former colonies in the 1960s when it ended its official colonisation of African countries (and commenced its unofficial colonisation of the same countries). Is this not the same logic used by white commercial farmers in Zimbabwe who lost 'their' farms to the state during the highly disputed land reform programme which commenced in 2000 (Nhemachena et al. 2018, p. 18).

The African (post) colonial state is therefore still extroverted and serving the agenda of the colonisers, a situation which needs to be reserved. This reversal requires that Africa base its justice logics, human rights underpinnings and leadership ethos on itself and its people. In the next section, I explain how the processes which created the colonial states in Africa created a brutal, resilient, transformative and hugely disguising colonial state. In their relationship with their (former) colonies, the (former) colonisers perform three central functions; they discipline, dispense and co-opt. Gaddafi was dispensed because he wanted to free Africa, Museveni, Mobutu Sese Seko Kuku Ngbendu Wa Za Banga, José Eduardo dos Santos, Abdel Fattah El-Sisi were co-opted.

The Creation of the Colonial State

The manner in which the colonial state was created in Africa is a key in any attempt at explaining the perennial lack of African development. The creation of the colonial state must be traced back to the Berlin conference where Europe consolidated the state sovereignty of its member states while at the same time proceeding to conquer and subdivide Africa, thereby denying Africa and Africans the same state sovereignty which they had just bestowed on themselves. Hence, the creation of the colonial state was part of the endeavour by European powers to create a mercantilist colonial unsovereign state. This type of state still exists everywhere in Africa today. Thus, Mbembe was correct in positing that the myth of decolonisation as one of the greatest myths in the nationalist agenda and served as a poison to the ideals of pan-Africanism.

The contests between nationalism and pan-Africanism form the part of Africa's problems. The relationship between nationalism and pan-Africanism can be characterised as one of mutual accommodation with nationalism emerging as the dominant one. This is where Africa's problems partly emanate from. Nationalism, which forms the base of Africa's response to national challenges, is a fake and cancerous base. As alluded to earlier on, African nationalism is a dangerous form of nationalism.

In terms of identity, it can be argued that Africanism, as a form of identity, occupies the bottom tier with Africans identifying themselves first with the tribe, the ethnic group, the nation, the region and finally the continent. For example, one can identify her/himself as a Khumalo, Ndebele, Zimbabwean, Southern African and finally, as an African.

Inflictions and afflictions bedevilling Africa have long been treated from a nationalistic and rarely from a continental perspective. The continental view, also referred to as the Africanist view, is traceable to Check Anta Diop who argued that Africa's many shared cultures and pre-colonial civilisations must be used as the reference point for solving Africa's problems (Anta Diop 1974, 1987, 1989). I argue in this article that the nation in Africa is a colonial product, one manufactured to meet colonial demands. As such, basing Africa's response to its plethora of challenges on nationalism is not only futile but misplaced because such challenges are rarely nationalistic in nature but purely continental, of which the nation is fake and the continent is real. African nationalism is counter pan-Africanism; it is a colonial idea meant to incubate colonialism and take it beyond decolonisation.

The Systems of the Colonial State and How They Trapped Africa

When the colonial state was created at the Berlin conference, it was engineered in such a way that it will only function as a satellite of the centre, a function which Africa fulfils to date. Africa's raw materials fuel the world economy, its people provide cheap labour both at home at abroad, and the continent remains the medical training ground of choice for pharmaceutical conglomerates. It is therefore not in the best capitalist interest of the centre to have a free and prosperous periphery.

The Institutionalisation of Coloniality

Coloniality operates at a global scale through the institutionalisation of all spheres of life. At the zenith of this system sits the five veto-welding victors of the Second World War. Essentially, the five veto-wielding members of the United Nations Security Council control global affairs. With them in charge, a victors' justice system ensues and is manned by the International Criminal Court and the International Court of Justice. Far from ensuring and enforcing global justice, these multilateral justice institutions perpetuate coloniality by safeguarding the interests of their creators, who are also their major funders.

On the Resilience of the Colonial State

The colonial state continues, because of a plethora of reasons, to thrive even after the official end of apartheid and colonialism in Africa. The chief reason being that the post-colonial colonial state is sustained by an African elite which effectively masquerades as nationalists. In reality, these elites are a front for Western capital and colonial gatekeepers. These are the same elite that hijacked genuine colonial moves by the peasants and turned them into their own fight for after the colonisers had refused them their demands not to be treated by the rest of Africa but rather to be treated as whites on the grounds that they were educated and had accumulated substantial wealth. Today, these same elites rule most of Africa with the same fate which the colonial subjects faced.

These elites are guilty of short-changing their subjects at various levels. First, they appear to be fighting for the cause of the majority, yet they fight for their own benefit. The masses blindly follow and believe in them, yet they Nicodemously wine and dine with Western capital, which they publicly denounce during the day. Wayne Reilly terms this the Hombe thesis, which is the ability of the African manager to skilfully mismanage the economy so that they benefit from the mismanagement. Second, they directly repress their citizenry if they demand genuine development and democracy (Reilly 1987). Third, these ruling elites became masters of articulating the problems of the people as if they are their own problems, thereby effectively muzzling the actual victims. Moeletsi Mbeki has to this to say about these black elites:

> Nationalism in Africa has always paraded itself as a movement of the people fighting for their liberation. The reality is, in fact, rather different. African nationalism was a movement of the small Westernised black elite that emerged under colonialism. Its fight was for the inclusion in the colonial system so that it, too, could benefit from the spoils of colonialism. (Mbeki 2009: 6)

Fourth, they facilitate and front of the extraction and exportation of raw materials from the periphery to the centre, thereby perpetuating Africa's mercantilist, peripheral and marginal position in the global economy. Fifth, they directly and indirectly syphon huge sums of money from state coffers to offshore accounts mainly in Switzerland and other havens such as the Isle of Man.

Prior to the official ending of apartheid and colonialism, the colonial state was buttressed through the formation of institutions and mechanisms, which ensure the continuity of the colonial interest and influence well into the post-colonial state. Such institutions and mechanisms include passports, identity documents, visas, and negotiated constitutions. Thus, if one does not have an identity document, they legally do not exist. Similarly, without a passport and or visa, one cannot enter certain countries. The constitutions of both Zimbabwe and South Africa were a result of protracted negotiations from which the colonisers got away with huge concessions, which made a mockery of the claims about the end of colonialism and apartheid.

Decoloniality Is the Answer

While presenting his inaugural full professorship lecture at the University of South Africa, Ndlovu-Gatsheni spoke about the need to decolonise the academic discipline of development studies. He ended by suggesting that the most credible way to end Africa's marginalisation and peripheral status in the world economy is perhaps decoloniality. Decoloniality makes a clear distinction between the processes of colonisation, decolonisation and coloniality. While decolonisation is the physical removal of the coloniser from the colony to the metropolis, coloniality is the continued presence of a sophisticated power matrix which continues to tilt power in favour of the coloniser and at the experience of the colonised. Decoloniality argues that the processes of colonisation did not end with the decolonisation of Africa as the colonial state simply indigenised itself and began the processes of masquerading as the post-colonial state, a situation which persists until today. The first step in ending the African problem is therefore one which involves the unmasking of the colonial state. This must be preceded by a realisation by the colonised people that we still exist in a colonial state. The onus is on the slave to first realise his/her slavery and start making taking action to end the situation. The slave master cannot be blamed for not freeing the slave from who he is deriving so many benefits.

One way of decolonising Africa is to charter a completely different developmental path often that is not Euro-American centred. Enrique Dussel calls this notion transmodernity (Dussel 1993). Eurocentrism is characterised by notion of "a unilateral and unidimensional form of democracy, citizenship, liberty, human rights, authority and economy" (Maldonado-Torres 2006). A transmodern world—a world beyond modernity—is open to a diversity of definitions of democracy, citizenship, liberty, human rights, authority and economy from the ethical-epistemic perspectives/historical projects (Maldonado-Torres 2004) of the silenced, subalternised and dominated side of the colonial difference.

Conclusion

In conclusion, and as a way of setting up the next seven chapters, I want to reiterate that the overarching aim of this chapter was to postulate that there can never be justice, human rights and good leadership in a colonial state precisely because it is yet to inhibit these three-core characteristics, thereby perpetuating colonialism in every form. The colonial state, together with its infrastructure such as the borders, parliaments and Westernised courts of law, is still effective today as it was when they were inaugurated. One way of overcoming this to have a level of the African Union and the various regional organisations that are solely constituted by African traditional leaders. Admittedly, African traditional leaderships of incumbency practice have been infiltrated, polluted and hijacked by (former) colonisers. There are aspersions over traditional authorities in Africa, as some of them became extensions and allies of the (former) colonisers.

How then do we solve this structural and lethal crisis of Africa? In line with the theme of this book, it is time for the continent to look in what even though it is still structurally and functionally colonised. Rwanda's President Paul Kagame argued that it is time for Africa to move away from seeking aid, assistance and development from elsewhere noting that it was time to gather like-minded people who will champion a much-desired shift in mindset. Kagame argued that Africa has reached a stage where it asks for aid even for things that it already has. This demonstrates the extent to which Africa created extroverted economies not only in terms of human development but also in terms of justice, leadership and human rights. In peroration, the logic, which got Africa to be a zone of injustice, bad leadership and poor human rights, is not capable of getting Africa from this problem.

References

Alexander, J., and J. McGregor. 2013. Introduction: Politics, Patronage and Violence in Zimbabwe. *Journal of Southern African Studies* 39 (4): 749–763.
Amin, S. 1976. *Unequal Development: An Essay on the Social Formations of Peripheral Capitalism*. New York: Monthly Review Press.
Anta Diop, C. 1974. *The African Origin of Civilization: Myth or Reality?*. Westport, CT: Lawrence Hill Books.
Anta Diop, C. 1987. *Precolonial Black Africa: A Comparative Study of the Political and Social Systems*. Westport, CT: Lawrence Hill Books.
Anta Diop, C. 1989. *The Cultural Unity of Black Africa: The Domains of Patriarchy and of Matriarchy in Classical Antiquity*. London: Karnak House.
Beach, D. 1998. Zimbabwe: Pre-colonial History, Demographic Disaster and the University. In *Inaugural Lecture of Professor David Beach, Department of History, University of Zimbabwe*. Harare: University of Zimbabwe.
Benyera, E. 2016. Expected Yet Uncomprehendible: Unpacking Death Through Nikolas Zakaria's Rufu Chitsidzo. *Gender & Behaviour* 14 (2): 7171–7181.
Benyera, E. 2017. Towards an Explanation of the Recurrence of Military Coups in Lesotho. *Air & Space Power Journal—Africa and Franchophonie, 8* (3), 56–73.

Chafer, T. 2002. Franco-African Relations: No Longer So Exceptional? *African Affairs* 101 (404): 343–363.
Cheng, C., and D. Zaum. 2013. *Corruption and Post-Conflict Peacebuilding: Selling the Peace*. London: Routledge.
Cobbe, J. 1983. The Changing Nature of Dependence: Economic Problems in Lesotho. *The Journal of Modern African Studies* 21 (2): 293–310.
Cruz, C., and C.J. Schneider. 2015. Foreign Aid and Undeserved Credit Claiming. *American Journal of Political Science* 61 (2): 396–408.
Dersso, S. 2012. The Quest for Pax Africana: The Case of the African Union's Peace and Security Regime. *African Journal on Conflict Resolution* 2: 137–158.
Diaby, A., and K. Sylwester. 2015. Corruption and Market Competition: Evidence from Post-Communist Countries. *World Development* 66: 487–499.
Dussel, E. 1993. Eurocentrism and Modernity (Introduction to the Frankfurt Lecturers). *Boundary 2*, *20* (3), 65–76.
Eckert, A. 2016. Re-examining Colonialism: The Past Is Never Dead.
Frank, A. G. 1966. *The Development of Underdevelopment*. Boston: MA: New England Free Press.
Frank, A.G. 1978. *Dependent Accumulation*. New York: McGrawhill Publishers.
Gaddafi, M., et al. 1976. *The Green Book. Evaluation*. Octavo: Martin, Brian & O'Keeffe.
Grimm, S., N. Lemay-Hébert, and O. Nay. 2014. 'Fragile States': Introducing a Political Concept. *Third World Quarterly* 35 (2): 197–209.
Grosfoguel, R. 2007. The Epistemic Decolonial Turn: Beyond Political-Economy Paradigms. *Cultural Studies* 21 (2–3): 211–223.
Grzymala-Busse, A. 2008. Beyond Clientelism: Incumbent State Capture and State Formation. *Comparative Political Studies*, (April 2007), 638–673.
Gu, J., C. Zhang, A. Vaz, and L. Mukwereza. 2016. Chinese State Capitalism? Rethinking the Role of the State and Business in Chinese Development Cooperation in Africa. *World Development*, *81*.
Hall, R., and T. Kepe. 2017. Elite Capture and State Neglect: New Evidence on South Africa's Land Reform. *Review of African Political Economy* 44 (151): 122–130.
Hellsten, S. K. 2012. Transitional Justice and Aid. *UNU-Wider*, 1–25.
Igreja, V. 2010. Traditional Courts and the Struggle against State Impunity for Civil Wartime Offences in Mozambique. *Journal of African Law* 54 (01): 51.
Johnson, T.H., R.O. Slater, and P. McGowan. 1984. Explaining African Military Coups d'Etat, 1960-1982. *The American Political Science Review* 78 (3): 622–640.
Jones, S., and F. Tarp. 2016. Does Foreign Aid Harm Political Institutions? *Journal of Development Economics*, *118*.
Kagame, P. 2014. Rebooting Rwanda: A Conversation With Paul Kagame. *Foreign Affairs* 93 (3): 40–48.
Lenin, V. 1963. *Imperialism, the Highest Stage of Capitalism*. Moscow: Progress Publishers.
Lonsdale, J. 2015. Have Tropical Africa's Nationalisms Continued Imperialism's World Revolution by Other Means? *Nations and Nationalism*, *21* (4).
Maldonado-Torres, N. 2006. Césaire's Gift and the Decolonial Turn. *Radical Philosophy Review* 9 (2): 111–139.
Mamdani, M. 2015. Political Identity, Citizenship and Ethnicity and Post-colonial Africa. In *Keynote address at the Arusha Conference "New Frontiers of Social Policy"* (pp. 1–18). Arusha.
Mandela, N. 1993. South Africa's Future Foreign Policy. *Foreign Affairs* 72 (5): 86–97.
Mandela, N. 1994. *Long Walk to Freedom: The Autobiography of Nelson Mandela*. Boston, MA: Little, Brown and Company.
Mawere, M. 2013. Traditional Environment Conservation Strategies in Pre-Colonial Africa: Lessons for Zimbabwe To Forget or To Carry Forward Into the Future? *Afro Asian Journal of Social Sciences* 4 (4): 1–23.

Mazrui, A.A. 1977. Early Struggles against Dependency: Nkrumah Versus de Gaulle. *Africa's International Relations: The Diplomacy of Dependency and Change*, 41–66. Boulder: Westview Press.

Mazrui, A.A. 1982. Africa Between Nationalism and Nationhood: A Political Survey. *Journal of Black Studies* 13 (1): 23–44.

Mazrui, A.A. 1995. The Blood of Experience: The Failed State and Political Collapse in Africa. *World Policy Journal* 12 (1): 28–34.

Mbeki, M. 2009. *Architects of Poverty. Why African Capitalism Needs Changing*. Johannesburg: Picador África.

Mbeki, T. 1998. *Statement of Deputy President Thabo Mbeki at the Opening of the Debate in the National Assembly, on "Reconciliation and Nation Building, National Assembly Cape Town, 29 May 1998*. Cape Town: South African History Online.

Mbembe, A. 2000. *On Private Indirect Government: State of the Literature Series Number 1*. Dakar, Senegal: CODESRIA Books.

McGregor, J. 2013. Surveillance and the City: Patronage, Power-Sharing and the Politics of Urban Control in Zimbabwe. *Journal of Southern African Studies, 39* (4).

McIntosh Keech, S., and R. J. McIntosh. 2011, March 13. Jenne-jeno, An Ancient African City. *Nairaland Forum*.

McIntosh, S. K. 1995. *Excavations at Jenné-Jeno, Hambarketolo, and Kaniana (inland Niger Delta, Mali), the 1981 Season*, ed. S. Keech McIntosh. University of California Publications in Anthropology. Berkeley, Los Angeles & London: University of California Press.

Mlambo, A.S. 2013. Becoming Zimbabwe or Becoming Zimbabwean: Identity. *Nationalism and. Africa Spectrum* 48 (1): 49–70.

Moyo, D. 2009. Why Foreign Aid Is Hurting Africa. *Wall Street Journal*, 1–6.

Mpofu, W. 2014. A Decolonial, "African Mode of Self-Writing": The Case of Chinua Achebe in Things Fall Apart. *New Contree* 69 (July): 1–25.

Mudenge, S. G. 1988. *A Political History of Munhumutapa, c.1400–1902*. Harare: Zimbabwe Publishing House.

Mudimbe, V. Y. 1988. *The Invention of Africa: Gnosis, Philosophy and the Order of Knowledge*. Bloomington & Indianapolis: Indiana University Press.

Mudimbe, V.Y. 1991. *Parables and Fables: Exegesis, Textuality, and Politics in Central Africa*. Winscinsin: University of Wisconsin Press.

Mudimbe, V. Y. 1994. *The Idea of Africa*. Bloomington & Indianapolis: Indiana University Press.

Museveni, Y. 2000. *What is Africa's Problem?*. Minneapolis: University of Minnesota Press.

Muzodidya, J., and S. Ndlovu-Gatsheni. 2007. "Echoing Silences": Ethnicity in Post-Colonial Zimbabwe, 1980-2007. *African Journal on Conflict Resolution* 7 (2): 275–297.

Ndlovu-Gatsheni, S. J. 2010. Do 'Africans' Exist? Genealogies and Paradoxes of African Identities and the Discourses of Nativism and Xenophobia. *African Identities, 8*(March 2015), 281–295.

Ndlovu-Gatsheni, S.J. 2011. The World Cup, Vuvuzelas, Flag-Waving Patriots and the Burden of Building South Africa. *Third World Quarterly* 32 (2): 279–293.

Ndlovu-Gatsheni, S.J. 2015. Decoloniality as the Future of Africa. *History Compass* 13 (10): 485–496.

Nhemachena, A., T.V. Warikandwa, and S.K. Amoo. 2018. Identity, Originality and Hybridity in Jurisprudence and Social Theory: An Introduction. In *Social and Legal Theory in the Age of Decoloniality: (Re-)Envisioning African Jurisprudence in the 21st Century*, ed. A. Nhemachena, T.V. Warikandwa, and S.K. Amoo, 1–72. Bamenda, Cameroon: Langaa.

Niu, Z. 2014. China's Development and Its aid Presence in Africa: A Critical Reflection from the Perspective of Development Anthropology. *Journal of Asian and African Studies* 51 (2): 199–221.

Nkrumah, K. 1965. *Neo-Colonialism: The Last Stage of Imperialism*. New York: International Publishers.

Nyerere, J.K. 1968. *UJAMAA—Essays on Socialism*. Dar es Salaam, Nairobi, London and New York: Oxford University Press.

Nyerere, J. K. 2008. African Studies: A United States of Africa A United States of Africa, (1963), 1–6.
Nyika, N. 2014. Discourses of Ethnicity in Zimbabwe: Deliberative Democracy or Online Misogyny? *Language Matters* 45 (3): 342–359.
Nzongola-Ntalaja, G. 1985. The National Question and the Question of Crisis. *Alternatives* 26: 533–563.
Nzongola-Ntalaja, G., and A. Olukoshi. 2001. *Africa in the New Millennium*, ed. R. Suttner. Uppsala: Nordiska Afrikainstitutet.
Nzongola-Ntalanja, G. 1997. The Role of Intellectuals in the Struggle for Democracy, Peace and Reconstruction in Africa. *African Journal of Political Science* 2 (2): 1–14.
Ogunmola, D. 2009. Redesigning Cooperation: The Eschatology of Franco-African Relations. *Journal of Social Scinces* 19 (3): 233–242.
Pikirayi, I. 1999. David Beach, Shona Histry and the Archaeology of Zimbabwe. *Zambezia*, *xxvi* (ii), 105–116.
Ranger, T. 1984. Missionaries, Migrants and the Manyika: Ethnicity in Zimbabwe. *Witwatersrand African Studies Seminar*, (146).
Ranger, T. 1989. Missionaries, Migrants and the Manyika: The Invention of Ethnicity in Zimbabwe. In *The Creation of Tribalism in Southern Africa*, ed. L. Vail, 118–151. London and Berkeley: Currey University of California Press.
Reilly, W. 1987. Management and Training for Development: The Hombe Thesis. *Public Administration and Development* 7 (1): 25–42.
Reno, W. 2000. Clandestine Economies, Violence and States in Africa. *Journal of International Affairs* 53 (2): 433–459.
Rotberg, R. 2010a. *Failed States, Collapsed States, Weak States: Causes and Indicators*. Princeton: Princeton University Press.
Rotberg, R. 2010b. *Weak States: Causes and Indicators. When States Fail Causes & Consequences*. Princeton: Princeton University Press.
Rotberg, R. 2012. *Transformative Political Leadership: Making a Difference in the World*. London and Chicago: Chicago University Press.
Sachikonye, L. 2011. *When a State Turns on Its Citizens: 60 Years of Institutionalised Violence in Zimbabwe*. Johannesburg: Jacana Media.
Saunders, R. 2014. Geologies of Power: Blood Diamonds, Security Politics and Zimbabwe's Troubled Transition. *Journal of Contemporary African Studies*, *32* (3).
Shivji, I.G. 2009. *Accumulation in an African Periphery: A Theoretical Framework. World*. Dar es Salaam: Mkuki na Nyota Publishers.
Sithole, M. 1980. Ethnicity and Functionalism in Zimbabwe Nationalist Politics 1957–79. *Ethnic & Racial Studies* 3 (1): 17.
Southall, R. 2013. *Liberation Movements in Power. Party & State in Southern Africa*.
Suberu, R.T. 2013. Prebendal Politics and Federal Governance in Nigeria. In *Democracy and Prebendalism in Nigeria: Critical Interpretations*, ed. W. Adebanwi and E. Obadare, 79–101. New York: Palgrave Macmillan.
Tafira, C.K., and S.J. Ndlovu-Gatsheni. 2017. Beyond Coloniality of Markets-Exploring the Neglected Dimensions of the Land Question from Endogenous African Decolonial Epistemological Perspectives. *Africa Insight* 46 (4): 9–24.
Vail, L. 1989. *The Creation of Tribalism in Southern Africa*. Berkeley, Los Angeles and Oxford: University of California Press.
van Wyk, J.-A. 2007. Political Leaders in Africa: Presidents, Patrons or Profiteers? *ACCORD Occational Paper Series*. Durban: The African Centre for the Constructive Resolution of Disputes.
Verheul, S. 2013. 'Rebels' and 'Good Boys': Patronage, Intimidation and Resistance in Zimbabwe's Attorney General's Office after 2000. *Journal of Southern African Studies* 39 (4): 765–782.
Wamba dia Wamba, E. 1992. Beyond Elite Politics of Democracy in Africa. *Quest*, *6* (2), 55–69.

Winters, M.S., and G. Martinez. 2015. The Role of Governance in Determining Foreign Aid Flow Composition. *World Development* 66: 516–531.

Wiredu, K. 1998. Toward Decolonizing African Philosophy and Religion. *African Studies Quarterly* 1 (4): 18–45.

Everisto Benyera is Associate Professor of African Politics in the Department of Political Sciences at the University of South Africa in Pretoria, South Africa. He is Decolonial Reader and holds an M.Sc. in International Relations from the University of Zimbabwe and a Ph.D. in African Politics from the same university. He researches on transitology and transitional justice focusing on indigenous, traditional and non-state reconciliation, peacebuilding and healing mechanisms. He is Editor of the journal *Politeia*, Journal of Political Sciences and Public Administration and Management and his publications are accessible via: https://orcid.org/0000-0002-2706-9097 and https://independent.academia.edu/EveristoBenyera.

Part II
Justice

Chapter 3
The Tyranny of the Coloniality of Nature and the Elusive Question of Justice

Romain Francis

Abstract This chapter alleges that attempts to frame a universal environmental ethic to accommodate the varied experiences of social groups in the Global South struggling against ecological injustices are based on a hegemonic Euro-American conception of human–nature relations. It contends that critical approaches that reveal how non-Europeans and subsequently the natural world were excluded from the evolving discourse of environmentalism, whilst claiming to reconcile "brown" with "green" issues actually conceals a more fundamental pattern of power that reproduces ecological injustice. The main point of departure is that environmental degradation and efforts at conserving and protecting nature are ostensibly part of a process of dehumanization born of western imperialism that continues to define not only our ecological past, but our ecological futures as well—what is referred to here as the tyranny of the coloniality of nature. By historicising, theorising and applying the coloniality of nature as an analytical tool to demonstrate the inextricable link between oppression of the subaltern and nature, this chapter will also through a personal experience, propose an alternate path to ecological justice. This represents a decolonial turn in forging an authentic environmental ethic, which is informed by the knowledge, experiences, cultures and practices of the oppressed.

Keywords Justice · Ecology · Coloniality of nature · Dehumanisation · Environmental ethic and decolonial turn

Introduction

Ethical considerations underpinning efforts at arriving at a just environmentalism is often presumed to have a universal appeal and relevance that accommodates cultural, religious, social, national and economic difference. They are mainly predicated on the principle of plurality that advances multiculturalism encouraging competing

---

R. Francis (✉)
University of South Africa, Office 23, 7th Floor Theo van Wijk Building, Pretoria 0003, South Africa
e-mail: francr@unisa.ac.za

ideas and perspectives on nature and creating a dialogic epistemic platform for an interdisciplinary (and transdisciplinary) approach towards effective environmental management and protection. In short, it is premised on the idea that the ecological crisis is global and therefore transcends national borders and identities, the effects of which are indiscriminate and tangible. Few issues, if any, have the potential to galvanize humanity around a common struggle and ideal than that of the environment, more especially climate change. In reality, however, environmental ethics is essentially a product of Western frames of thought that evolved within a particular spatio-temporality and became ubiquitous with the advent of European colonisation. The particularity of the Euro-American subject's experience, knowledge and culture assumed a dominant status in the articulation of discourses on nature by virtue of the imposition of an ontological dichotomy that rendered non-Europeans as sub or non-human. Consequently, other cosmologies and modes of understanding and representing human–nature relations beyond the borders of the occident were not only dismissed, misinterpreted, misrepresented and misappropriated, but also relegated to the margins of ethical reasoning and practice. Although attempts have been made by radical schools of thought to establish an ethics that reconcile social justice concerns of vulnerable peoples in the Global South with the destruction of the natural environment culminating in a more inclusive ecological justice that is neither anthropocentric or biocentric, this simply serves to reproduce an exclusiveness that is endemic to environmentalism.

This does not only point to the fact that environmentalism can be construed as elitist, but also is a project of Western domination that perpetuates the subjugation of people and environments (more aptly ecologies). It emphasises that environmental degradation and efforts at conserving and protecting nature are ostensibly part of a process of dehumanisation born of western imperialism that continues to define not only our ecological past, but our ecological futures as well—what is referred to here as the tyranny of the coloniality of nature. In addition to historicising, theorising and applying the coloniality of nature as an analytical tool to demonstrate the inextricable link between oppression of certain people and nature and how this undermines establishing a universal ethic that is authentically inclusive, this chapter will also, by way of example of a personal experience, propose an alternate path to ecological justice. This epitomises the decolonial turn which advances an environmental ethic that is directly informed by the knowledge, experiences, cultures and practices of people from the alterity and that also has the potential to contribute to the establishment of a more inclusive environmentalism.

Environmentalism as a Discourse of Power: Eurocentricity and Environmental Justice Struggles

For most ecophilosophers, the exponential increase in ecological degradation is symptomatic of the moral decadence of modern industrial society. There is a growing consensus that human–nature relations need to be re-evaluated and a "new" environmental ethic is required to ensure the survival of the future generations. The biocentricity of traditional environmentalism, which advances a conception of justice exploring the extension of rights and freedoms to both sentient creatures and inanimate objects of nature, is esoteric. Besides the impracticability of establishing a legislative and judicial framework for justice predicated on a normative dimension that affords nature a similar degree of ethical value as humans, it places conservation and preservation of flora and fauna (conservation and preservation) ahead of the social justice concerns of the poor (or "brown" issues). Postmodernists therefore criticised traditional environmentalism for being misanthropic, romanticising nature (or, more appropriately, wilderness), ostensibly circumventing the discourses on environmental racism and sexism masking human oppression, making 'disputed values non-essential, eternal and innate' (Cronon 1995: 36). The postmodernist approach influenced the formation of the environmental justice movement (EJM) as a response to environmental racism in the 1980s. It emphasised the centrality of geopolitics as its ethical basis advocating for subjective self-conscious constructions of environment. Hence, the EJM defined the environment through a strictly anthropocentric lens as where 'we live, work and play' reducing nature to a container through which social processes occur, rather than something that we (humans) interact with as a subject of political and economic processes (Rangan and Kull 2009: 32; Bryner 2002: 40).

Attuned to this critique, poststructuralists argued that the postmodernist approach to environmental justice does not consider how the subject imposes itself onto the objective or real environment and how this in turn determines consciousness of her/his surroundings. Whether natural or unnatural, environments are very much human constructions influenced by significant historical processes that conceal structures of power determining not only how specific groups relate to other subjects and objects in their immediate locus (or *habitus*), but how they came to see, experience, value, understand and interact with the natural world. Consequently, the poststructuralist approach to environmentalism portends that before contemplating a universal ethics that includes a plurality of justice struggles across spatio-temporalities accommodating different interpretations of "environment", it is necessary to understand the instrumental role that massive project of modernity and capitalism has played in separating humans from nature.

In bringing humans closer to nature through aesthetics, science and natural history, these "technologies" of modernity have paradoxically pulled us further away. Transformations of ecologies and landscapes, and the knowledge we possess of human relations with them, are products of a dominant Western philosophical tradition and culture. The values afforded to nature, borne out of a strictly Cartesian logic and Judeo-Christian belief system, have imposed a moral imperative on environmental ethics (Lane and Clarke 2006: 63; Rolston 2004: 94). Under the guise of a broader humanism, efforts at extending instrumental value to nature within an anthropocentric utilitarian intergenerational framework for justice have exacerbated ecological degradation and the unequal distribution of environmental benefits and burdens. Poststructuralists allude to the concealment of truth, emphasising how supposedly just solutions to the ecological and development crisis through market-based, political and social institutions have actually perpetuated rather than remedied injustices against people and nature. Protests highlighting discontent with climate change mitigation policies implemented at recent meetings of the United Nations Framework Convention on Climate Change (UNFCCC) reflect civil society's awareness of the inauthenticity of existing environmental justice frameworks. Carbon sequestration strategies claiming to promote sustainable development through carbon sinks, the distribution of carbon credits and ecological modernisation for vulnerable peoples and environments, are seen as instruments of ecological and social oppression, rather than agents for justice (Bond 2012: 51). Marginalised people, as designated beneficiaries of environmental justice, know that plantations are not forests and that supposedly clean development mechanisms lead to the "greening" of the North and the "browning" of the South—blacks, indigenous peoples, women and children shoulder the burden of development and conservation without reaping the rewards.

Ironically, environmental conscientisation has not translated into a robust environmental justice movement that is able to reconcile the broad intersection of environmental interests across race, class, ethnicity and culture. The failure of the Environmental Justice Networking Forum (EJNF) of South Africa[1]—that was meant to serve as an umbrella body for a myriad of grassroots organisations, community-based organisations, social movements, worker organisations and women's rights organisations since its inception in 1992—is testament to this. The historical dichotomy between conservation and quality-of-life or needs-based environmental concerns has made the task of bringing these issues together extremely difficult in terms of promoting a holistic approach to environmental justice. Mainstream white-dominated environmental organisations such as the National Parks Board and the Wildlife Society opposed the construction of development-oriented projects meant to create employment opportunities for disenfranchised black South Africans, such as the Saldanha steel plant in 1995, because it posed a threat to wildlife in the nearby West Coast National Park and the Langebaan lagoon. The surrounding black communities, on the other hand, were in full support of this proposed development as a viable source of employment providing much-needed relief from their state of poverty (Khan 2002: 38). This complex conflict of interests and value over the distribution of, and access to, environmental benefits and burdens across racial lines has characterised the environmental discourse not only in post-apartheid South Africa, but also in former colonies throughout the world.

The source of this problem is based on the fact that discourses on environmental justice and social mobilisation efforts in the developing world are universally

---

[1] http://www.ngopulse.org/article/environmental-justice-networking-forum [Accessed on 5 September 2018].

determined by international environmental non-governmental organisations (NGOs) from Europe and America, such as *Greenpeace* and *Friends of the Earth*, which are unable to address the particularity of unique socio-political and historical *loci*. As Richard Grove (1990: 11) had the insight to note more than two decades ago in his commentary on *The Origins of Environmentalism*, 'most attempts to understand the roots of conservationist responses to the destructive effects of man on nature have been largely confined to Europe and North America'. This claim to universality of the environmental justice discourse is based on power effects. It advocates a human-centred approach to environmental justice, creating political and intellectual spaces for marginalised peoples to articulate their realities, whilst the epistemic roots of environmental thinking and activism within these spaces are firmly entrenched in the particularism of the dominant Euro-American viewpoint that has been universalised. In other words, formalised institutional platforms such as local environmental organisations and movements in the Global South ostensibly risk advocating a western-centric environmental agenda rather than one tailored to their own needs since they are heavily reliant on donor funding and human resources from global eNGOs and political parties based in the Global North. A scenario is created where we end up speaking *about* the subaltern *with*, but not *from* the subaltern. As Ribeiro (2011: 286) alludes, when attempting to address a common challenge like that of the environment in a globalised world:

> ... the problem is the imperial pretension to hegemony, the imposition of viewpoints that are disseminated through painless structures of prestige diffusion from global or national hegemonic centres. (Ribeiro 2011: 286)

Hence, the main concern with postmodern and poststructuralist strategies towards establishing an environmental ethic is that, in claiming to be committed to revealing the truth about modernity and being self-critical, they conceal the darker side of modernity, which is a *coloniality of nature*. The *coloniality of nature* infers the commoditisation of nature resulting in profligate exploitation and conspicuous consumption dismissing its phenomenological and ontological value in the cultural, epistemic and identity formation of the subaltern. Escobar (2007: 197) argues that the environmental crisis represents the limits of a modern instrumental rationality indicative of 'modernity's failure to articulate biology and history save through the capitalisation of nature and labour'. Through this regime of the capitalisation of nature, other articulations of biology, history and the relationship between society and nature (representing cosmological ties between local cultural practices, the natural world and the supernatural) have been subalternised. Hence, the *coloniality of nature* reflects the hegemony and cultural monotony of one particular knowledge, understanding and experience of human–nature relations—that of Western Europe and North America, the primary agents of modernity.

The Euro-American perspective is therefore endemic to ideological, theoretical and sociological discourses on nature with the occident established as the epistemological and ontological centre of the world (Coronil 1996: 60). Inevitably, no matter how subversive postmodernist and poststructuralist critiques (including radical forms of environmental ethics like Arne Næss' utopian deep ecology approach that affords equal rights to all sentient and non-sentient entities in the biosphere) appear to be, they are still recognised. The knowledge and experiences of indigenous peoples on environmental thought and practice from Africa, Latin America and Asia, are wilfully ignored. This dismissive attitude is predicated on indigenous people, blacks and women as beings incapable of generating morals and producing knowledge, but as moral subjects and knowledge consumers. People on the exteriority, therefore, belong to the *anthropos* and not the *humanitas* (Mignolo 2011: 275). It is this binary of the *anthropos/humanitas* that presents the greatest challenge to achieving a true and sustainable environmental ethics that is able to avert the oppression of nature and people.

Othering Nature and Peoples: Unveiling Cartesian Logic

The epistemic origin of human–nature relations is grounded in Cartesian logic. Since nature is incapable of reason, it is therefore not a moral agent to which rights and freedoms can be afforded (Doppelt 2002: 396). Through the lens of the Cartesian subject or *cogito*, the natural world only possesses epistemic value in so far as it can be measured in terms of mathematical formulae and logic. The neutral consciousness of the *cogito* reduced nature to an object of study using an empirical method that formed the epistemic foundations of the natural sciences through the blind belief that the application of universal categorical imperatives will always produce truth (Padrutt 1992: 20). Radical interventions questioning the universality of scientific knowledge from the enlightenment onwards, emerged in Thomas Kuhn's magnum opus, *Structure of Scientific Revolutions* in the 1960s (Harding 2008). Although it served as seminal text challenging Western science as a linear, progressive discourse pointing to significant paradigm shifts subverting universal truths, it offered its critique within the logocentric and phallocentric paragon of the *cogito*—what Nelson Maldonado-Torres (2006: 123) refers to as 'subversive complicity'. Hence, it did not raise ontological questions that attempted to extend greater cultural and moral value to the natural world. Instead, it reified the notion that our relationship with nature is therefore purely mechanistic and material and does not have ontological relevance or worth (Paterson 2006: 147). Nature is therefore an object of reason and is not related to our "being". By universalising Cartesian logic, humans placed nature firmly in the exteriority and justified the need to control and order it.

Besides othering nature, the Cartesian subject or *Cogito* excludes certain people from the realm of reason and moral judgement. Not all peoples have the benefit of God's eye view of the Cartesian subject. In fact, it conceals an insidious racism which Descartes himself inferred, that justified an objective subjectification of non-Europeans. Descartes repudiated the perceivably primitive thought and barbarism of people outside the occident. In his, *Discourses on Colonialism*, Aimé Césaire (1972: 56) highlights this exception, referring to Descartes' statement, the charter on universalism, that 'reason . . . is found whole and entire in each man' and that 'where individuals of the same species are concerned, there may be degrees in respect

3   The Tyranny of the Coloniality of Nature ...

of their accidental qualities, but not in respect of their forms, or natures'. Quijano (2007: 173–174) elucidates how these 'differences were admitted primarily above all as inequalities in a hierarchical sense', relegating non-Europeans to objects rather than subjects of reason. Blacks and indigenous people thus needed to be civilised because they lacked ontological density. They were deemed devoid of a soul and without a God; prerequisites to assume the objective consciousness of the all-knowing Cartesian subject (Mills 2007: 18).

Ironically, later critiques of the exclusivity of Cartesian logic by European scholars through existential phenomenology that attempted to bring together language, land/soil or nature as part of a broader national liberation discourse, ostensibly reified Cartesian racist underpinnings, whilst establishing ontological connections to nature (Maldonado-Torres 2004: 33). Heidegger (2014), whose work exploring metaphysics provided the philosophical basis for German nationalism, also spawned a 'new-age' conservationism emphasising the organic link between "being" and nature. Under fascist Germany, nature conservation assumed a deeper meaning. Any acts considered to be damaging to conservation areas such as the Black Forest were seen as inimical to German nationalism and warranted extreme forms of punishment. Indigenous flora and fauna became symbols of nationalism, but closely enmeshed in their own epistemic liberation from the cultural hegemony of the French and British philosophical literary tradition. However, this form of conservationism was linked to a type of ecofascism that emphasised the superiority of its own people, experiences and ecologies. Conservation thinking and practice in Germany followed the imperial scientific tradition of the British Royal Geographic Society, as well as the French School of Forestry in Nancy, which was imbued with Cartesian logic (Grove 1997: 31). Germany was in a race with former colonial powers to establish itself as a leader in conservation science paradoxically affirming the logocentric and technologic order of the Cartesian subject. Natural sciences, which began in enlightenment Europe in the eighteenth century through the taxonomy of various species of plants and animals, were shaped by an empirical-scientific method or logic strictly endemic to the European experience.

As we will come to see, knowledge of ecologies outside Europe with the onset of colonisation was only considered credible if filtered through the European cultural prism using "superior" Western scientific methodologies (Beinart 2000: 298). Since non-Europeans were objects of Cartesian logic and not subjects, they too were on the exteriority. Unlike the all-knowing European, they were incapable of reason and lacked morals; hence, their knowledge of nature was based on superstition, folklore and myth and the practices informed by them were therefore inherently flawed and pejorative to the natural world (Walsh 2007: 225).

Prominent libertory black scholars such as Frantz Fanon and Lewis R. Gordon infer how environmental determinist discourses emanating from scientific racism, colonial domination and white European superiority as part of the Cartesian legacy, metaphorically attributed certain animal characteristics to the colonised people belonging to the *anthropos*. Within this context, 'Africans could be interpreted as creatures of nature, exhibiting the indolence induced by the tropics, or subject to 'primitive' impulses born of a non-technological society' (Beinart and McGregor

2003: 7). These people were seen as savages and, like the "wilderness" (nature), in need of taming as part of the broader civilising mission of colonisation. The othering of nature was synonymous with the othering of colonised people (*anthropos*); both on the exteriority of the *humanitas*. As this chapter illustrates, the forceful imposition of a hegemonic Western scientific knowledge on conservation and Euro-American viewpoints of ecologies, coupled with a dismissal of indigenous people as producers of knowledge on nature and their ontological connections with it, entrenched a *coloniality of nature* which has perpetuated the current destruction of peoples and nature.

Tracing the Coloniality of Nature

The *coloniality of nature* can be traced back to the single most significant turning point in history, the colonisation of the Americas in 1492. Industrialisation in Europe precipitated colonial expansion into the New World in search of exotic places providing a cornucopia of natural resources and fertile lands to fuel a bourgeoning capitalist system (Guha and Martinez-Allier 1997: 82). The colonisation of the Americas not only marked the creation of the modern world system based on imperial designs representing a coloniality of power, it was justified on the pretext of a civilising mission, to save the souls of savages and to tame "wild" lands—what Rudyard Kipling referred to as the 'white man's burden' (Beinart 2000: 270). On the pretence of spreading civility, ethics and justice, the colonial encounter sardonically led to the massacring of indigenes. The modernising and "civilising" mission of Europeans was defined by a suspension of ethics. As people without a soul, a history and reason belonging strictly to the *anthropos*, the unleashing of brutality and diversion from morals was an accepted practice—they needed to be rescued from their nothingness:

> The paradox of 1492 is posited in the increasingly sharp conflict which interprets it as a "glorious achievement", a heroic deed of discovery, "a triumph of the Christian West" on one hand, and on the other hand, as a brutal invasion and conquest which led to the genocidal extinction of large numbers of indigenes as well as set in train the now looming prospect of an ecological catastrophe (Wynter 1991: 258).

Crucially, this genocide of indigenes was made possible not only through material violence, but with the assistance of what Crosby (2004:162), in his groundbreaking work on ecological imperialism, refers to as a 'portmanteau biota'. In addition to guns, Europeans brought pathogens and alien plant and animal species to the New World. With the establishment of empire, they attempted to create 'neo-Europes', taking with them plants and domesticated animals to other regions of the world which were nostalgic remnants of the landscape and ecology they had left behind in Europe. The effects were devastating: unknown diseases such as smallpox-decimated indigenous populations who had no immunity (Crosby 2004: 200). Besides destroying people, this 'portmanteau biota' coupled with the avarice of settler communities steeped in a modern economy that commoditised nature and saw landscape as private property, also resulted in an ecocide. Alien invasive species threatened to wipe out a significant number of indigenous flora and fauna, erasing the "memory" that the landscape and ecologies had of themselves, in some instances leading to mass extinctions of certain species.

Debunking Imperial Scientific Myth

Most pertinently, the colonial encounter laid the foundations for a *coloniality of nature* that survived colonisation and continues to shape current discourses on environmental ethics that are disingenuous and intensify (rather than ameliorate) the oppression of people and nature. Colonisation was accompanied by a particular imagination of primitive people and wilderness in the New World that itself was a construct, ironically informed by myth, instead of scientific facts. The colonial imagination of nature in peripheral regions such as Africa viewed it as being virgin lands and pristine wilderness untouched by humans—informed by what J. M. Blaut referred to as a 'diffusionist myth of emptiness' (Maldonado-Torres 2004: 37). This imagination culminated in a colonial conservation discourse that vilified indigenous peoples as destroyers of nature and portrayed white settlers as defenders of it (Beinart 2000: 271). Conservation thinking was therefore informed by an authoritarian racial discourse. This reflected the *hubris of zero point*, a particular arrogance unique to the superiority of colonial science based on a proclaimed neutrality and epistemic authority. Colonial scientists, upon witnessing indigenous people utilising fire for hunting and agricultural purposes, based their judgements on scientific discourses on the use of fire and its impact on ecology from the European experience. As Pyne (1997: 25) argues, the use of fire by peasant communities in Europe was a heretical practice, which was seen to deplete soil nutrients and encourage desertification and species extinction.

Hence, when early European explorers came across unfamiliar ecologies and witnessed what appeared to be destructive practices (such as the use of fire), it was based on a wilful ignorance of the landscape and ecologies and, more significantly, the knowledge indigenous people had of them. When John Croumbie Brown, the Scottish missionary and colonial botanist, was assigned the task of establishing the botanical gardens in Cape Town, South Africa, he misread the unique ecology of the region and ignored the agency of the indigenous San (who frequently employed slash-and-burn techniques for hunting purposes) in shaping this ecosystem. He implemented draconian conservation policy measures banning the use of fire by the indigenous San. Through his later research, Croumbie Brown discovered that the unique flora in the Cape region, the *fynbos*, was a fire-propagated biota that relied almost exclusively on anthropogenic fire (Grove 1997: 149). Contrary to the "scientific facts" disseminated throughout the empire by early European colonial botanists, scientists and naturalists who associated the fire burning practices of indigenes with desiccation in the colonies, later scientific evidence illustrated how unique biomes such as the Cape *fynbos* evolved over millennia to adapt and subsequently rely on indigenous people for its survival. Indigenous 'fire communities' were therefore agents of conservation, rather than destruction. Curiously, it was the broad-based introduction of exotic plant species (such as *hakea* and *eucalyptus*) as part of forestry conservation efforts by colonial botanists to prevent desiccation, that invaded and threatened to decimate the indigenous *fynbos*, than the traditional fire practices of the San (Beinart and Coates 1995: 41).

Nature and National (*Dis*)unity

Conservation practice in the colonies, governed by an inherently racist logic, was perpetuated by settler communities between the late eighteenth and early nineteenth century. In the process of establishing a national identity, settler communities such as the Afrikaners (*trekboers*), as part of their liberation from colonial dominance, emphasised the need to form cultural ties with the land. The demarcation of national game reserves such as the Kruger National Park and the implementation of draconian hunting and gathering laws under the auspices of the Afrikaner Republic (and later the apartheid regime) were used as instruments of appropriation, which separated indigenous blacks ontologically from nature. Carruthers (1994: 268) argues that the creation of game reserves was essentially based on political considerations rather than an ingenuous commitment to protecting wildlife and nature. The proposed demarcation of a game reserve area under the auspices of Paul Kruger in the South Eastern Transvaal, in the gorge of the Pongola River, containing seven small farms at the confluence of the Swaziland, Transvaal, New Republic and Tongaland borders, was portrayed as the primary solution to preserving diminishing wildlife. However, it served the strategic interests of the Transvaal government, instead, providing access to the sea through Tongaland, which gave the Afrikaner Republic greater control over access to the territory and the authority to evict Africans from the land (Carruthers 1994: 268).

The national parks and nature conservation served an even bigger purpose as an ideologue of Afrikaner nationalism (Carruthers 1997). Whilst Afrikaners were undergoing an indigenisation process, forming symbolic cultural relations to the South African environment, precipitating a rich frontier and conservation history, it simultaneously led to the disindigenisation of black communities. Indigenous blacks were forcibly removed from designated nature reserve areas and relocated to native reserves or Bantustans, as their primitive hunting and gathering and farming practices were perceived as inimical to natural flora and fauna (Cock and Fig 2002: 132). Besides being denied material access to certain plants and animals pivotal to their livelihoods, the memory of natural landscapes and cultural identities (defined by their experiences and interactions with the natural world) was also being erased. Even within the extremely limited confines of the Bantustans, the agricultural practices of blacks were often the subject of blame for soil erosion and the subsequent loss of biodiversity (Beinart 2000: 298).

In most instances, indigenous traditional animal husbandry methods, notably open veld (field) or rangeland grazing combined with overstocking, were cited as the primary cause of soil erosion. As Yngstrom (2003: 177–178) illustrates, 'Africans were constructed as "unscientific exploiters" with a poor understanding of the local ecology and production techniques, in contrast to colonial agricultural knowledge generated from its own modern "scientific" research base'. Agricultural practices following normal European farming models forcefully implemented through betterment schemes in the 1930s (such as straight-line cropping) were meant to protect indigenous flora from the perceivably pejorative mound-cropping and shifting agricultural techniques of black farmers. However, scientific research conducted at the time proved that traditional methods of farming using fire as a catalyst for soil rejuvenation were far more effective than straight-line agricultural methods relying on the application of organic and chemical fertilisers (Tilley 2003: 120). White administrative officers managing the native reserves or Bantustans failed to acknowledge the impact that policies such as the Native Lands Act of 1913 and 1936 had in contributing to environmental degradation (Beinart and Coates 1995: 66). Prior to European colonisation and the imposition of land as private property based on European legal convention, contrary to the indigenous understanding of land as 'commons', there was an abundance of grazing land available for African pastoralists such as the Khoisan to exploit. The open veld or rangeland grazing techniques employed by indigenous pastoral communities, in a context where land was sparsely populated and could support large herds of livestock, promoted conservation of the landscape and sensitive ecologies. The constant movement of cattle over vast areas ensured that land was never overgrazed and that indigenous flora recovered quickly. In fact, this technique assisted in the propagation of biota, rather than contributing to the denudation of the landscape (Beinart 2000: 279).

Interestingly, agricultural scientists who undertook their own research in native reserves often found scientific evidence indicating the superior effectiveness and ecological relevance of indigenous agricultural practices compared to modern scientific techniques that, in certain instances, led some colonial scientists to question the wilful ignorance of modern science in recognising indigenous people as primary authentic knowledge producers. H. R. Hosking, a botanist in Uganda's Department of Agriculture, stated that 'the question of improving native food crops is beset with difficulties' since with such 'long established crops it is probably true to say that the native can teach us more than we can teach him' (Tilley 2003: 116).

Perpetuating Oppression of Nature and Peoples Through Justice

Postcolonial science in the modern democratic context has exacerbated environmental degradation and underdevelopment in former colonies. Witt (2010: 300–301) alludes to how the biotechnology revolution that defined the 'last decade of the twentieth century ushered the promise of a new age in agricultural productivity whereby genetically engineered crops would be potentially powerful aids to sustainable agriculture, improved food security and profitability within agriculture in general'. These genetically modified crops which contain the *Bacillus thuringiensis* (*Bt*) bacteria produce insecticidal and herbicidal proteins meant to limit or prevent the use of chemical pesticides and herbicides that affect the natural environment, whilst increasing crop yields as an instrument of promoting sustainable development. In fact, the introduction of genetically engineered (GE) *Bt* maize and cotton through seed programmes by the global agribusiness, Monsanto, in developing countries has increased food insecurity, destroyed the biodiversity of local ecosystems and created chronic indebtedness amongst small-scale farmers, leading to incidents of farmer suicides (Tokar 2001). GE crops have become ubiquitous, penetrating isolated rural regions, externalising the cost of development on subaltern groups (notably small-scale farmers, especially women) who are traditionally responsible for food production and ensuring household food security. The natural pests of these crops have mutated into 'super pests', which have reduced crop yields dramatically and placed increasing financial pressure on households to pay back loans used to purchase seed packages.

To address the pest explosion, agribusinesses encourage the use of pesticides, which have not only worsened farmer indebtedness but also poisoned and reduced the natural predator population, affecting the synchronic balance of local ecosystems. The integration of 'terminator technology' rendering the seeds produced by *transgenic* GE crops sterile, together with the patents issued on them, has prevented farmers who historically functioned within a 'closed agricultural' system from storing their own seed varieties used to propagate new crops in the next growing season (Chataway et al 2000: 22). These unwanted genes have been transferred through the natural process of cross-pollination to traditional crop varieties that have been developed through trial and error by indigenous people based on their interactions and experiences with nature prior to Western scientific intervention.

Traditional crop varieties that have been selected for desired characteristics authentically suited to specific ecologies have lost their "ecological memory", which has drastic consequences for the preservation of biodiversity (McNeely and Scherr 2002). Crucially, generations of indigenous knowledge employed to establish ecologically relevant crop varieties have been erased. By controlling the reproductive cycle of these crops, agribusinesses have claimed an epistemic monopoly over food production, increasing dependency on canonical Western scientific knowledge and technologies. Through patenting, indigenous knowledge employed over generations has been wrongfully appropriated by agro-monopolies without recognition, which is referred to as *biopiracy*. As a result, indigenous farmers are impelled to purchase seeds from agro-monopolies which are essentially products of their own knowledge, but can only be "legitimised" by the application of Western scientific knowledge. Furthermore, those indigenous farmers who have resisted this injustice by continuing to preserve and grow such seeds have been subject to "legal" punishment for claiming proprietorship of a product of their own knowledge.

Paradoxically, whilst contributing to the demise of agricultural systems, food regimes and ecologies amongst the *anthropos*, Western scientists have been assigned the task of identifying and researching natural phenomena in their geographical regions that could have an inimical effect on local food security and agricultural productivity. For example, 'the US Department of Homeland Security, enacting a Presidential Directive to defend the agriculture and food system against terrorist attacks and other emergencies, has put the collapse of bee populations on its agenda' (Kosek 2010: 651). Intensive research by geneticists, toxicologists and insect pathologists into the honeybee genome, to isolate certain viral strains or chemicals that indicate a possible "environmental terror" attack on the *humanitas*, reflect the utilitarian Western bias invoking investigations into human–nature relations. In his work, *Ecologies of Empire: On the New Uses of the Honey Bee*, Kosek (2010) argues that few researchers exploring the crisis of the collapsed state of honeybees, whatever its cause, have actually situated it within historical, political and economic relationships between people and nature.

Whilst he provides an insightful exegesis of how the changing relationship between humans and bees has made bees vulnerable to new threats, he unwittingly inferred how the occident consciously uses nature as an instrument of war, genocide and torture to maintain a coloniality of power. Thus, confining the subaltern to what Gordon (2007) refers to the 'hellish zone of non-being' where ethics, law and rights do not apply. During the Korean War, the USA dropped plague-infested fleas in North Korea and used mosquitoes and bees to torture the Vietcong in Vietnam. More recently, in the Western-initiated *War on Terror*, due to their sensory capacity, bees have assumed a more sophisticated role, serving as intelligence and surveillance instruments gathering evidence on potential terror threats. Hence, they are able to enter spaces too dangerous for human investigation and can gather evidence without being detected. Bees have been conditioned to associate food (nectar) with nuclear trace elements and their behavioural patterns have been analysed as indicators of radioactive material (Kosek 2010: 657–658). However, exposure to high radiation levels and manipulation of their genetic structure have had a dire effect on global bee populations, which are the most essential propagators of ecologies. In fact, the extinction of the honeybee is the single most profound event that would mark the death of humans.

This example of the honeybee does not refer exclusively and parochially to the need for an environmental ethics to protect nature from the destructive practices of humans, nor does it imply that we naively call for a revision of the ethical practice in war (*just in bellum*), where countries with superior scientific knowledge of nature should not gain an unfair advantage in war or undermine individual state sovereignty with the aid of environmental non-human agents, or merely challenge the 'inhumanity' of using animals as instruments of torture. Rather, it points to the discursiveness of the ecological crisis and illustrates why it is interwoven into a broader nexus of injustice and oppression of people and nature that cannot be disentangled. We need to shift beyond existing paradigms of ethics towards nature and people seen through a hegemonic Euro-American perspective that categorically separates nature from people and, when it suits it, claims to strive for an all-embracing ethics that reflects the experiences, ideas and needs of the occident that has problematically become a universal moral imperative. However, before this can be achieved the subaltern must negate their negation by the Western world as not being producers of knowledge, whilst duplicitously appropriating their knowledge to infer a separation of their being from knowledge. Crucially, ecologies and traditional varieties of indigenous seeds are not simply products of indigenous knowledge created independently of nature in the realm of thought, but are born out of their experiences and close interactions with unique ecologies. They are therefore organic representations of the individual histories of peoples and nature.

Beyond a Philosophy of Ethics: Making the Decolonial Turn

A truly just and sustainable environmental ethics can only be achieved if we strive for an overarching ethics of liberation based on an ecology of knowledge that explores the knowledge of ecologies. As Shiva (1993: 61–62) argues, a truly cosmopolitan world culture would consist of many local cultures existing together, mutually and respectfully exchanging and learning from one another. De Sousa Santos (2007: 39) infers that this objective can only be realised if we shift beyond the level of the *logos* predicated on the universal positivistic Western philosophical and scientific tradition and explore the exterior force of the *natura naturans*. Making this decolonial turn involves analysing human–nature relations through the lenses of the excluded "others" that are able to speak from where they are, or as Kwasi Wiredu states, from the locative 'there' using their own languages and drawing from lived experiences and histories that have wilfully been ignored, appropriated without recognition and erased from 1492 to the present. What is required is not a repudiation of modern science and Western environmental ethical discourse, but a decortication of the Euro-American viewpoint, removing the blindness, prejudice, violence and injustice that inform its epistemic and philosophical tradition. Indigenous people should be free to employ 'border thinking', applying their own knowledge whilst extracting ideas and practices from Western knowledge to understand their own contexts, without adopting the perspective that informs them.

The functionality and efficacy of 'border thinking' rely, however, on the willingness of indigenous people to maintain and revive oral traditions that articulate their ontological relations to nature, as embedded in pre-colonial history. It also requires significant introspection where indigenous people need to ask difficult questions of themselves. For example, how do they reproduce a *coloniality of nature* through daily consumption patterns which make them complicit in erasing the memory of the cultural ties with authentic ecologies and the knowledge they have of them? Nineteenth-century French gastronomer and epicurean philosopher Brillat-Savarin's provocative statement of '*tell me what you eat and I will tell you who you are*' serves as a heuristic device enabling indigenous people to think about what they eat and how it is related to the historical construction of their identities. With the spread of GE food crops (maize, rice and wheat) in Africa, Latin America and South East

Asia, traditional food crops endemic to these regions (varieties of millet, sorghum and pulses) are seen as archaic relics of an "uncivilised" past (Friedmann 2004).

Indeed, the modern diet of marginalised people worldwide contains GE varieties of either rice, maize or wheat as a food staple. These grains are nutritionally limited and do not provide the diverse range of vitamins, proteins and minerals that indigenous food crops and traditional varieties do. Hence, they do not assist in ameliorating malnutrition and preventing disease. Furthermore, marginalised people blindly and wrongfully accept these staples as a symbol of who they are, which is an outcome of the colonial encounter and the intervention of modernity, rather than a product of their own histories. For example, maize was introduced to Africa through the slave trade and has since become the primary staple of people across the continent, particularly in southern Africa. Although indigenous agriculturalists over the years have managed to develop traditional varieties of maize, the memory of pre-colonial traditional food crops (millet and sorghum) and their ontological significance in the identity construction of these people, has been erased (Middleton 2003: 46). The food we therefore choose to consume is also a sign of our ontological connection to food and the ecologies that sustain them. Reviving these histories does appear to be an almost impossible task, especially when the green movement influencing the emergence of the organic food revolution (dominated by middle- to upper-class whites who claim ownership of indigenous eco-agricultural methods) commercialise and industrialise organic food production, catering exclusively for a bourgeoning global market for traditional organically grown food crops. The duplicity of this intervention, where indigenous knowledge is owned and applied, and whose benefits accrue to everyone except the original producers and practitioners of that knowledge, reifies the *coloniality nature*. As Walsh (2007: 227) intimates, this therefore begs the question: 'Who produces critical knowledge, for what purposes, and with what recognition? Asked differently: Whose critical knowledge? For whom? Why and for what uses? And, what in fact is meant by "critical"?'

Independent community-based or grassroots organisations that articulate the experiences and realities of indigenous people are pivotal to achieving ecologically relevant sustainable agricultural and conservation practices. These structures serve as locatives for reviving, sharing and operationalising indigenous knowledge. An example of such an organisation is the Deccan Development Society (DDS) based in the Medak District in Andhra Pradesh, India. In January 2009, I had the good fortune of accompanying a group of small-scale farmers from northern Maputaland, South Africa, on a two-week visit to witness, first hand, the successes of the DDS, where I was given the task of documenting their experiences.[2] The objective of this visit was to expose the South African farmers to the subsequent benefits of "returning" to growing traditional crops using eco-agricultural practices. Most of these small-scale farmers, at the time, were exclusively growing *Bt* maize and cotton on their

---

[2]This visit was part of a farmer exchange between *Bt* cotton farmers from Mboza and Ndumo in Northern KwaZulu-Natal and farmers from India, facilitated by the *African Centre for Biosafety* in coordination with the *Deccan Development Society* (DDS). I had the task of documenting these exchanges between the farmers and our daily experiences. I captured all these experiences in a document entitled *A Reflection of Maputaland Farmers' Visit to India*.

smallholdings with increasing difficulty. In that time, I noticed that the DDS worked closely with women-based traditional village-level associations for the poor called *sangams*. These served as minor centres of knowledge production emphasising the conservation of traditional crop varieties through the establishment of village seed banks and shared experiences on natural pest management systems and mixed pattern intercropping.[3] Seed banks containing traditional crop varieties are managed by a designated village seed keeper who distributes a container of seeds to a farmer on the principle that once s/he has reaped her/his first crop s/he must return two containers of that seed to be redistributed to other farmers who are in need. Since its inception over two-and-a-half decades ago, in response to the chronic indebtedness, food insecurity and lack of food sovereignty caused by the introduction of GE crops such as *Bt* cotton, it has witnessed an unprecedented improvement in food security, food sovereignty and the recovery of biodiversity across villages in the Medak District. A major part of its success can be ascribed to its commitment to an all-embracing ethical framework which extends beyond a simple land ethic centralising the role of low-caste *dalit* women whose knowledge and experience of ecological agricultural practices have been exteriorised.

Its ethical framework is not influenced by the Eurocentricity endemic to ecofeminist, Marxist, deep ecologist or postmodernist discourses imported from the West. In other words, their struggles are not exclusively articulated in terms of the commoditisation of women's labour and nature or romanticising women's ontological relationship to nature sharing similar traits of nurturing life, or the creation of apparent spaces for them to express their realities. Instead, it is informed by specific viewpoints based on their own experiences and interpretations. This programme is not merely motivated by recovering traditional varieties of food crops that romanticise indigenous knowledge and the traditional eco-agricultural practices of women. By extension, it enables women to diversify their functions beyond the farm and use "spaces" created and normally dominated by a Western viewpoint to disseminate their own viewpoints. For example, these women are responsible for documenting their own experiences of eco-agricultural farming using modern technological aids. They have scheduled slots on community radio stations to speak on topically relevant social, political and farming issues. Biodiversity festivals are annually held across villages, celebrating and connecting the cultural, spiritual and material dimensions of human–nature relations. Sacred animals (cows, elephants) are venerated through the adornment of gifts and dress, whilst poems on nature and traditional crops are recited, and testimonies of the successes of *returning* to indigenous lifeways and traditions are shared. In addition, they have established mobile farm stalls that are operated by women from local villages selling traditional food crops in city centres. Prices for the respective crops are collectively determined by the farmers, thus eliminating competition between them and mitigating against the vagaries of the market. The DDS represents the practical possibilities of 'border thinking' for subaltern groups around the world.

---

[3] See http://www.ddsindia.com/www/default.asp.

The turning point for me came when I was documenting the afternoon cultural exchange meeting on 14 January 2009 at Tekur during the Biodiversity Festival when one of the farmers, Mrs. Manukuze from Maputaland, shared her reflection on the day's events:

> I have seen a path of farming. I recall our traditional methods of farming in South Africa. Young girls when scattering seeds would sing to the princess of the heavens. In those days there was community involvement in agricultural production. Everyone helped the other; this is how people would gain profit. People would work on each other's farms without being paid. Instead, after a day's work people would drink sorghum beer and celebrate. They even built houses together. I am glad to see that people in India are keeping their culture and I would like a similar event back home to celebrate our traditional crops and farming practices.

This session demonstrated the effectiveness of a *transcultural* approach enabling subaltern groups from different regions to share and learn from the experiences of one another in intellectual, social and cultural spaces established, influenced and managed by themselves. The reflection of Mrs. Manukuze illustrates the importance of reviving and renewing oral tradition as a means of preserving the memory of the cosmological links between the supernatural or *mythos* and sustainable agricultural and conservation practices. Unlike the Euro-American viewpoint that attempts to universalise models of environmental ethics, the transcultural experience allows subaltern groups to independently draw from the experiences of others to articulate their own realities. It emphasises a mode of learning based on the renewal of memory, invoking the power of testimony and sovereign interpretation—a *decolonial turn* that calls on us to look beyond the existing philosophy informing environmental ethics and focus on a broader ethics of liberation that speaks from and to subaltern people and nature.

Bibliography

Beinart, W. 2000. African History and Environmental History. *African Affairs* 99 (395): 269–302.
Beinart, W., and P. Coates. 1995. *Environment and History: The Taming of Nature in the USA and South Africa*. London: Routledge.
Beinhart, W., and J. McGregor. 2003. Introduction, ed. W. Beinart and J. McGregor, 1–24. Ohio: Ohio University Press.
Bond, P. 2012. *Politics of Climate Justice; Paralysis Above, Movement Below*. Scottsville: University of KwaZulu-Natal Press.
Bryner, G. 2002. Assessing Claims of Environmental Justice. In *Justice and Natural Resources: Concepts, Strategies and Applications*, ed. K. Mutz, G. Bryner, and D. Kenney, 31–56. Washington, DC: Island Press.
Carruthers, J. 1994. Dissecting the Myth: Paul Kruger and the Kruger National Park. *Journal of Southern African Studies* 20 (2): 263–284.
Carruthers, J. 1997. Nationhood and National Parks: Comparative Examples from the Post-imperial Experience. In *Ecology & Empire: Environmental History of Settler Societies*, ed. T. Griffiths and L. Robin, 125–138. Pietermaritzburg: University of Natal Press.
Césaire, A. 1972. *Discourses on Colonialism*. New York: Monthly Review Press.

Chataway, J., L. Levidow, and S. Carr. 2000. Genetic Engineering of Development? Myths and Possibilities. In *Poverty and Development in the 21st Century*, ed. T. Allen and A. Thomas, 469–487. Oxford: Oxford University Press.

Cock, J., and D. Fig. 2002. From Colonial to Community-Based Conservation: Environmental Justice and the Transformation of National Parks (1994–1998). In *Environmental Justice in South Africa*, ed. D.A. McDonald, 131–155. Cape Town: University of Cape Town Press.

Coronil, F. 1996 February. Beyond Occidentalism: Toward Non-imperial Geohistorical Categories. *Cultural Anthropology*, 11 (1): 51–87.

Cronon, W. 1995. Introduction. In *In, Uncommon Ground: Rethinking the Human Place in Nature*, ed. W. Cronon, 23–56. New York and London: Norton.

Crosby, A. 2004. *Ecological Imperialism: The Biological Expansion of Europe, 900–1900 2nd edition*. Cambridge: Cambridge University Press.

De Sousa Santos, B. 2007. Beyond Abyssal Thinking: From Global Lines to Ecologies of Knowledges. *Review*, 30 (1): 45–89.

Doppelt, G. 2002. Can Traditional Ethical Theory Meet the Challenges of Feminism, Multiculturalism and Environmentalism? *Journal of Ethics* 6 (4): 383–405.

Escobar, A. 2007 March. Worlds and Knowledges Otherwise. *Cultural Studies,* 21 (2/3): 179–210.

Friedmann, H. 2004. Remaking Traditions: How We Eat, What We Eat and the Changing Political Economy of Food. In *Women Working the NAFTA Food Chain: Women, Food and Globalisation*, ed. D. Barndt, 35–60. Toronto: Sumach Press.

Gordon, L. R. 2007. Through the Hellish Zone of Nonbeing: Thinking through Fanon, Disaster, and the Damned of the Earth. *Human Architecture: Journal of the Sociology of Self-Knowledge* (Special Double Issue), pp. 5–12.

Grove, R. 1990. The Origins of Environmentalism. *Nature* 345: 11–14.

Grove, R. 1997. Scotland in South Africa: John Croumbie Brown and the Roots of Settler Environmentalism. In *Ecology and Empire: Environmental History of Settler Societies*, ed. T. Griffiths and L. Robin, 139–153. Pietermaritzburg: University of Natal Press.

Guha, R., and J. Martinez-Allier. 1997. *Varieties of Environmentalism: Essays North and South*. London: Earthscan.

Harding, S. 2008. *Sciences from Below: Feminisms, Postcolonialities and Modernities*. London: Duke University Press.

Heidegger, M. 2014. *Introduction to Metaphysics,* 2nd ed. Revised and expanded translation by G. Fried and R. Polt. London: Yale University Press.

Khan, F. 2002. The Roots of Environmental Racism and the Rise of Environmental Justice in the 1990s. In *Environmental Justice in South Africa*, ed. D.A. McDonald, 15–48. Cape Town: University of Cape Town Press.

Kosek, J. 2010. Ecologies of Empire: On the New Uses of the Honeybee. *Cultural Anthropology* 25 (4): 650–678.

Lane Jr., J.H., and R.R. Clark. 2006. The Solitary Walker in the Political World: The Paradoxes of Rousseau and Deep Ecology. *Political Theory* 34 (1): 62–94.

Maldonado-Torres, N. 2004. The Topology of Being and the Geopolitics of Knowledge: Modernity, Empire, Coloniality. *City* 8 (1): 29–56.

Maldonado-Torres, N. 2006. Césaire's Gift and the Decolonial Turn. *Radical Philosophy Review* 9 (2): 111–138.

Mazel, D. 2000. *American Literary Environmentalism*. Georgia: University of Georgia Press.

McNeely, J.A., and S.J. Scherr. 2002. *Ecoagriculture: Strategies to Feed the World and Save Wild Biodiversity*. Washington, DC: Island Press.

Middleton, K. 2003. The Ironies of Plant Transfer: The Case of Prickly Pear in Madagascar. In *Social History & African Environments*, ed. W. Beinart and J. McGregor, 43–59. Ohio: Ohio University Press.

Mignolo, W.D. 2011. Geopolitics of Sensing and Knowing; On (De)coloniality, Border Thinking and Epistemic Disobedience. *Postcolonial Studies* 14 (3): 273–283.

Mills, C. 2007. White Ignorance. In *Race and Epistemologies of Ignorance*, ed. S. Sullivan and N. Tuana, 11–38. New York: SUNY Press.
Padrutt, H. 1992. Heidegger and Ecology. In *Heidegger and the Earth: Essays in Environmental Philosophy*, ed. L. McWhorter, 11–36. Kirksville, MO: Thomas Jefferson University Press.
Paterson, B. 2006. Ethics for Wildlife Conservation: Overcoming the Human-Nature Dualism. *BioScience* 56 (2): 144–150.
Pyne, S.J. 1997. Frontiers of Fire. In *Ecology and Empire: Environmental History of Settler Societies*, ed. T. Griffiths and L. Robin, 19–34. Pietermaritzburg: University of Natal Press.
Quijano, A. 2007. Coloniality and Modernity/Rationality. *Cultural Studies* 21 (2): 168–178.
Rangan, H., and C.A. Kull. 2009. What Makes Ecology 'Political'? Rethinking 'Scale' in Political Ecology. *Human Geography* 33 (1): 28–45.
Ribeiro, G.L. 2011. Why (Post)colonialism and (De)coloniality Are Not Enough: A Post-imperialist Perspective. *Postcolonial Studies* 14 (3): 285–297.
Rolston III, H. 2004. Ralph Waldo Emerson, 1803–82. In *Fifty Key Thinkers on the Environment*, ed. J.A. Palmer, D.E. Cooper, and P.B. Corcoran, 93–100. London: Routledge.
Shiva, V. 1993. *Monocultures of the Mind: Perspectives on Biodiversity and Biotechnology*. London: Zed Books.
Tilley, H. 2003. African Environments & Environmental Sciences: The African Research Survey, Ecological Paradigms & British Colonial Development 1920–1940. In *Social History & African Environments*, ed. W. Beinart and J. McGregor, 109–130. Ohio: Ohio University Press.
Tokar, B. 2001. *Redesigning Life: The Worldwide Challenge to Genetic Engineering*. London: Zed Books.
Walsh, C. 2007. Shifting the Geopolitics of Critical Knowledge. *Cultural Studies* 21 (2/3): 224–239.
Witt, H. 2010. Agrarian Interventions: Corporate Biogenetics on the Makhathini Flats. In *Development Dilemmas in Post-apartheid South Africa*, ed. B. Freund and H. Witt, 299–324. Scottsville: University of KwaZulu-Natal Press.
Wynter, S. 1991. Columbus and the Poetics of the *Propter Nos*. *Annals of Scholarship* 8 (2) (Spring): 251–286.
Yngstrom, I. 2003. Representations of Custom, Social Identity & Environmental Relations in Central Tanzania 1926–1950. In *In, Social History & African Environments*, ed. W. Beinart and J. McGregor, 175–196. Ohio: Ohio University Press.

Romain Francis is Lecturer in the Department of Political Sciences at the University of South Africa (UNISA). He teaches modules at undergraduate and postgraduate levels exploring a range of disciplinary themes including inter alia political development, political economy, political theory, philosophy and ideology and contemporary South African political issues. In 2008, he obtained a Masters of Social Sciences Degree (MSocSc) in Political Sciences from the University of KwaZulu-Natal (UKZN). The title of his Master's research was '*The extent of environmental conscientisation and social mobilisation in the context of environmental racism: a case study of the residents of Merebank*'. He is currently registered for and working towards the completion of a Ph.D. at the University of the Witwatersrand (Wits). Evolving from his master's project, his primary research interest falls within the discourse of *Environmental Racism and Environmental Justice*. His passion and interest in the discursive *nexus* between social justice and environmental issues emanate from his positionality of living in a community of colour in South Africa grossly affected by toxic pollution and a deep-seated fascination and love for the natural world. In fact, this experience informed his desire to precipitate meaningful societal or more aptly, ecological change, translating into his early involvement in social activism and community development that has subsequently manifested in his intellectual endeavours. His research assumes a political theory approach interrogating the interrelationship between the following specialised areas within the inherently transdisciplinary subject of environmental racism and justice, namely recognition, justice and ethics. Romain Francis is an advocate of the school of decoloniality, and his research is centred on the philosophical and practical precepts of this intellectual and ethical project.

Chapter 4
Don't Develop Us Without Us! Inclusion of Indigenous Ethnic Minorities in Sustainable Development Goals in Africa

Paul Mulindwa

Abstract The adoption of Sustainable Development Goals (SDGs) in 2015, with a pledge of "no one will be left behind" was greeted with optimism, and ushered in hopes and promise of all-inclusive approaches to development. However, the implementation of SDGs has remained elusive and the effects not reaching the very vulnerable and marginalised communities. The 18 SDGs will be achieved effectively, if serious attention is given to the needs and human rights of vulnerable ethnic minorities; improve on strategies for achieving the goals (particularly at the national level); and reduce the barriers, such as discrimination, exclusion and inadequate processes, which challenge participation of ethnic minorities in SDGs processes. Many human rights instruments and legal frameworks emphasise that states have to devise means to enable ethnic minorities to participate fully in economic, social, political progress and development affairs of their country. Inclusion and effective participation of ethnic minorities in development processes is crucial to sustainable development. The question is whether SDGs will deliver development to vulnerable groups such as ethnic minorities in Africa [which Millennium Development Goals (MDGs) failed to do] without their inclusion? Inclusion of ethnic minority implies efficient and accountable institutions that promote development; protect human rights; respect for the rule of law, as well as ensure that people contribute to decision-making processes on issues that affect their lives.

Keywords Sustainable development · Ethnic minority · Participation · Inclusion · Discrimination

Introduction

The right to participation has evolved as part of the democratic discourse deemed fundamental for the development of any society. A founding principle of the

---

P. Mulindwa (✉)
Department of Politics and International Relations, SARChI: African Diplomacy and Foreign Policy, University of Johannesburg, B Ring 211, Auckland Park, Johannesburg 2006, South Africa
e-mail: paul.mulindwa@gmail.com

© Springer Nature Switzerland AG 2020
E. Benyera (ed.), *Reimagining Justice, Human Rights and Leadership in Africa*, Advances in African Economic, Social and Political Development, https://doi.org/10.1007/978-3-030-25143-7_4

Universal Declaration of Human Rights (UDHR) (Brown 2016) is the recognition that all individuals are of equal value, and must effectively participate in the cultural, religious, social and economic affairs of their states (Article 2, paragraph 2). In the preamble, in paragraph 6, the UDHR denotes that the inclusion of indigenous ethnic minorities in decision-making processes is an integral part of (sustainable) development and a "condition *sine qua non*" to maintaining or building harmonious and respectful relations among society's various components.

The United Nation's Sustainable Development Goals (SDGs) started from where the Millennium Development Goals (MDGs) ended, conceding that ethnic minorities in Africa had not adequately benefited from the latter. Arguably, the drafters of SDGs did not learn much from the MDGs and how the issues of ethnic minorities had been (mis)managed (i.e. their (non)participation and inclusion/exclusion in all processes). The African Commission on Human and Peoples' Rights (ACHPR) (2006) notes that the exclusion of, and discrimination against, ethnic minorities in development processes exacerbated their plight, which is characterised by *inter alia*, poverty, illiteracy and landlessness. This chapter interrogates how SDGs can effectively deliver development to indigenous ethnic minorities in Africa only if these marginalised "Others" participate in their own development. The overarching argument of the chapter is that in order for development to work for ethnic minorities in Africa, the minorities have to be included. Their participating must not be tokenism by empowered participation where they make binding decisions as opposed to rubber stamping development programmes imposed on them.

The Concept of Ethnic Minority in an African Context

The concept of ethnic minority remains contentious among state leaders, with reports of their exclusion from, and discrimination against them, when it comes to development processes in countries such as Burundi, the Democratic Republic of the Congo (DRC), Ethiopia, Gabon, Kenya, Nigeria, Rwanda and Uganda (Forest Peoples Programme 2014b). In Africa, indigenous ethnic minorities are often poorly represented, face barriers in accessing social services and live in poor or more remote regions that offer limited prospects for their economic development (McDougall 2011). Equally, large-scale economic and development projects, implemented in their lands without their participation, have led to displacements, impoverishment and, in some cases, violence (McDougall 2010) in Burundi, the DRC, Kenya, Uganda and Tanzania. In a case before the ACHPR, presented by Centre for Minority Rights Development (Kenya) on behalf of the Endorois Welfare Council, the commission found that the Kenyan government had violated the Endorois' rights to property and development, under the *African Charter* (Articles 8, 14, 17, 21 and 22) by displacing them without consulting them and not involving them in decision-making processes leading to their eviction (ACHPR 2009).

The term "minority" has been used in international and human rights discourse, but interestingly none of the international instruments on minority rights has offered an explicit legal definition of the concept.[1] Similarly, despite Africa being home to many ethnic minority communities, and given the work dedicated to related issues by both scholars and practitioners, there is no generally acceptable definition of which ethnic minorities are. Individual states in Africa specifically consider a wide range of groups domestically as minorities, based on shared characteristics (using objective and subjective criteria). Objectively, ethnic minorities are identified based on the shared features of the group (ethnicity, national origin, culture, language, religion)—categories derived from the only global standard on minorities (United Nations [UN] 1992). Subjectively, their identification is based on self-identification and the desire to preserve their identity (UN 1992).

States such as Burundi, Ghana, Morocco, Rwanda and Uganda have found it difficult to fully recognise the issues facing minority communities, believing that the minority "problem" is essentially European and thus showing a reluctance to admit that Africa is *not* immune to ethnic concerns (Slimane 2003). For instance, while appearing before the ACHPR, in response to a question whether there was domination of one people by another, the Ambassador of Ghana answered: "Well, I must say, the obvious answer in the case of Ghana is no. There is no domination of one people, one ethnic group against the other. That is quite obvious" (ACHPR 1993). Similarly, Gabon reported to the UN Human Rights Committee that "there is no problem of minorities in Gabon [because] the population is fully integrated socially" (UN 1998). However, many minorities (including indigenous ethnic minorities in Africa) continue to suffer exclusion, discrimination, poverty and a lack of recognition/attention from their states when it comes to protecting their rights—including the rights to human dignity, equality and non-discrimination.

In addition to continuing ambiguity and negative attitudes about the concept of "minorities" (in relation to their specific concerns and needs), unanswered questions remain about what would be the appropriate approach to their development—a major factor underlying the development issues which many countries on the continent are grappling with. Selassie (1992/1993, 1, 5) observes that no issue is more critical than how African societies understand minority issues and treat their ethnic minorities. Negative attitudes have resulted in minority issues either being ignored deliberately or the selected approaches not appropriately addressing their problems. Those issues will, for the foreseeable future, remain the central problem of postcolonial African statecraft (Okafor 2005). Rwanda, for instance, has suppressed ethnic identity and their demands, in the interest of forging national unity and fostering loyalties beyond the confines of ethnicity.

There is a tendency to focus on UN human rights regimes when considering the issues facing ethnic minorities in Africa—perhaps since not much has been done to protect them. It is thus critical to focus on those African legal and policy frameworks

---

[1] One of the primary sources of minority protections in international law is the International Covenant on Civil and Political Rights, art. 27, 19 December 1966, formulated "in an extremely cautious, vague manner" and "leaves many questions open, for which an answer must be found by way of interpretation". See Manfred Nowak, UN Covenant on Civil and Political Rights—CCPR Commentary 485 (1993). See also Articles 31 and 32 of the Vienna Convention on the Law of Treaties, 23 May 1969, 1155 UNTS 331, *reprinted in* 8 I.L.M. 679, *entered into force 27* January 1980.

whose mandates are to protect ethnic minorities on this continent. African human rights systems lack specific frameworks dedicated to specifically addressing minority issues, compared to Europe, for instance. While the *African Charter* brings in the concept of "peoples" (meant to include all categories, such as ethnic minorities), it falls short of making robust and explicit mention of ethnic minorities and/or devoting a specific clause related to issues. A lesson could be learnt from the framework of the Council of Europe, which promotes and protects human rights and the rule of law: it has a number of relevant frameworks, bodies and approaches designed to ensure equality and minority protection, including the Venice Commission, the European Commission against Racism and Intolerance (ECRI), the Framework Convention for the Protection of National Minorities (FCNM) and the Lund recommendations. Although inferences can be drawn from such instruments to protect the rights of ethnic minorities in Africa, the argument put forward here is that the challenges facing Africa ethnic minorities differ (socially, economically, politically) from those of other continents. Specific instruments are needed to meet the unique needs of African ethnic minorities.

African ethnicity issues are complex, and the question of minority status—especially in terms of the non-dominance of particular groups—is complicated by the way in which many elites exploit ethnic differences for political ends (Slimane 2003). Adekeye (2010), Venkatasawmy (2015) and Deng (2008) opine that most of the recent conflicts in African states (Burundi, Chad, the DRC, Mali, Niger, Nigeria, Rwanda, Uganda, South Africa and Sudan) were ethnically based. Often numerically weaker groups have, through alliances, gained dominance in the political arena, but in Nigeria, historically dominant minorities such as the Efik or Ijaw now find themselves marginalised politically. Deng (2008) states that such dominance is not sustainable because it thrives on the political fortunes of the allies: should there be a change in political dimensions or a breakdown in the alliance, the ethnic group will likely return to its non-dominant status. Conversely, numerically large groups such as the Hutu in Rwanda and the Oromia in Ethiopia have been largely excluded from power. It is against this backdrop that SDGs should be aligned to concerns around recognition which will facilitate national unity and cohesion and foster sustainable development.

Minority Rights and Their Specific Concerns

Human rights and fundamental freedoms are universal to all human beings, including ethnic minorities (either as individuals or in groups). Although this applies to every human being, because of their specific concerns and status, the emphasis should be on minorities' culture, religion and language (Henrard 2007a). Further, as internationally coded under the *Universal Declaration of Human Rights* (Brown 2016) (Articles 1, 2, 7 and 23), all human beings are born free and equal in dignity and rights and are entitled to all rights without distinction or discrimination of any kind. Other human rights treaties and declarations have subsequently explicitly coded the fundamental rights and freedoms of ethnic minorities as indivisible, interdependent and interrelated, to include the right to development which fully realises human rights and fundamental freedoms (UN 1985).

Another guarantee that is accorded to minorities is special rights (UN 1994), which are not privileges but rights granted to facilitate and enable minorities to preserve their identity, characteristics and traditions. Special rights are important in achieving equality of treatment for minorities in situations where they are not recognised and/or not integrated into the community. Only when minorities are able to use their own languages, benefit from services they have themselves organised and take part in the political and economic life of their nation, will they achieve the status which majorities take for granted. Differences in the treatment of such groups/individuals are deemed justified if implemented to promote effective equality and the welfare of the community as a whole (UN 1998). This form of affirmative action may have to be sustained over a prolonged period, to enable minority groups to reap social benefits on an equal footing with majority groupings. Other rights which ethnic minorities enjoy include the right to participate effectively in all public issues affecting them and in shaping decisions and policies concerning their group/community at the local, national and international levels (Altenhoener 2009; Henrard 2007b).

While ensuring the protection and promotion of the rights and fundamental freedoms of minorities, it is important to acknowledge their situation in Africa. The recognition of minorities will facilitate their protection and entrench their rights. There is no right to recognition per se under international law since the existence of minorities is a matter of fact, rather than law. Their recognition by the state is thus not a necessary condition for claiming minority protection, but where it is taken into consideration, recognition facilitates the protection of minority rights. The recognition of minorities in any given location facilitates (a) development: if minorities are not recognised, steps to ensure that they benefit equally from development cannot be implemented easily or directly; (b) peaceful coexistence: failure to recognise minorities and the marginalisation they face can create inter-communal tensions and even conflict; (c) democratic governance: participatory and multicultural states acknowledge the diversity of communities that constitute the polity (United Nations Development Programme [UNDP] 2010). Together, these factors create a favourable environment for sustainable development.

Minorities and the Right to Development

The ACHPR's charter is the only human rights treaty in which the right to development is legally binding on the African human rights system (Kamga 2018). Article 22 of the charter (ACHPR 2018) states:

(1) *All peoples shall have the right to their economic, social and cultural development with due regard to their freedom and identity and in the equal enjoyment of the common heritage of mankind.*
(2) *States shall have the duty, ... to ensure the exercise of the right to development.*

It is from this provision that member states derive obligations to fulfil the realisation of the right to development by all. On several occasions, ACHPR has asserted that the right to development of ethnic minorities (like other rights) falls under the obligation of the state to protect, respect and remedy, as noted by the UN (2008). For instance, ACHPR, while handling the Endorois case, observed that the eviction and displacement of the community from their ancestral lands contributed to their current social and economic vulnerability; and that the state, which bears the burden for creating conditions favourable to people's development, is obligated to ensure that the Endorois are not left out of the development process (ACHPR 2009).

"Development" has acquired a negative connotation for ethnic minorities, especially in Africa, as developmental strides often affect them negatively or leave them with miserable histories and traumatic experiences. In a number of instances, "development projects" have resulted in their eviction from their lands and seen them lose their property and resources. Notably, government-prompted developments are regarded as one of the root causes of ethnic minorities' problems in Burundi, Cameroun, the Congo, the DRC, Kenya, Rwanda, Uganda and Tanzania, where ethnic minorities such as the Batwa, Endorois, Masai, Tuareg, Mbororo, Baka, Yaka and Bambuti (ACHPR 2005) have been evicted from their ancestral lands to make way for government projects, or have lost valuable resources [through the commercial extraction of natural resources, logging, infrastructure construction, chemical-intensive agriculture, industrial deforestation and wildlife/biodiversity/environmental conservation (UN 2009a, b)]. Termed "development aggression" (Gilbert 2006), such projects, under the guise of modernisation, have been imposed on minorities without their involvement or participation. If the continuum of development is to be realised, there must be a paradigm shift in development processes to include minorities in all stages of development affecting them.

The right to development, which is hotly debated in international law, forms part of the third generation of human or "solidarity" rights, which espouse a shared/collective responsibility for the realisation of human rights around the globe. It is almost 32 years since the UN General Assembly (UNGA 1986) officially recognised the right to development in the United Nations Declaration on the Right to Development; about 23 years since a consensus involving all governments was reached on the same right to development (UNGA 1993), almost 19 years since the UN Working Group on the Right to Development was established (UN 1999) and subsequently appointed an independent expert on the right to development; and 15 years since the UN High-Level Task Force on the Implementation of the Right to Development was established (UN 2004), yet these rights remain controversial. Vandenhole (2003, 378) observes that despite the plethora of discussions and debates on the right to development, no clear consensus has been reached, even on basic issues. The topic is still not addressed in an international, legally binding document and is, consequently, still not a justiciable right at an international level (Vandenhole 2003, 378).

It is impossible to discuss minorities and development without looking at how such groups benefited from the MDGs. For instance, in juxtaposing ethnic minority issues and MDG 1 (which sought to eradicate extreme poverty and hunger), many minorities in Africa remain in abject poverty, and no country in Africa has endeavoured to provide opportunities in the 15 years of MDG implementation to enable them to achieve that goal. Studies by an independent expert on minority issues (Corpuz 2005) have shown that minorities failed to benefit from national strategies aimed at achieving the MDGs, which did not take into account their unique situations, or the impact of discrimination and exclusion. The norms and values embedded in the United Nations Millennium Declaration (UN 2000) and international human rights instruments are key to this endeavour: in particular, the human rights principles of non-discrimination, meaningful participation and accountability. In adopting the Millennium Declaration, heads of state and government recognised their "collective responsibility to uphold the principles of human dignity, equality and equity at the global level" (para. 2) and resolved to strengthen their capacity "to implement the principles and practices of democracy and respect for human rights, including minority rights" (para. 25). However, the reality on the ground, in most African countries, is far from the aspirations and spirit of this declaration.

Ethnic minorities, such as the Batwa of the Great Lakes Region, the Khoisan of South Africa, the San of Namibia and Angola, the Basarwa of Botswana, the Baka and Mbororo of Cameroon and Gabon, the Hadzabe of Tanzania, and the Ogiek, Elimoro, Endorois, Sengwer and Yakuu of Kenya, are poorer than their respective dominant population groups, having been disfranchised and lacking equal access to economic opportunities. Such disfranchisement is the result of them being evicted from their lands and thus being rendered landless. This has hindered the development of ethnic minorities and left in vulnerable situations which, unless dealt with, will be perpetuated by the next generation of ethnic majorities. Notably, at the time of drafting the MDGs, each country had its own specific set of challenges, though some broad trends and cross-cutting issues were identified as priorities. One critical priority was to ensure that ethnic minorities received targeted investments (substantive equality), for MDG 1 to be achieved sustainably or to be realised under the SDGs (UN 2005).

In African countries where economic growth is slow yet steady, ethnic minorities are often excluded from structural processes designed to ensure their development. As alluded to, many have become impoverished due to the fact that they have lost their cultures, beliefs and way of life. Many have not been resettled and/or compensated, while those who have been resettled live in hostile or infertile lands that cannot cope with their lifestyle and have been pushed to remote areas where infrastructure and service delivery are poor. As a result of such changes in lifestyle, many have resorted to begging and becoming squatters of the very people who took their lands. Examples include the Endorois (who lost their land to establish game reserves and tourist facilities in Kenya); the Ik in Karamoja, Uganda (dispossessed of natural resources that include gold and Gama Arabic and living impoverished lives reliant on the dominant ethnic groups extracting the natural resources); and the Batwa in Burundi, in the DRC, Rwanda and Uganda (evicted from their rich ancestral lands where mining and the extraction of natural resources such as timber, gold, diamonds now take place, or where tourist attraction centres are being built). Another case is the Ogoni people of Nigeria, where Shell (the petroleum giant) together with the government encroached on the land, leading to the widespread contamination of the soil, water and air; the destruction of homes; and the burning of crops and the killing of farm animals.

Paradoxically, development aid extended to government projects by intergovernmental development agencies such as World Bank (WB), International Monetary Fund (IMF) and the UNDP have contributed to the underdevelopment of ethnic minorities in Africa. An analysis by the International Fund for Agricultural Development (IFAD) (2003) indicates that the support received from these agencies sometimes reinforces or destroys the sustainable resource management systems of ethnic minority communities, disrupting their traditional systems and affecting their capacity to cope with development. Importantly, ethnic minorities are often not included in the initial planning and decision-making processes. For instance, the World Bank funded a biodiversity conservation project in Uganda that led to the evictions of the Batwa in 1991. While the bank had advised the Ugandan government to conduct an impact assessment and involve affected communities in the process, this was not done and the bank never followed up (World Bank 1995). Notwithstanding the failure to involve the Batwa in the process leading up to their eviction from their lands, the bank continued to support the government's project, without offering any compensation.

In a related case, in 2014 in Kenya, the police evicted the Sengwer community from their ancestral lands in Cherangany Hills. Like the Endorois and the Ogiek, who were evicted in 1970 and 2008, respectively, their eviction resulted in their properties being destroyed (Forest Peoples Programme 2014a). Shockingly, since 2007, the World Bank, through its Natural Resource Management Project (NRMP) has funded activities on biodiversity conservation in the Cherangany Hills, thus violating its policies on indigenous ethnic communities and failing to respect the dignity, human rights, economies and cultures of communities in which it implements its projects (World Bank 2005). The bank is further accused of funding a project that put the lives of the Sengwer in the hands of the Kenyan government. In a related manner, the Kenyan police, in implementing the United Nations' policy of Reducing Emissions from Deforestation and Forest Degradations (REDD), evicted the Sengwer from their land even after the Kenyan courts had twice ruled in favour of the Sengwer community and issued injunctions against their eviction (Amnesty International 2018).

There is growing awareness that ventures which do not involve the beneficiary ethnic minority communities and fail to consider their cultural beliefs, values, human rights and dignity, render such initiatives open to challenges and may not bring about the intended sustainable development. This calls for consultation and consensus building with the affected ethnic minorities, as well as the recognition and strengthening of local cultures and values that preserve their dignity and diversity and enhance their identity and social cohesion. Learning from the Great Lakes region experience, efforts to bring about developmental changes for ethnic minorities through forced social integration into mainstream society have failed, mainly because such efforts were not built on ethnic minorities' cultural strengths and did not entail their active participation.

Minorities and MDGs: Rhetoric and Reality

Although African countries faced challenges in achieving the MDGs by 2015, it is more challenging to relate their whole continuum to African ethnic minorities. While the MDG processes had some impact at a national level, ethnic minorities' exclusion increased the already wide political, economic and social gap between them and the rest of the population. Arguably, the problem started with the origination of the MDGs—they were formulated in a way that did not recognise the situation of minorities. For instance, MDG 2 advocates universal education for all, as if there are no obstacles or definitive boundaries in the definition of "all". Arguably, a "one-size-fits-all" approach cannot and will never work for vulnerable minorities who have been disfranchised and excluded from the very issues affecting them. Also, the MDGs mainly define poverty as economic deprivation, while for minorities social discrimination is a major factor contributing to poverty. In any development process, there is a need to address the exclusion of, and discrimination against, ethnic minorities if such initiatives are to be truly meaningful.

While progress has been made in some of the goals (notably goal 1) in countries such as India and Vietnam, Africa still lags behind the rest of the world in respect of most metrics, including inequalities in development due to socio-economic barriers. The MDGs have been criticised for using much of the data collected at a country/national level rather than the lower/grassroots levels when monitoring progress towards achieving these goals. While this method of data collection provides an easy-to-digest perspective, it misses critical trends occurring on the sub-national level, including among specific ethnic minority communities and similar vulnerable/challenged socio-economic groups on the margins. The main reason for the prevailing poverty amongst such groups is not only a lack of aid, as prescribed in MDG 1, but social barriers (such as discrimination) which make it difficult to reap the benefits of that aid. As a result, while some populations had seen progress in respect of the MDGs by 2015, many ethnic minorities in Africa did not, also due to a lack of recognition of ethnic minority issues by the MDGs themselves. For instance, while women-related issues are referred to in five of the eight development goals, ethnic minorities are not mentioned anywhere. Thus, despite their unique situations, ethnic minorities were never a direct target of the MDGs, thus the MDG indicators are not generalisable.

With lessons learnt in Rwanda, Uganda, South Africa and Botswana, there are compelling arguments for paying greater attention to disadvantaged minorities in any development agenda. Minorities in Africa remain among the poorest and most socially and economically excluded and marginalised communities in the world, subject to discrimination, exclusion, poverty and underdevelopment, which emphasises the need for greater targeted attention to their situations. The relationship between inequality, discrimination and poverty and their impact on disadvantaged minority groups cannot be ignored or underestimated. Change is possible if those groups are involved in the planning and implementation of any development plans affecting them.

In transitioning from the MDGs to the SDGs, those responsible for the latter arguably "learned nothing and forgot nothing" (Minority Rights Group International 2015): if the framers of SDGs had assessed the achievements of MDGs on minorities (which they ought to have done), any post-2015 development initiatives would have ensured, among others, an all-inclusive approach. However, most African countries did not do this, and thus, post-2015 national consultative processes did not bring on board ethnic minorities. In Uganda, for instance, while government conducted consultations and tried to involve various stakeholders, this mainly happened at a national level, not in local communities; in towns and hotels that are inaccessible to minorities, rather than in their own settings. Some civil society organisations have indeed tried to reach communities, but they are not accountable to the people—government is. This was confirmed by the UN Independent Expert on Minority Issues, Rita Izsák, who warned that many disadvantaged ethnic minorities in Africa were once again being left out of promising international development initiatives because of a lack of clear commitment by governments to address their development needs and human rights (UN 2014). Arguably, SDGs provide an important opportunity to refocus development agendas on inequality and put ethnic minority issues at the centre of these efforts, especially when it comes to implementation.

While the participation of ethnic minorities in development processes enhances their chances of benefiting from the same, we need to interrogate whether SDGs, in fact, offer a window through which ethnic minorities can realise their rights, before even addressing development. As Lattimer (2016) observes, SDGs do not present a model for future development that is radically different from that envisaged by the MDGs, adding that perhaps what has changed is an increase in the number of goals and an extension of the targets focusing on sustainability. Stakeholders of SDGs must ensure that the means to end inequality and poverty are changed and that a more robust and friendlier equal partnership between north and south is encouraged. Without such adjustments, the SDGs remain an extension of the very MDGs that failed to benefit ethnic minorities. Today, poverty is increasingly reflecting an ethnic dimension: according to the World Bank (2011), during MDG implementation, countries such as India and Vietnam saw poverty rates lowering amongst ethnic minorities. However, for similar vulnerable groups in Africa, poverty levels have continued to rise or have remained static (UN 2015).

Securing Sustainable Development for Ethnic Minorities

Before involving ethnic minorities in activities aimed at developing or benefiting them, it is important that they access information and have the capacity to engage on issues pertinent to them. This has been advanced by scholars such as Sen (1993) and Nussbaum (1997) who, in their notion of capability, posit that only informed citizenly can effectively participate in issues affecting them. Ethnic minorities must therefore be capacitated in an appropriate way, to enable them to show meaningful involvement in the implementation of SDGs. Such an approach is likely to enhance the sustainability of development goals since capacity building gives minorities greater awareness of what kind of claims they can make and how, while holding accountable their leaders.

Linked to this is the proposal by activists such as Rita Izsák to strengthen local and community-based mechanisms aimed at supporting the advancement of their issues (UN 2014). In most African countries, ethnic minorities have established initiatives aimed at bringing them together, including community-based organisations, local networks and national NGOs such as the United Organisation for Batwa Development in Uganda (UOBDU); the *Communauté des Autochtones Rwandais* (CAURWA); *Unissons-nous pour la Promotion des Batwa* (UNIPROBA) in Burundi; *Centre d'Accompagnement des Autochtones Pygmées et Minoritaires Vulnérables* (CAMV) in the DRC; Pastoralists Indigenous NGOs (PINGOS) in Tanzania; and the Mbororo Social and Cultural Development Association (MBOSCUDA) in Cameroon (International Work Group for Indigenous Affairs 2018). Strengthening such unifying organisations is crucial for sustainable development: these structures reinforce the participation of the communities themselves in decision-making processes/negotiations with any party that proposes development plans that will affect them directly or indirectly. There is sufficient evidence that demand-driven and participatory approaches which emphasise the empowerment of the beneficiaries of any given development plans become more sustainable.

Another initiative aimed at securing the sustainable development of ethnic minorities is to use the rights-based approach, as advocated by the UN Statement of Common Understanding on Human Rights-Based Approaches to Development (UN 2009a, b) when dealing with issues concerning ethnic minorities. This approach represents a critical element of a new design in development. Involving ethnic minorities in all plans and processes related to SDG implementation will ensure free, prior and informed consent, thus those communities will be implementing their own goals, and ensuring the sustainability of those goals.

In every situation involving minority communities, the government has the sole responsibility for protecting and promoting the former's rights, as given in International Covenant on Civil and Political Rights (ICCPR) Article 27 (UN 2018).[2] It is therefore essential to initiate engagements/dialogues on ethnic minority rights and related issues with governments and to exploit any international obligations on their part, such as international or regional treaties that they have ratified.

Another way of ensuring sustained development for ethnic minorities is to recognise and respect their specific rights, even in Africa, where some governments refuse to acknowledge indigenous minorities. As stated, what those minorities need, is the recognition of their rights and entitlements in terms of social, cultural and economic resources (land, forests), which are not only assets for livelihood security but also the context supporting their continuing existence as a community. Working out

---

[2] Article 27 states that in those states in which ethnic, religious or linguistic minorities exist, persons belonging to such minorities shall not be denied the right, in community with the other members of their group, to enjoy their own culture, to profess and practice their own religion or to use their own language.

innovative mechanisms to ensure minority recognition will help address the various challenges they experience in their unique contexts. Learning from what most African governments have done with affirmative action regarding, for instance, the empowerment of women and other historically disadvantaged groups could work for ethnic minorities. Addressing historical injustices and/or imbalances and recognising their rights is an excellent starting point.

Challenges of Including Ethnic Minorities in Sustainable Development

While various efforts at the international level have put in place legal frameworks to ensure the promotion and protection of ethnic minority rights, not much is being done at the national level to ratify these instruments. For instance, by the end of 2017, only one African country—the Central African Republic—had ratified Convention No. 169 of the International Labour Organisation concerning Indigenous and Tribal Peoples in Independent Countries (ILO 1989). Domesticating those other ratified instruments remains a challenge: the lack of a framework to implement international conventions and declarations for the protection of minorities, at national levels, is hampering the task of harmonising constitutional rights for ethnic minorities with international standards in particular and complicates the enforcement and monitoring of those rights. The same applies to SDGs.

A common characteristic among most African ethnic minorities is limited formal education and training (OHCHR 2008), which results in a lack of adequate skills and knowledge—deficits which are compounded by high poverty levels and landlessness. While countries such as Rwanda, Ethiopia and Burundi have devised means to ensure that minorities are brought on board through public participation, many have not utilised such programmes and opportunities due to structural and systemic challenges (McDougall 2010). The right to effective participation is pointless if a group does not have the necessary ability, access and resources. The capacity of ethnic minorities to participate is an important precondition for sustainable development, and this should be reflected in a broad range of issues.

A central challenge in respect of sustainable development is ethnic minorities' marginalisation from effective participation. For instance, the Batwa (Lewis 2000) in Burundi, the DRC, Rwanda and Uganda and Kenya's Endorois (Africa Peace Point 2012) have found it difficult to participate effectively in development processes in their countries, due to marginalisation and discrimination from different sectors of society. Discrimination takes different forms and manifests in terms of political exclusion, widespread prejudice among dominant groups, failure to include minorities' voices in public discussions and media hostility towards minority concerns and participation (Kabananukye and Wily 1996).

The recognition of minorities is essential for securing their rights in a state, including the right to effective participation. Since non-recognition hinders their enjoyment of internationally established rights, it ultimately aggravates their marginalisation and exclusion from political processes. Recognition based on self-identification is the first step in the process of securing minority rights and safeguarding individuals' positions as equal members of society. While Burundi has launched initiatives to include minorities, there are few effective institutions and structures to safeguard their representation and participation, as well as a seeming lack of political will from the government to establish such mechanisms. The lack of mechanisms hinders minorities' optimal involvement in sustainable development programmes, while their presence provides a platform for minorities to have their voices heard (either through representation or direct participation) and includes them in decision-making structures at various levels, empowering them and enhancing their capacity, thus making them stronger and more prepared to participate equally.

Conclusion

Ethnic minority issues worldwide have different socio-historical origins, assume different forms and are expressed differently. Almost all states have one or more minority groups within their territories, characterised by their own ethnic, linguistic or religious identity that differentiates them from the majority population. Three key pillars of human rights and minority legal protection are fundamental to addressing the challenges impeding minorities from optimal participation in projects aimed at sustainable development: the right to non-discrimination; the right to effective participation in decision-making; and the implementation of special measures/affirmative action to address the effects of long-standing and entrenched discrimination. To ensure a sustainable approach, any structural factors facilitating the marginalisation and exclusion of minorities must be addressed. To achieve the SDGs sustainably, it is vital to concede that MDGs largely failed minorities and did not mainstream their rights into all goals. Especially adapted indicators and programmes to overcome barriers to realising SDGs must be implemented, otherwise those goals will not place ethnic minorities at the centre of their own development.

References

ACHPR. 1993. *Ghana: Examination of State Report.* http://hrlibrary.umn.edu/achpr/sess14-complete.htm. Accessed 25 Aug 2018.

ACHPR. 2005. *Indigenous Peoples in Africa: The Forgotten Peoples?.* Denmark: African Commission's Working Group of Expert on Indigenous Populations/Communities.

ACHPR. 2006. *Indigenous Peoples in Africa: The Forgotten Peoples?.* Copenhagen: Transaction Publishers.

ACHPR. 2009. *Centre for Minority Rights Development and Another vs. Kenya Government: No. 276/03.* http://www.achpr.org/communications/decision/276.03/. Accessed 27 Aug 2018.

ACHPR. 2018. *African Charter on Human and Peoples' Rights*. http://www.achpr.org/instruments/achpr/. Accessed 25 Aug 2018.

Adekeye, A. 2010. *The Curse of Berlin: Africa After the Cold War*. Durban: University of KwaZulu-Natal Press.

Africa Peace Point (APP). 2012. *Contesting Local Marginalization through International Instruments: The Endorois Community Case to the African Commission on Human and Peoples' Rights*. Nairobi: APP.

Altenhoener, C. 2009. Promoting Effective Participation of National Minorities in Economic, Social and Cultural Life through Project Activities. *International Journal on Minority and Group Rights* 16 (4): 583–592.

Amnesty International. 2018. *Families torn apart forced eviction of indigenous people in Embobut Forest, Kenya*. London: Amnesty International Ltd.

Brown, G. 2016. *The Universal Declaration of Human Rights in the 21st Century: A Living Document in a Changing World*. Cambridge, UK: Open Book Publishers. https://doi.org/10.11647/obp.0091.

Corpuz, V. T. 2005. *Millennium Development Goals and Indigenous Ethnic Communities*. Report submitted to United Nations Economic and Social Council, New York. May 16–27.

Deng, F. 2008. *Identity, Diversity, and Constitutionalism in Africa*. Washington: United States Institute of Peace Press.

Forest Peoples Programme. 2014a. *Securing Forests, Securing Rights* [Report of the International Workshop on Deforestation and the Rights of Forest Peoples.]. London: FPP.

Forest Peoples Programme. 2014b. *Forced Eviction by Kenya Threatens Minority Communities' Human Rights and Ancestral Forests* [Press release, 6 January.]. http://www.redd-monitor.org/2014/01/07/forced-eviction-by-kenya-threatens-indigenous-communities-human-rights-and-ancestral-forests/. Accessed 24 Aug 2018.

Gilbert, J. 2006. *Indigenous Peoples' Land Rights Under International Law: From Victims to Actors*. Ardsley, NY: Transnational.

Henrard, K. 2007. *Equal Rights Versus Special Rights; Minority Protection and the Prohibition of Discrimination*. Luxembourg: European Commission.

Henrard, K. 2009. Minorities and Socio-economic Participation: The Two Pillars of Minority Protection Revisited. *International Journal on Minority and Group Rights* 16 (4): 549–576.

International Fund for Agricultural Development (IFAD). 2003. Indigenous Peoples and Sustainable Development. Roundtable Discussion Paper for the 25th Anniversary Session of IFAD's Governing Council, Rome, February.

International Labour Organization. 1989. *Indigenous and Tribal Peoples Convention*. https://www.ilo.org/dyn/normlex/en/f?p=NORMLEXPUB:12100:0::NO::P12100_ILO_CODE:C169. Accessed 25 Aug 2018.

International Work Group for Indigenous Affairs (IWGIA). 2018. *Partnerships*. https://www.iwgia.org/en/partners. Accessed 24 Aug 2018.

Kabananukye, K., and L. Wily. 1996. *Report on a Study of the Abayanda Pygmies of South West Uganda*. Kampala: Mgahinga and Bwindi Impenetrable Forest Conservation Trust.

Kamga, S.D. 2018. *The Right to Development in the African Human Rights System*. London: Routledge.

Lattimer, M. 2016. *The Forgotten Minority*. London: Minority Rights Group International. http://www.sustainablegoals.org.uk/the-forgotten-minority/. Accessed 28 May 2018.

Lewis, J. 2000. *The Batwa Pygmies of the Great Lakes Region*. London: Minority Rights Group International; see also Wairama, B. 2001. *Uganda: The Marginalization of Minorities*. London: Minority Rights Group International.

McDougall, G. 2010. *Minorities and Effective Participation in Economic Life*. Geneva: Human Rights Council. http://www.ohchr.org/Documents/HRBodies/HRCouncil/MinorityIssues/Forum_On_Minority_Pub_en_low.pdf. Accessed 17 July 2018.

McDougall, G. 2011. *Report of the Independent Expert on Minority Issues. Addendum: Mission to Rwanda (A/HRC/19/56/Add.1)*. Geneva: United Nations Press.

Minority Rights Group International. 2015. *Minorities, indigenous peoples and the post-2015 framework*. London: Minority Rights Group International.

Nussbaum, C. M. 1997. Capabilities and Human Rights. *Fordham Law Review* 66 (23). http://ir.lawnet.fordham.edu/flr/vol66/iss2/2. Accessed 3 Mar 2018.

Office of the High Commission for Human Rights. 2008. Forum on Minority Issues. 2008. *Inaugural Session of the Forum on Minority Issues: The Right to Education*. https://documents-dds-ny.un.org/doc/UNDOC/GEN/G09/118/19/PDF/G0911819.pdf?OpenElement. Accessed 25 Aug 2018.

Okafor, O.C. 2005. Righting, Restructuring, and Rejuvenating the Post-Colonial African State: The Case for the Establishment of an AU Special Commission on National Minorities. *African Yearbook of International Law* 13 (1): 43, 464.

Selassie, A. G. 1992/1993. Ethnic Identity and Constitutional Design for Africa. *Stanford Journal of International Law* (Fall): 1, 5.

Sen, A. 1993. Capability and Well-being. In *The Quality of Life*, ed. M. Nussbaum and A. Sen, 30–53. Oxford: Clarendon Press.

Slimane, S. 2003. *R Recognizing Minorities in Africa*. London: Minority Rights Group International. http://www.minorityrights.org. Accessed 25 May 2018.

United Nations (UN). 1985. *United Nations Declaration on the Right to Development*. http://www.un.org/documents/ga/res/41/a41r128.htm. Accessed 25 Aug 2018.

United Nations. 1999. *Consideration of Reports Submitted by States Parties Under Article 40 of the Covenant: Gabon*. Report No. CCPR/C/128/Add.1. Available at https://tbinternet.ohchr.org/_layouts/15/treatybodyexternal/Download.aspx?symbolno=CCPR%2FC%2F128%2FAdd.1&Lang=en.

United Nations. 1992. *Declaration on the Rights of Persons Belonging to National or Ethnic, Religious and Linguistic Minorities*. http://www.ohchr.org/Documents/ProfessionalInterest/ccpr.pdf. Accessed 25 Aug 2018.

United Nations. 1994. *UN Human Rights Fact Sheet No. 18 (Rev.1). Minority Rights*. Geneva: United Nations Press.

United Nations. 2000. *United Nations Millennium Declaration*. https://www.un.org/millennium/declaration/ares552e.htm. Accessed 25 Aug 2018.

United Nations. 2004. *High-Level Task Force on the Implementation of the Right to Development*. https://www.ohchr.org/EN/Issues/Development/Pages/HighLevelTaskForce.aspx. Accessed 5 Apr 2018.

United Nations. 2005. *UN Millennium Project, Investing in Development: A Practical Plan to Achieve the Millennium Development Goals*, 32. New York: UN.

United Nations. 2008. *The UN "Protect, Respect and Remedy" Framework for Business and Human Rights*. https://www.business-humanrights.org/en/un-secretary-generals-special-representative-on-business-human-rights/un-protect-respect-and-remedy-framework-and-guiding-principles. Accessed 24 Aug 2018.

United Nations. 2009a. *State of the World's Indigenous Peoples*. http://www.un.org/esa/socdev/unpfii/documents/SOWIP/en/SOWIP_web.pdf.

United Nations. 2009b. *UN Common Understanding on Human Rights-Based Approaches to Development*. https://hrbaportal.org/the-un-and-hrba. Accessed 24 Aug 2018.

United Nations. 2014. *Report of the UN Independent Expert on Minority Issues, Rita Izsák*. https://www.ohchr.org/Documents/HRBodies/HRCouncil/MinorityIssues/Session7/GAReport_SR_MinorityIssues_en.pdf. Accessed 25 Aug 2018.

United Nations. 2015. *The Millennium Development Goals Report 2015*. http://www.un.org/millenniumgoals/2015_MDG_Report/pdf/MDG%202015%20rev%20(July%201).pdf. Accessed 15 June 2018.

United Nations. 2018. *ICCPR*. https://www.ohchr.org/en/professionalinterest/pages/ccpr.aspx. Accessed 25 Aug 2018.

United Nations Development Programme (UNDP). 2010. *Marginalized Minorities*. New York: UN Bureau for Development Policy.

United Nations General Assembly (UNGA). 1986. *Adoption of Declaration on the Right to Development by UN General Assembly, Resolution 41/128 of 1986-12-04.* New York. http://www.un.org/documents/ga/res/41/a41r128.htm. Accessed 25 Aug 2018.

United Nations General Assembly. 1993. *Vienna Declaration and Programme of Action 1993-06-14-25.* Vienna, Austria. https://www.ohchr.org/en/professionalinterest/pages/vienna.aspx. Accessed 25 Aug 2018.

Vandenhole, W. 2003. The Human Right to Development as a Paradox. *Verfassung und Recht in Übersee (Law and Politics in Africa, Asia and Latin America)* 36 (3): 377–405.

Venkatasawmy, R. 2015. Ethnic Conflict in Africa: A Short Critical Discussion. *Transcience Journal* 6 (2): 26–37. http://hdl.handle.net/1959.13/1330910. Accessed 20 May 2018.

World Bank. 1995. *Uganda: Bwindi Impenetrable National Park and Mgahinga Gorilla National Park Conservation.* Global Environment Facility, Project Document 12430—UG. Washington, DC: Global Environment Coordination Division, World Bank.

World Bank. 2005, July. *Operational Manual OP 4.10 for Indigenous Peoples.* https://policies.worldbank.org/sites/ppf3/PPFDocuments/090224b0822f89d5.pdf. Accessed 20 May 2018.

World Bank. 2011. *Improving the Odds of Achieving the MDGs: Heterogeneity, Gaps, and Challenges.* Global Monitoring Report.

Dr. Paul Mulindwa is a Post-Doctoral Fellow in the Department of Politics and International Relations under SARChI: African Diplomacy and Foreign Policy, at the University of Johannesburg, South Africa. He holds a Master's degree in Human Rights from Makerere University in Uganda and Bachelor's of Philosophy from Pontifical Urbaniana University, Rome. Dr. Paul Mulindwa previously worked with the Centre for Conflict Resolution (think-tank) based in Cape Town, South Africa as Senior Project Officer. He also worked with the United Nations Population Fund, Minority Rights Group International, Amnesty International and Rule of Law Association. His research interests are focusing on indigenous ethnic minorities in development. His academic interests are: human rights, governance, peacekeeping and peacebuilding. He has 18 years' experience in governance, development, human rights and peacebuilding work in Africa.

Part III
Human Rights

Chapter 5
Theorising the Direct Effect Doctrine of International Law in Human Rights Enforcement

Torque Mude

Abstract This chapter theorises the direct effect of international law in human rights enforcement in the *Campbell* and *Von Abo* cases. Since international law has assumed a significant role in relation to securing the rights of individuals in domestic and international courts, it suffices to explore a theoretical framework that provides analytical insight into the competence of international law in this endeavour. For the purpose of this chapter, the triangulation of the realist and transnational legal process theories are explored to provide theoretical grounding upon which the competence of international law in human rights enforcement in the cases in question will be understood. The theories in question were propounded by scholars from across the sister disciplines international politics and international law. Even though they largely diverge in assumptions, both explain why states comply or do not comply with international law at both international and domestic levels. The realist theory focuses on political processes and factors in analysing compliance with international law while transnational legal process focuses on legal processes and factors in examining compliance. Hence, realism deals with how politics influence why states obey international law while transnational legal process is concerned with how international law influences why states obey.

Keywords International law · Direct effect · Human rights enforcement · *Campbell* case · *Von Abo* case

Introduction

This chapter explores the Direct Effect Doctrine as a theoretical and conceptual framework that guides the chapter and also as a subject whose effect is examined in the chapter. It is a narrative, descriptive and analytical chapter. The chapter is narrative because it outlines and gives an account of what Direct Effect entails. It

---

T. Mude (✉)
Department of Politics and Public Management, Midlands State University, Zvishavane, Zimbabwe
e-mail: mudet@staff.msu.ac.zw

is descriptive because it explains what the doctrine seeks to achieve and analytical since it critically analyses the functional applicability of the doctrine in securing the welfare of individuals in the Campbell and Von Abo cases. Furthermore, the realist and transnational legal process approaches are analytically explored in this chapter as the theoretical foundations of this chapter.

The *Campbell (Pvt) Limited and Others versus The Republic of Zimbabwe (SADC (T) 02/2007)*, hereinafter, referred to as the Campbell case was decided by the SADC Tribunal on 28 November 2008. It emanated from the land conflict that resulted from the land reform and resettlement program that Zimbabwe embarked on in the year 2000. Mainly, white former farmers including Mike Campbell and others lost their farms and properties as a result of this policy. They sought relief from the Zimbabwean judicial system, but to no avail. In 2007, they lodged an application to appear before the SADC Tribunal and their application was successful. In November 2008, the SADC Tribunal delivered a ruling in favour of the white former commercial farmers.

Like the Campbell case, the Von Abo case, *Von Abo v Government of the Republic of South Africa and Others: Case Number ZAGPHC 226/2008*, had roots in Zimbabwe's land reform. The Von Abo case was concerned with a South African national, Crawford von Abo, who took the South African government to the North Gauteng High Court for failure to provide him with diplomatic protection in respect of the violation of his property rights in Zimbabwe due to the land reform programme in that country. The North Gauteng High Court decided the case on the basis of International Law and delivered a judgment in favour of the applicant. It ordered the South African government to take appropriate measures to remedy the violation of its national's rights by the Zimbabwean government. Hence, a national court compelled the state to perform an international act governed by International Law which impacted on foreign relations between South Africa and Zimbabwe. The court invoked diplomatic protection which is an institution of the branch of International Law called State Responsibility. Even though direct effect is not a common practice in the African context due to lack of clear provisions of the principle, it can be argued that the North Gauteng High Court gave direct effect to diplomatic protection irrespective of the absence in South African of a provision to give direct effect to diplomatic protection.

Both cases illustrate the encroachment of International Law into the domestic arena in challenging states and governments for failing to protect their nationals in need. To this end, International Law's Direct Effect in achieving the intended objectives in domestic affairs warrants investigation. Hence, this chapter examines the strength of the Direct Effect of International Law in securing the rights of individuals in domestic affairs by cross-examining the Campbell and Von Abo cases. The conclusion drawn from the two cases is that the Direct Effect of International Law is potent in human rights enforcement, but the national interests of states and other political considerations inhibit its success.

The Campbell and Von Abo cases illustrate the interest International Law has developed in securing the welfare of individuals in domestic affairs. Hence, Zimbabwe and South Africa's patterns of compliance with International Law in their internal affairs warrant investigation pertaining to the strength of the direct effectiveness of International Law in their national affairs. The theoretical grounding of the process through which International Law was used to compel these states to protect their nationals, how the states perceived the processes and the outcome of the cases in respect of compliance with the rulings are examined in this chapter.

The justification for basing the Direct Effect of International Law on domestic affairs on compliance with rulings is that complying with a ruling can be a good measure of the efficacy of the direct effect of International Law. Tyler (1997: 2440) asserts that 'for law to be effective in fulfilling its role of minimising the occurrence of socially damaging behaviours, people must comply with the dictates of the law…the law must be obeyed'. Using this argument, this chapter considers compliance with International Law as the fulfilment of obligations dictated by a national court. However, the cases are analysed from the determination, ruling and post-ruling levels of a case in order to eliminate subjectivity and to widen the horizons of understanding the potency of Direct Effect in human rights protection. Compliance with International Law is used as a benchmark to examine the final effects the Direct Effect of International Law had in the two cases. At this juncture, it is imperative to unpack the concept of Direct Effect of International Law. Prior to unpacking this concept, it suffices to diagrammatically present the nexus between Direct Effect, human rights enforcement and compliance with Direct Effect rulings.

The transnational legal process through which individuals in the Campbell and Von Abo cases is presented as human rights enforcement in the diagram below. The diagram presents the ABC of how the Direct Effect of International Law in domestic affairs is examined in this chapter. It is presented as human rights enforcement because the ultimate purpose of human rights litigation in these cases was to achieve the protection of the individuals in question. As indicated in the diagram, the applicability of International Law in the human rights enforcement process and compliance with International Law-based decisions are used as yardsticks for measuring the potency of the Direct Effect of International Law in Zimbabwe and South Africa. Both the acceptance of International Law in human rights enforcement and compliance with rulings illustrate the strength of the direct effectiveness of International Law in domestic affairs.

Diagram 1

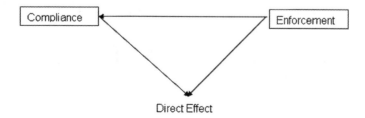

Direct Effect of International Law in Domestic Affairs: A Conceptual Analysis

The Direct Effect of International Law is twofold. First, it denotes that the international legal system engenders obligation on states to protect their citizens. Second, it gives individual rights to directly influence enforcement of their rights by directly invoking International Law before national courts (Olivier 2014: 168; Nollkaemper 2014: 105; Weiler 2014: 95). Direct Effect has two varieties; vertical and horizontal Direct Effect. Both horizontal and vertical Direct Effects are concerned with human rights enforcement. For the purpose of a succinct comparison and explanation of the varieties of Direct Effect and dynamics thereof in human rights enforcement, the chapter commits the next sub-section towards that.

Varieties of Direct Effect Explained

Horizontal Direct Effect is concerned with relations between individuals. In accordance with horizontal Direct Effect, an individual can invoke International Law in relation to another individual in the interests of redressing violated rights of the former (Eurofound 2016). For instance, a natural individual can depend on Direct Effect of treaty provisions which confer individual rights to make legal claims against a legal or private individual such as firm or organisation before national courts. The effectiveness of the horizontal Direct Effect has been noticeable in areas related to employment and industrial relations because few treaty provisions confer rights to individuals in those issue areas (Ibid.). More so, it can be argued that horizontal Direct Effect does not attract much attention because, in many cases, issues to do with individual conflicts regarding employment and industrial relations are not as sensitive as state-individual conflicts relating to human rights involving vertical Direct Effect.

Unlike horizontal Direct Effect, vertical Direct Effect deals with relations between individuals and states. Accordingly, vertical Direct Effect empowers citizens to apply vertical Direct Effect in claims against states of one's nationality or foreign states to enforce their rights (Eurofound 2016). With vertical Direct Effect, an individual can directly invoke International Law against a government to enforce his/her rights. This chapter is premised on vertical Direct Effect since individuals in the Campbell and Von Abo cases invoked International Law against Zimbabwe and South Africa regarding the human rights of applicants. It is argued that political considerations of states have made the Direct Effect of International Law—almost a phantom on the horizon. This is attributable to the complex nexus between International Law and political considerations, especially national interests which this chapter expounds in a multidimensional manner.

The Origins of the Doctrine of Direct Effect

Direct effect emerged in the jurisprudence of the ECJ in 1963 in the famous Van Gend en Loos case. The case is concerned with the abrupt change in the classification of goods for custom purposes resulting in the subjection of goods to various import duty tariffs that affected Dutch importers (Berski 2016: 5). Relying on Article 12 of the European Community Treaty (presently Article 30 of the Lisbon Treaty), the importers questioned the decision by the government before the ECJ. In part, the regional court decided that:

> The community constitutes a new legal order of international law for the benefit of which the states have limited their sovereign rights, albeit within limited fields, and the subjects of which comprise not only member states but also their nationals. Independently of the legislation of member states, community law therefore not only imposes obligations on individuals but is also intended to confer upon them rights which become part of their legal heritage. These rights arise not only where there are expressly granted by the treaty, but also by reason of obligations which the treaty imposes in a clearly defined way upon individuals as well as upon the member states and upon the institutions of the community.... [European Court of Justice: Judgment in Van Gend en Loos versus Netherlands Inland Revenue Administration: Case 26-62 (1963) ECR].

It is the above determination of the ECJ ruling that introduced the doctrine of Direct Effect. Fifty years (2018) since the decision in the case, Direct Effect is still considered as one of the significant achievements of the ECJ (Craig 1992: 453). The iconic nature of Van Gend en Loos has been acknowledged by scholars who have concluded that it was a legal game changer (Nollkaemper 2014: 105) that shaped and constituted the new international legal order (Olivier 2014: 165; Weiler 2014: 94). Since the ECJ ruling, judicial practice of Direct Effect proliferated throughout the world to over 1 100 cases (Oxford Reports on International Law in Domestic Courts in Nollkaemper 2014: 106). Hence, the doctrine gained momentum as a proxy for governance (Weiler 2014: 98) not only in the European context but also in non-European contexts. It is this judicial practice of Direct Effect, even though without explicit reference to the doctrine, as well as the hybrid nature it assumed in the African context, coupled with the dismissal of its compatibility with African legal systems that prompted this chapter to examine the potency of the phenomenon in the Campbell and Von Abo cases.

It is explicitly indicated in the ECJ ruling that EU law constitutes a new legal order of International Law characterised by limited state sovereignty for the benefit of individuals in the context of human rights. By making reference to the implications of EU law on International Law with regard to Direct Effect, it is not farfetched to interpret the ruling to imply that Direct Effect could be diffused to other parts of the world for the same benefits to individuals as implied in the Van Gend en Loos case. Furthermore, with the level of interconnectedness of the world in all aspects of life including the political, economic and legal facets, it would be minimalistic to argue that Direct Effect has exclusive relevance in the European context.

While some scholars have concluded that Direct Effect is a potent proxy tool for human rights enforcement (Nollkaemper 2008: 1) that represents an effective and seductive bottom-up human rights enforcement approach (Weiler 2014: 96–97), some have argued that it presents a dilemma by limiting state sovereignty by piercing territoriality which gives states the monopoly over the effects of International Law within their domestic legal orders (Chalmers and Barroso 2014: 3). Against such a background, it suffices to indicate that the traditional understanding of state sovereignty has undergone remarkable change to embrace the rights of individuals. Consequently, Direct Effect evolved a legal and socio-legal mechanism to spearhead the human rights cascade. As a socio-legal phenomenon, Direct Effect attaches the political, social and economic interests of the individual in asserting those rights to the public interests of warranting the rule of law at the transnational level (Weiler 2014: 96). As a legal phenomenon, Direct Effect denotes the mutual obligation among states as rights owed by states to individuals which national courts must protect (Ibid.).

Therefore, since the ECJ was the first international tribunal to adjudicate in a state-individual dispute in the Van Gend en Loos case in which the ruling was in favour of the individual, the precedence is that individuals have been elevated as subjects of International Law. Apart from being instrumental in the emergence of the doctrines of Direct Effect and the supremacy of community law over national law, the jurisprudence made the individual a 'legal vigilante' of the rule of law in the international legal system (Weiler 2014: 96). As a result of Direct Effect, individuals have been able to rely on International Law to enforce their own rights; the practice commonly discouraged by traditional political theorists such as Thomas Hobbes and Niccolo Machiavelli on the basis of sovereignty. The incorporation of international rules in domestic law through direct applicability also emanated from the ECJ jurisprudence. At this juncture, it suffices to illuminate on the distinction between Direct Effect and direct applicability.

Direct Effect and Direct Applicability

Since the two concepts are usually conflated, it is important to clarify their interplay. Direct applicability and Direct Effect are different yet interconnected doctrines that describe and explain the dynamics through which International Law operates in the EU legal order. Direct Effect refers to the mechanism through which individuals could obtain rights in national courts based on International Law, whereas direct applicability relates to whether EU law or International Law in general become part of national law without the need for implementing legislation such as an act of parliament (Winter 1972). For instance, EU Treaties and regulations are directly applicable in the national law of member states because once a treaty is signed or a regulation is passed in Brussels by the Council of Ministers it automatically becomes applicable in all EU member states (Ibid.). Put simply, Direct Effect is concerned with the reliance on International Law in domestic courts by individuals and direct applicability is when International Law becomes part of national law without measures or procedures at the national level to incorporate international rules into domestic law. The premise of this chapter is on Direct Effect.

Brief Scope of Direct Effect

From the configurations of Van Gend en Loos, Direct Effect is concerned with whether the provision of a Treaty could be relied on as a source of individual rights that national courts protect. Broadly understood, the doctrine is designed for the enforcement of human rights by individuals in national courts. According to the ECJ, Direct Effect limits the sovereign rights of states to pave way for the enforcement of their rights directly by individuals concerned [European Court of Justice: Judgment in Van Gend en Loos vs. Netherlands Inland Revenue Administration: Case 26-62 (1963) ECR]. It suffices to indicate that Direct Effect is not contained in treaties but is evident in judicial practice. Furthermore, it ought to be stressed that Direct Effect does not have operational parameters in relation to which rights have Direct Effect in domestic courts. Since its emergence, the doctrine has been used and in many cases without direct mention of the concept.

Challenges Confronting Direct Effect

Direct Effect has attracted conceptual and practical criticism from across the legal and political frontiers. According to Olivier (2014: 181), Direct Effect results in role splitting as national judges are required to apply both International Law and national law in national courts. One challenge relating to role splitting is that national courts lack the professional capacity to correctly apply international norms as most judges have little, if any, International Law experience or training and the politicisation of proceedings in politically sensitive and legally complex cases (Shany 2012: 206).

In continuation of the above, judges in both the case considered in this chapter have been criticised for politicising cases or incorrectly concluded their cases. For instance, Tladi (2009) argued that Prinsloo's judgment in the Von Abo case could have possibly been in protest against South Africa's policies towards Zimbabwe. In other words, Tladi inferred that judges can be influenced by political dynamics to decide cases in favour of those they sympathise with or against those they despise.

Another challenge associated with Direct Effect is its incompatibility with the Westphalia notion of state sovereignty whose contemporaneous understanding many states, especially in Africa, appear not willing to embrace. Chalmers and Barroso (2014: 3) have advanced the argument that Direct Effect limits the very foundations of state autonomy and state sovereignty. Arguments on the implications of International Law on state sovereignty are more profound in Third World states largely because they associate the international legal system with Western imperialism and hegemonic foundations of capitalism (Chimni 2006; Anghie 2005; Chinkin and Charlesworth 2000; Cass 1996). Indeed, International Law can is a lawfare mechanism by the Western countries to subject African countries to their imperialist political agendas.

Hence, in light of the decolonisation agenda, nationalism and the need to erase the notion of Western superiority complex, it has become the national objectives of African states to embark on a political and constitutional transformation agenda resulting in their disdain of International Law machinations including human rights. Part of this anti-colonial movement has been evidenced by the trajectory of embattled Africa-International Criminal Court (ICC) relations in which African states have contemplated withdrawing from the ICC en masse citing its selective application of international criminal law against Africans. Evidently, dissociating and viewing International Law, including Direct Effect whose foundations are Western, with contempt has become more of African states' national interests. In the end, compliance with Direct Effect-related rulings is arguably a mammoth task largely due to such political considerations.

Interplay Between Direct Effect and Political Considerations

The nexus between the Direct Effect of International Law in domestic affairs and political choices of governments is complex. Direct Effect can be used both as a tool for human rights protection and as a shield for protection of domestic political institutions or a government from judicial review predicated on International Law (Nollkaemper 2014: 17). As a tool for the protection of human rights, it circumscribes government powers and transposes the ability of individuals to invoke International Law as the basis for the protection of their rights. As a 'shield', Direct Effect can be used as a smokescreen by dualist states to restrict International Law from influencing internal affairs of the state, particularly on issues of human rights enforcement. Exhaustion of local remedies, the requirement to incorporate International Law into domestic law, non-liquet, the principle of non-justiciability and national interests are usually invoked to shield the government from the functional applicability and enforceability of rules of International Law in national affairs.

The above justifies the assertion by Morgenthau (1985: 26) that when confronted by political interests, International Law has no effect on state behaviour. Hence, political decisions are usually employed to moderate the influence of International Law in domestic affairs. It can therefore be argued that once political interests intercept the direct effect of International Law in domestic affairs, its functions in the protection of individual rights become redundant. This can largely be attributed to the extent of separation of powers in a state. While the doctrine of separation of powers suffices to prevent the executive from interfering with judicial issues, the practice in pseudo-democratic states like Zimbabwe reduces separating powers to a mere charade.

Unlike in the Zimbabwean context, the judiciary in South Africa appears independent. Nonetheless, it can be argued that South Africa's political interests in terms of the significance of Zimbabwe-South Africa diplomatic, political and economic ties contributed to the South African government's reluctance to heed the ruling by the North Gauteng High Court to provide Von Abo with due diplomatic protection.

Consequently, securing the welfare of individuals becomes problematic and the blame is usually directed towards the voluntary nature of the international legal system and its inability to impose forceful measures against the derelict conduct of states.

However, the influence of political decisions does not always suffice to make the functions of International Law in domestic affairs redundant. Due to the increasing influence of transnational legal practices, individuals are now able to successfully take governments to task for failing to protect them as in the Campbell and Von Abo cases. Nevertheless, reprimanding governments and compliance with human rights enforcement rulings are totally different processes and inquiries. Whereas individuals can seek legal recourse against governments in national courts, states as sovereigns are at the helm of decision-making with regard to compliance with rulings. Such decisions often reflect political preferences of states to the detriment of protection of individuals. This practice was evident in Von Abo and Campbell cases.

Conceptualising Compliance with International Law

The term compliance is used differently in different circumstances. Broadly defined, compliance is an act of doing what you have been asked to do (Merriam-Webster Dictionary Online), an act of conforming, submission, obedience or conformance (Black's Law Dictionary 1990: 285). The Black's Law Dictionary uses the terms compliance, conformity and obedience interchangeably. Although the three can be used interchangeably, there exists a pronounced difference. In How Is International Human Rights Enforced? Koh (1999: 1400) gave a precise distinction between the three terms.

For him, conformity happens when a state conforms its conduct to a rule when it is convenient to do so, compliance is when a state accepts being bound by a rule due to fear of punishment or to get rewards and obedience is when a state adopts the conduct that is prescribed by a rule because of internalisation of a rule in the state's value system (Koh 1999: 1400). Basing on Koh's interpretation, states practice more of conformance and compliance and very little obedience. This chapter refers to compliance with International Law as complying with court orders obliging Zimbabwe and South Africa to abide by rules of International Law.

Varying reasons have been cited to explain why states sometimes comply with International Law while disregarding it in other instances. States comply with International Law to protect their national interests (Guzman 2002: 1825; Wallace and Ortega 2009), pursue their interests (Koh 1997:2652), because International Law is effective (Raustiala and Slaughter 2002: 539) and because they risk losing the incentives that follow obeying it (Dixon 2013: 13; Hillebrecht 2014: 969). These same reasons may be invoked to explain the direct effect of International Law in domestic affairs because compliance with a ruling influenced by International Law can be a good measure of its direct effectiveness.

This chapter treats compliance not as a once-off event, but as a gradual process that emanates from the determination level of the case, decision level and the post-decision level vis-à-vis the objectives of the case. According to Bilder (2003: 66); and Haas (2003: 45), compliance is a process and it is not an 'on–off switch' (Mayntz 2002: 1964).

Many studies delved on states' perceptions of International Law vis-à-vis their domestic laws which are largely explained by the monist, dualist and harmonisation theories to analyse motivation for compliance. While accepting some of the explanations advanced by monist, dualist and harmonisation theories in analysing the relationship between International Law and domestic law in influencing compliance, this chapter interrogates factors which transcend the nexus between the two legal systems. Therefore, a realist perspective suffices to explore this phenomenon which dualists, monists and harmonisation theorists eclipse.

The following sections lay the theoretical framework upon which this chapter hinges. The theoretical framework provides insights into the potency of the direct effectiveness of International Law in securing the welfare of individuals in domestic affairs using the realist theory and transnational legal process. Compliance with International Law is considered as one of the intriguing and controversial questions in International Law (Guzman 2002: 1842). However, no theoretical paradigm has adequately explained what motivates compliance or non-compliance with International Law. Since the direct effect of International Law in domestic affairs is largely determined by the decisive influence of international rules in national affairs, as well as on obedience with judgments predicated on international rules, this chapter delves on the triangulation of the realist and transnational legal process theories to provide theoretical grounding upon which the potency of direct effect of International Law will be examined.

The realist theory is a rationalist theory while the transnational legal process theory belongs to the normative category of international legal theory. These theories were propounded by scholars from across the sister disciplines of international politics and International Law in explaining why states comply or do not comply with International Law at the international level. This chapter employs these theories to explain the competence of the Direct Effect of International Law in domestic affairs in issues involving state preferences vis-à-vis individual interests.

Justification for triangulating realism and transnational legalism is that realism focuses on political processes and factors in analysing compliance with International Law while transnational legal process focuses on legal processes and factors in examining compliance. Realism deals with how politics influence why states embrace rules of International Law. Transnational legal process is concerned with how International Law and related legal practices influences why states comply. The next section discusses the assumptions of the realist theory and the transnational legal process theory and their usefulness in this chapter in explaining the potency of the Direct Effect of International Law in securing the welfare of individuals in the Campbell and Von Abo cases.

The Realist Theory

The realist theory is understood as an international political theory that explains human nature in comprehending the political behaviour of political actors (Forsyth 2006: 267). It has its roots in the writings of Italian Renaissance politician, historian, philosopher, diplomat and humanist Niccolo Machiavelli who, because of his 1513 political treatise, *The Prince*, was labelled the father of political realism. *The Prince* gave birth to Machiavellianism which is the employment of cunning and duplicity in statecraft or in general human interaction. Political realism is therefore premised on 'what is' or reality. It views states as rational, self-interested and unitary actors that calculate the benefits and costs of their actions in their interaction with other actors. Political realism maintains that power is the primary end of all political action. Other philosophers like Thomas Hobbes have also significantly influenced the development of political realism.

Modern proponents of political realism are Hans J. Morgenthau, Reinhold Niebuhr George Kennan, Henry Kissinger and Edward H. Carr among others. A reformulation of the classic realist tradition of Morgenthau, Carr and Niebuhr culminated into Kenneth Waltz's neorealist theory. Outlined by Waltz in his 1979 book, *Theory of International Politics*, neo-realism, which is also known as structural realism, has the same tenets as classical realism. This chapter is informed by classical realist assumptions, especially the tenet that power exigencies eliminate ethical considerations.

Political realism should not be confused with legal realism. Legal realism upholds that judges decide cases by considering factors that transcend pre-existing law (D'Amato 2010: 1). This chapter is not guided by legal realism. The following section delves on justification for the use of realism in this chapter.

Justification for Using an International Relations Theory

Despite being an international relations theory, the realism also touches on International Law because international relations and International Law cover much of the same scholarly territory. In fact, International Law is a subfield of international relations. The two have been oddly estranged (Koh 1997: 2615) by pervasive academic insularity (Beck 1996: 3) stemming from the omnipresent international relations–International Law divide. Though contestable, the two share identical ontological and epistemological affinities. First, it should be mentioned that both disciplines are largely state-centred even though they embrace the significance of non-state actors. Second, International Law and international relations share the same core interests including peace and security, traditionally the preserve of the state and contemporaneously for individuals as well. At this juncture, it suffices to briefly conceptualise international relations and international law to illustrate how interrelated the two disciplines are.

On the one hand, the discipline of international relations is concerned with the relations between and among states and non-state actors such as international organisations, multinational corporations, non-governmental organisations and individuals. It is concerned with the analysis of the dynamics, complexity and unpredictability of events in the world. Events such as war, cooperation, political and economic competition among others are the focus of international relations analysis. On the other hand, international law governs international relations. Therefore, the conceptual and theoretical collaboration between international relations and international law is clear.

Consequently, this chapter treats realism as an international legal theory drawing substantially from the idea of International Law–international relations interdisciplinary collaboration supported by Abbott (1989: 172), Keohane (1992: 180), Young (1992: 175) and Burley (1993: 205). The 'two cultures problem' (Beck 1996: 18) of analysing International Law and international relations theories as absolutely distinct is not appreciated in this chapter. Many political scientists have habitually left International Law to lawyers while legal scholars have unceremoniously downplayed the conceptions of political scientists on international rules, compliance and related analyses. Against this disciplinary insularity, Henkin (1968: 6) has also lamented over the unprecedented phenomenon which has driven the student of politics and the student of law to look at the same world from different point of views.

The Nexus Between International Relations and International Law Theories

Since International Law and international relations are sister disciplines, theoretical approaches to them are explicitly interwoven. Hence, realism, liberalism, international legal process and rational choice theories are classified as international relations–International Law approaches in international legal theory. It is apparent that there is no way international legal theories can ignore political factors and their interplay with legal norms. Similarly, political theories cannot overlook the influence of the law on political behaviour. Legal scholars largely draw from political science and international relations worldviews including realists, liberalists and institutionalists. These approaches are quintessentially useful to the international legal order because they address key political-legal issues of power, legal personality and dynamics of state perceptions of and compliance with, international rules.

Realism as an International Law–International Relations Theory

Since time immemorial, both international politics and International Law scholars have always addressed similar issues including peaceful coexistence of states, security, international rules, human rights and justice among others. The demarcation between International Law and international politics as well as differences in their theoretical foundations emerged during the Cold War (Koh 1997: 2615). Such a synthetic separation of the two fields generated confusion and distorted conceptions regarding their theoretical premises. The works of legal and political philosophers intersect both disciplines. For instance, the works John Austin, a legal philosopher, English philosopher and political radical Jeremy Bentham as well as political philosopher Thomas Hobbes influenced both classic and modern political realist assumptions on the legal qualities and effectiveness of International Law in relation to state behaviour and variations power.

Those who uphold a positivist realist strand opined that states do not obey International Law because it lacks the qualities of law. Austin's argument that International Law is not law is, however, disputed in this chapter. Jeremy Bentham, whose writings influenced Austin, argued that states obey International Law due to the persuasion from other states participating in a discursive international legal process. Bentham's process-oriented assertion resonates with Koh's transnational legal process. However, the former negates the contribution of non-state actors, whereas the latter acknowledges their contribution to influencing compliance with International Law. Furthermore, Hobbes maintains the rationalist perspective which asserts that states observe International Law only when it serves their short-term or long-term interests. Recent scholarship has also observed the intersection between political and legal theory. Hence, Burley (1993: 205) maintains that political theorists scrutinise constitutions and legal theorists inquire into the nature and substance of political issues. It is without doubt, therefore, that one can use a political theory such as realism to analyse the dynamics of International Law.

When applied to the international legal system, realism is viewed as one of the principal rationalist theories of compliance with International Law. Realists view International Law as epiphenomenal and argue that considerations of power, more than law, determine compliance (Morgenthau 1985: 26). Morgenthau further posits that International Law is premised on power and when confronted with actions of determined states, it is rendered weak and ineffectual (Ibid.). This conception dismisses the relevance of International Law and views International Law as utopian that has no effect on state behaviour. While this view has some measure of truth, it can be argued that the role of International Law in altering state behaviour cannot be discredited. For instance, states have always observed the law of diplomatic relations by respecting each other's diplomatic officials and premises. On the human rights front, even though political interests have a bearing on compliance, international rules are influential is setting standardised parameters guiding how states treat individuals.

Political realists such as Carr (1946: 179) argue that International Law should not be comprehended independent of the political foundations on which it anchors and of the political interests of states which it seeks to serve. For Carr, International Law largely represents the interests of states. Applied to this chapter, the encroachment of International Law in domestic affairs to promote human rights could be dismissed, by realists, as an idealist waste of time because state preferences always supersede issues of individual human rights enforcement. Against this background, realism is ideal for this chapter because it hints on the factors which could have influenced or hindered Zimbabwe and South Africa from complying with International Law; human rights law and diplomatic protection, respectively. Such factors have a bearing on the competence of the Direct Effect of International Law in human rights enforcement in domestic affairs.

For instance, Zimbabwe's rejection of the SADC Tribunal's judgment in the Campbell case was justified based on the existential quandary of state sovereignty which empowers a state to govern its territory, including treatment of its nationals, the way it pleases. Furthermore, South Africa invoked the principle of non-justifiability and successfully appealed against the North Gauteng High Court's ruling that ordered the South African government to exercise diplomatic protection on behalf of Von Abo following the expropriation of his properties in Zimbabwe.

The influence of political interests on the Direct Effect of International Law in domestic affairs is not peculiar to Zimbabwe and South Africa. The Abbasi case explicitly illustrates the superiority of political interests over the welfare of individuals. In the Abbasi case, Feroz Ali Abbasi's appeal against the British government's failure to grant him diplomatic assistance in respect of his unlawful detention by the United States (US) government at Guantanamo Bay in Cuba, was dismissed by the British Court of Appeal which held that it did not have jurisdiction over a case on diplomatic protection because this was a foreign policy issue belonging to the Executive. Wallace and Phillips (2009: 263) cited the Anglo-American 'special relationship' that characterises Britain's foreign policy towards the USA as a contributing factor to ITS refusal to espouse diplomatic claims on behalf of Abbasi.

However, when it comes to European Union's (EU) supranational law, European states, at least in theory, recognises the supremacy of EU Community law over national interests. Like the doctrine of Direct Effect, the supremacy of European Union law evolved through the jurisprudence of the European Court of Justice (ECJ) in the Van Gend en Loos and Costa-ENEL cases during the early years of the ECJ. While this is not a comparative chapter, it suffices to argue that the SADC Tribunal failed to create jurisprudence fostering the importance of human rights over national interests and sovereignty. Consequently, Zimbabwe could not heed the tribunal's ruling as it invoked the primacy of her sovereignty over the welfare of Campbell and others.

Like the European Court of Justice, the EACJ also established its case law in its first case to arrogate to itself the authority to ascertain the commitment of member states in human rights enforcement. In the Katabazi case decided in 2005, the EACJ ignored efforts by member states to backlash against its human rights rulings based on sovereignty (Gathii 2013: 252). This defies Posner and Yoo's (2005: 966) view which dismisses the compatibility of the functions of International Law in domestic politics in Africa.

How the ECJ and the EACJ dealt with the resistance of states to allow International Law to conform their domestic affairs to international understandings of legality and failure by the SADC Tribunal to do the same is explained by the transnational legal process theory. The theory disaggregates national interests and highlights the role of morality in inducing compliance with International Law. However, the theory admits the influence of state interests in determining compliance with International Law. Koh categorically stated that states comply with International Law to get external incentives and to avoid adverse results or actions.

In the context of this chapter, the shortcoming of realism in explaining the Direct Effect of International Law in domestic affairs is its state-centric foundations. It views states as the primary subjects of International Law (Smith 1986: 219; Jennings and Watts 1992). This conflicts with the mixed actor view that recognises the importance of non-state actors including individuals in International Law (Nijman 2010: 10). This chapter upholds the mixed actor conception that recognises legal personality of individuals. In the contemporary international legal system, individuals are recognised as subjects of International Law (McDougal 1994: 160–162; Higgins 1994: 49–50; Waldron 2009: 10). To fill the gap left by realism in conceptualising some of the dynamics, this chapter uses Koh's transnational legal process theory to comprehend the use of International Law to resolve domestic problems, the status of individuals in International Law and to complement the rigidity of realism regarding the influence of International Law on state behaviour. The transnational legal process theory is normative, non-statist, dynamic, non-static and non-traditional (Koh 1996: 184).

Realism also upholds the supremacy of politics over law. The Campbell and Von Abo cases confirm this tenet. The ruling of the SADC Tribunal in the Campbell case against Zimbabwe culminated in Zimbabwe's withdrawal of her membership of the court and the subsequent unanimous dissolution of the regional court by SADC states pending reforming the court's mandate. The dissolution of the tribunal to revise its mandate to limit its jurisdiction is a clear indication of the realist assumption that states are not constrained by International Law in circumstances of paramount political interests. That could partly explain why Morgenthau (1985: 295) calls International Law primitive and ineffective. More so, the statist nature of diplomatic protection which the South African government cited as the basis for dismissing the North Gauteng High Court's ruling in the Von Abo case, arguably to maintain her relations with Zimbabwe, illustrates that International Law is part of political reality. Hence, states are unitary actors who maximise their own preservation even to the detriment of their own nationals (Waltz 1979: 118).

The Campbell and Von Abo cases illustrate that International Law reflects the interests of states. First, International Law is not mandatory because state consent is the foundation of International Law (Henkin 1995: 27). A state may choose to accept certain principles of International Law and deny others. A state may also choose whether or not to be party to proceedings involving International Law. National interests influence these decisions made by governments. Zimbabwe chose to withdraw her membership of the SADC Tribunal when the tribunal delivered a ruling which had negative implications for the country's land reform policy. The Von Abo case exposed the state-centeredness of diplomatic protection which makes it an exclusive state right which the state decides whether, when and how to use depending on the nature of its relations with the offending state. Hence, states are primarily concerned with their survival (Legro and Moravcsik 1999).

Even though International Law is based on national interests, its competence in securing the protection of individuals should not be downplayed. Aust (2005: 3) observed that the true nature of International Law is disfigured by those who concentrate on its breaches. The adjudication of the SADC Tribunal in a domestic conflict between Zimbabwe and her nationals could be interpreted as an indication of the competence of International Law in domestic affairs. However, an analysis of Zimbabwe's reception of the SADC Tribunal's ruling in the Campbell case gives the impression that International Law failed to secure the rights of Campbell and other white farmers. Therefore, it can be argued that the direct effect of International Law should be measured beyond compliance with court judgements. The transnational legal process theory therefore becomes useful in comprehending the merits of the process and practice through which International Law was invoked as the basis for decisions against Zimbabwe and South Africa.

Transnational Legal Process Theory

The transnational legal process theory was propounded by Harold Hongju Koh who is (as of 2016) the Sterling Professor of International Law at Yale Law School. Koh is a renowned American lawyer and legal scholar. While realism considers using International Law to influence state behaviour as utopian, the transnational legal process offers a flexible, accommodative and moralistic approach to the comprehension of the direct effect of International Law. Transnational legal process is understood as a process and theory. Koh (1996: 183–184), defines the transnational legal process as the theory and practice through which state and non-state actors interact in a variety of fora including domestic and international to make, interpret, enforce and internalise norms of International Law. Even though the theory does not mention the term Direct Effect, the process it expounds is an explicit replication of Direct Effect.

As a theory, it holds that states comply with international rules when they internalise the norms and incorporate them into their value systems (Koh 1997: 2646) and to avoid undesirable outcomes or to attract certain incentives (Koh 1999: 1400). Hence, states act in accordance with international rules and decisions when the benefits of complying exceed the cost. Like realism, Koh's theory sheds light on why states comply with International Law; albeit from a moralistic perspective. As a process, it examines how actors provoke an interaction which forces an enunciation of international norms which may be applied to a particular situation and the internalisation of the new global norm into states' value systems.

The encroachment of International Law in domestic affairs for the protection of individuals has become a twenty-first-century global phenomenon that many states have embraced but are resisting conformity at the levels of compliance. Those that are resisting, Koh's theory submits, cannot insulate themselves forever from complying with international rules because regular participation in the transnational legal process will produce internalised compliance (Ibid., 199). There is a measure of truth in Koh's assumption of ultimate compliance. The Zimbabwean government's announcement in 2014 of its commitment to compensate white former farmers who lost their land since year 2000, a retraction of its declaration in 2008 that it had no obligation to compensate these individuals, bears testimony to Koh's assumption. Koh's theory acknowledges and accepts that states sometimes resist obeying International Law. Like realism, it also indirectly recognises the centrality of national interests. However, the theory is more inclined to the process through which International Law intersects with power through a complex process of rational self-interest and norm-internalisation to achieve internalised compliance. The theory provides useful insight into the strength of the Direct Effect of International Law as it expounds on how states end up complying with International Law despite being driven by national interests.

Transnational legal process is of fairly recent origins. Its development was largely influenced by interdependence and transnationalism. It has its roots in transnational law which emerged in 1956 and in Henry Steiner and Detlev Vagts' transnational legal problems concept contained in the 1968 casebook as well as the concept of international legal process. At this juncture, it is imperative to define transnational law, international legal process and international legal problems. Transnational law refers to the law whose operation transcends national frontiers; it is a mixture of domestic and International Law that has assumed dominance in modern societies (Koh 2006: 745). Transnational law may be formal or informal. Good examples of formal transnational law are European Union law, SADC law, East African Community law, ECOWAS law and Inter-American law.

International legal process is a theory propounded by Chayes, Ehrlich and Lowenfeld in 1968. It is a theory used in analysing how International Law is practically applied in international affairs and the means through which it can be improved. International legal problems refer to a mix of all international and domestic problems including issues related to human rights, trade and law among other important related issues. The terms international legal problems and transnational legal problems can be used interchangeably. Problems that befell Von Abo in Zimbabwe and Campbell and other farmers in the same country due to the 2000 land reform fall within the transnational legal problems category.

To understand the puzzling void in international legal scholarship and the near dogmatic dichotomy between international and domestic legal scholarship, Koh propounded the transnational legal process theory. His theory was influenced by the shortcomings and grey areas in international legal process, international legal problems and transnational law particularly an unclear explanation of how and why states obey International Law (Koh 1996: 183).

According to Koh (2002), a complex new order has supplanted the realist world order of sovereign states in this era of globalisation. Indeed, the advent of the human rights discourse, the emergence of new threats which are neither purely domestic nor international but rather transnational and other recent developments in governance have seen a shift, not complete change, in both domestic and international political and legal processes and practices. The increasing intervention of International Law in domestic politics to pursue the preferences of the individual is notable of these changes in the contemporary world order. While Koh acknowledged the increasing visibility of intense state centrality (Ibid.), he also observed that the new order has embraced the importance of non-state actors and a plethora of new decisional fora.

For instance, it can be observed that the last decade of the twentieth century witnessed an increase in the number of international courts than any other decade. As a result, there are now more than 20 judicial bodies that are increasingly being used and international judicial activity has since increased (Alter 2002: 4). The proliferation of international courts and tribunals has thus consolidated the standing of individuals in transnational legal practices. Until 2012, the jurisdiction of tribunals such as the SADC Tribunal was limited to inter-state disputes. The ECOWAS Court of Justice and East African Court of Justice, among others, permitted the *locus standi* of individuals in human rights litigation.

More so, the adjudication of the SADC Tribunal in Zimbabwe's domestic issues could be identified as an example of new decisional fora in the new world order because until recently, only states could appear before international courts under traditional International Law. However, the realist world order dominated by sovereign states still resonates. For instance, a nation depends on his or her state of nationality for diplomatic protection and as illustrated in the Von Abo, Abbasi, Van Zyl and other cases, states decide whether, when and how to exercise diplomatic protection based on their national interests. While this may be worrisome, the further development of the transnational legal practices could redress the traditional foundations sustaining the constraining effects of national interests. So far, the flexibility, non-statism, dynamism and normativity that characterise Koh's transnational legal process have introduced a ray of hope in defying mainstream realist assumptions that puts the state above individuals.

Koh's transnational legal process has four characteristics. First, it is non-traditional in that it does not recognise the traditional dichotomy that demarcated what constitutes domestic and international in the international legal and political systems (Koh 1996: 184). Traditionally, International Law and domestic law as well as international politics and domestic politics were analysed independent of each other. The traditional gulf separating these disciplines began to clear in the second half of the twentieth century when the importance of the multidisciplinary approach emerged at the instigation of multidisciplinarism. In accordance with the multidisciplinary approach, the transnational legal process treats international and domestic law and international and domestic politics as intrinsically intertwined. The increasing role International Law has assumed in domestic affairs bears testimony to transnationalism which is a manifestation of the multidisciplinary approach. Hence, the Von Abo case was cabined within neither domestic law nor International Law as a combination of national law and International Law was invoked in the North Gauteng High Court.

Second, transnational legal process has a non-statist approach to International Law (Ibid.). It defies the traditional realist view that states are principal subjects in the international arena. The transnational legal process embraces proactive non-state actors including individuals. Abbott (1989: 335) concedes that non-state actors are critical players in transnational legal process and Nijman (2010: 2) observed that non-state actors are agenda-setters of the future. Thus, International Law is no longer confined to inter-state relations only. It has assumed the responsibility of regulating intrastate relations; relations between governments and their citizens as evidenced in Campbell and Von Abo cases. However, states still maintain a considerable degree of power to determine the enforcement of International Law. Nonetheless, other subjects of International Law also have the power, albeit limited, to influence compliance through a variety of mechanisms including offering rewards.

Third, transnational legal process embraces dynamism. As a process, it is not static (Ibid.) because transnational law percolates and mutates from the domestic realm to the international realm, from state–state relations to state–citizen relations. In the Von Abo case, a national court invoked International Law to resolve a conflict between the state and its national and attempted to enforce diplomatic protection through compelling the South African government to act on behalf of Von Abo. In the Campbell case, a domestic dispute between the government and its citizens was heard in an international court because Zimbabwean law ousted the jurisdiction of national courts to entertain land cases against the government. Notably, both cases are concerned with International Law's effort to secure the welfare of individuals in domestic affairs through compelling governments to protect their citizens.

Fourth, Koh's theory is normative. It describes and explains the process of interaction through which international legal norms emerge and why states obey these norms. Koh argued that the process does not only generate new rules but also generate new interpretations of those rules and internalises them into national rules that guide the conduct of governments towards their citizens. The assumed role of International Law in domestic affairs could be construed as a new interpretation of rules designed for the protection of human rights. To this end, the extent to which Zimbabwe and South Africa gave direct effect to international rules by prioritising individual interests over national interests is what this chapter seeks to examine using transnational legal process and realist theories. While the theories have inherent differences, their explanations for the motivation for states to comply with International Law are intrinsically intertwined. Both emphasise the centrality of state interests in influencing compliance with International Law.

Rationale for Selecting Realism and Transnational Legal Process

Realism and transnational legal process were chosen because they complement each other in examining the strength of the direct effectiveness of International Law in domestic affairs. Transnational legal process is suitable in exploring the process through which International Law entered the domestic affairs of the states in question and why they reacted the way they did following decisions predicated on international rules. Realism is appropriate in explaining factors that determine the efficacy of direct effect of rulings in the Campbell and Von Abo cases. Realism has a rationalistic approach, whereas transnational legal process is normative in approach. However, their assumptions complement each other in explaining factors that determine the potency of the force and effect of International Law in human rights enforcement in internal affairs. This does not imply that this chapter analyses the reasons for compliance or non-compliance with International Law. Put simply, the Direct Effect of International Law in domestic affairs is partly measured by the extent to which the states in question enforced the rulings in fulfilment of the objective to secure the welfare of individuals.

Against the above background, it can be argued that by theory accumulation in this chapter, the two theories complement each other in examining the strength of the Direct Effect of International Law in securing the welfare of individuals in domestic affairs. On the one hand, the basic assumption of realism on the force and effect of International Law is that observance of International Law is a result of power dynamics. For realists, considerations of national interests rather than international rules determine obedience. On the other hand, the whole process of individuals taking their governments to court over failure or reluctance to protect them is explained by Koh's theory as transnational process of human rights litigation. Transnational legal process further posits that states observe International Law because their governments adopt standard operating mechanisms and other internal operating procedures that foster default patterns of habitual compliance with international legal rules.

Apart from this assumption, this chapter employs the basic tenets of transnational legal process that states observe international rules for incentives, to minimise costs of non-compliance and its illumination of the process through which International Law reaches domestic affairs. There is a point of agreement in these two theories; that decisions to allow the force and effect of International Law rests with states. It is this nexus that makes both of them appropriate for this chapter. At this point, it is imperative to examine the relationship between these two theories.

Nexus Between Realism and Transnationalism

Although the realism is rationalistic, whereas transnational legal process is normative, the two theories intersect in analysing the complex factors which determine the potency of Direct Effect of International Law in domestic affairs. It should be noted that the former underscores the politics of compliance while the latter focuses on when and how Direct Effect can be achieved. For realists, the force of International Law is largely driven by power dynamics and self-interests of states. For transnational legal process, key to the effectiveness of International Law is internalised compliance which emanates from norm-internalisation; the process through which states incorporate International Law into their municipal laws and practices. It is further submitted that norm-internalisation results from rational normative calculation of the benefits of compliance relative to costs. Both recognise the importance of national interests, but transnational legal process takes a step further in explaining how International Law overlaps national interests through the complex interaction between rational national interests and norm-internalisation spurred by transnational litigation that involves non-state actors.

Despite methodological differences, both reach for the same intuitive response with regard to why states may allow the Direct Effect of International Law in human rights enforcement in their internal affairs; voluntary observance not coerced compliance. In the final analysis, it is the state that determines whether what and when to permit the Direct Effect of International Law in its internal affairs. Thus, the direct effectiveness of International Law in securing human rights protection in domestic affairs is determined by a state's reception of International Law. However, transnational legal process broadens their focus of analysis to include the influence of non-state actors that is not reducible to rational calculations. Nevertheless, it does not assume away the rational calculations of states. In other words, the focus of attention in examining the Direct Effect of International Law in domestic affairs in this chapter will be whether, how, to what extent and for what reason did Zimbabwe and South Africa permit International Law's human-centric objectives in national affairs.

In both the Campbell and Von Abo cases, Zimbabwe and South Africa appeared to have the exclusive deciding powers on human rights litigation despite being compelled by both national and international courts to protect their citizens. This chapter does not interpret the decisive role of the state as an indication of the exclusive superiority of the politics over International Law. It rather accepts it as a foundational character of International Law which makes it consent-based. Moreover, this chapter does not construe the influential role of the state in observing International Law as a weakness of the international legal system. Nevertheless, the fact that International Law operates in state-centric system is accepted, but not to exaggerative levels.

International Law does not operate independently of political factors that determine order and security at both domestic and international levels. That is why realists maintain that states comply with International Law when compliance serves their interests. The same can be said of Koh's transnational legal process that explains habitual compliance with International Law as a result of the internalisation of international rules into a state's value system which depends on a cost-benefit analysis. Since the internationalisation of rules is a result of interactions that produce certain patterns of interpretations of international rules and lastly internalisation, there is no doubt that political factors also influence these processes. The political factors omitted by Koh in explaining motivations of internalising rules of International Law are therefore highlighted by realists; hence, the two theories meet half way in unpacking the dynamics inherent in this chapter.

Since its inception, International Law has always been dependent on states for formulation and compliance. It has always been made through the practice of states and by agreements entered into by states. The reality of it all is that the international legal system was designed to protect state rights. Only recently have rules emerged to advance the welfare of the individual. However, even human rights instruments depend on states for ratification and adoption. Furthermore, even though the emergence of human-centric international rules necessitated the encroachment of International Law in domestic affairs, the state is empowered with the authority to influence final decisions even in human rights litigation. However, this does not erode the effectiveness of International Law. Putting the state at the helm of International Law serves to protect the state from human rights litigations influenced by other states with a view to influence policies in another country in the pursuit of a foreign state's interests.

Therefore, history has shown that there is no way a state may be forced by a court to be part to proceedings or to allow International Law to influence its actions unless it willingly accepts to do so. Only states may directly force another state to protect human rights through humanitarian intervention. International organisations may also indirectly, at the instigation of states, use force in humanitarian intervention. The North Atlantic Treaty Organisation (NATO) forcibly intervened in Kosovo in 1999 to stop the killing of Serbs. The operation was based on the idea related to the initiative developed in the Pinochet decision that there are some crimes so egregious that a state responsible for perpetrating them, despite the principle of sovereignty, may be subject to military intervention (Roberts 1999: 102). However, such interventions are also influenced by the ulterior political interests of those states that intervene.

It can be argued that sovereignty is the source of state power to decide whether to allow the Direct Effect of International Law in its domestic affairs. Therefore, the direct effectiveness of International Law in domestic politics could be dependent on sovereignty. This is because sovereignty is dominant, but yet a contested concept in political and legal discourses. The Westphalia concept of sovereignty denotes the supreme and unlimited power of the state (Lake 2003: 305). However, contemporary state sovereignty has been observed to have been eroded by human rights (Weiss 2007: 97). In theoretical terms, Weiss's argument is correct because even individuals can now invoke International Law in challenging states in human rights litigation. Nonetheless, states still maintain their authority, except in circumstances where they voluntarily ratify human rights treaties, agree to be bound by human rights law and accept to be parties in human rights litigation as in the Campbell and Von Abo cases.

However, even in cases of invitational abrogation, states still maintain their final say in governance decision-making. Bartelson (2006: 465) noted that the sovereign state is likely to remain a potent source of authority even in the future. Moreover, Held (2003: 162) argued that due to internal sovereignty, governments, whether democratic or aristocratic, must enjoy the final and absolute authority within a given territory. As such, there is no doubt that states are still enjoying sovereign rights and it is analytically questionable to suggest that sovereignty has been eroded or undermined by human rights. More so, claims that sovereignty has been re-characterised, reconstructed and reformed lack realistic appreciation of what is on the ground that the sovereign state is still intact.

Back to the theoretical grounding of this chapter, Koh's internalised compliance implies voluntary surrendering of sovereignty. However, such submission of sovereign rights to courts either in human rights litigation or not cannot be separated from considerations of national interests. Most importantly, it suffices to mention that both theories are inclined to voluntary compliance. Consequently, it appears that the matrix of the competence of the Direct Effect of International Law in domestic affairs puts the state at the helm of decision-making. However, transnational legal process highlights how the final decision to obey International Law is influenced by a series of interactions which contribute to enunciation of an international norm and lastly to the internalisation of compliance into a state's value system. Nevertheless, all these processes are based on voluntary, not coerced decision-making in the sense of compliance with court decisions. Hence, this chapter applies realism and transnational legal process to gain insight into the competence of direct effect of international rules in the Von Abo and Campbell cases.

Conclusion

This chapter has fleshed out its theoretical and conceptual framework by analysing, describing and narrating the contours of the Direct Effect Doctrine of International Law. The chapter highlights that realism's compliance with International Law and Koh's transnational legal process are applicable in this research. The former is concerned with the rationalistic nature of the state in calculating the costs and benefits of obeying International Law. It places emphasis on the contribution of power dynamics and national interests as the driving factors behind compliance. The latter disaggregates the state and emphasises the role of non-state actors in influencing obedience with International Law. For Transnational legal process, the key to explaining obeying International Law is norm-internalisation into a state's value system. The chapter observed that the two theories have methodological differences in understanding compliance with International Law, but they concur on the centrality of the state in influencing the reception of the force and effect of International Law in domestic affairs. The chapter envisaged the Direct Effect of International Law in domestic affairs partly as a result of compliance with International Law.

References

Abbott, K.W. 1989. Modern International Relations Theory: A Prospectus for International Lawyers. *Yale Journal of International Law* 14: 335–411.

Alter, K.J. 2002. The European Union's Legal System and Domestic Policy: Spill over or Backlash? *International Organisations* 54 (3): 489–518.

Anghie, A. 2005. *Imperialism, Sovereignty and the Making of International Law*. Cambridge: Cambridge University Press.

Aust, A. 2005. *Handbook of International Law*. Cambridge: Cambridge University Press.

Austin, J. 1832. The Province of Jurisprudence Determined. In *Austin: The Province of Jurisprudence Determined*, ed. W.E. Rumble, 1995. Cambridge: Cambridge University Press.

Bartelson, J. 2006. The Concept of Sovereignty Revisited. *The European Journal of International Law* 17 (2): 463–474.

Beck, R.J., et al. 1996. *International Rules: Approaches from International Law and International Relations*. Oxford: Oxford University Press.

Berski, A. 2016. *Which Doctrine has had the Bigger Impact on EU Law Direct Effect or Supremacy?*, 1–12 Dublin Institute of Technology.

Bilder, R. 2003. Beyond Compliance: Helping Nations Cooperate. In *Commitment and Compliance: The Role of Non-Binding Norms in the International Legal System*, ed. D. Shelton, 2003. Oxford: Oxford University Press.

Black, H. C. 1990. Black's Law Dictionary. 6th ed. In *Black's Law Dictionary*, ed. H. Black, 1990. Minnesota: West Publishing Company.

Burley, A.M.S. 1993. International Law and International Relations Theory: A Dual Agenda. *American Journal of International Law* 87 (2): 205–239.

Carr, E.H. 1946. *The Twenty Year's Crisis, 1919–1939: An Introduction to the Chapter of International Relations*, 2nd ed. London: MacMillan.

Cass, D. 1996. Navigating the Newstream: Recent Scholarship in International Law. *Nordic Journal of International Law* 65: 341–383.

Chalmers, D., and L. Barroso. 2014. What Van Gend en Loos stands for. *International Journal of Constitutional Law* 12 (1): 105–134.

Chimni, B.S. 2006. Third World Approaches to International Law: A Manifesto. *International Community Law Review* 8: 3–27.

Chinkin, C., and H. Charlesworth. 2000. *The Boundaries of International Law: A Feminist Analysis*. Manchester: Manchester University Press.

Craig, P.P. 1992. Once Upon a Time in the West: Direct Effect and the Federalisation of EEC Law. *Oxford Journal of Legal Studies* 12 (4): 453–479.

D'Amato, A. 2010. Legal Realism Explains Nothing. Northwestern University School of Law Scholarly Commons, Faculty Working Papers, Paper 84, 1–20.

Dixon, M. 2013. *Textbook on International Law*, 7th ed. Oxford: Oxford University Press.

Eurofound. 2016. *Direct Effect*. http://www.eurofound.europa.eu/direct-effect. Accessed 24 July 2015.

European Court of Justice: Judgment in Van Gend en Loos versus Netherlands Inland Revenue Administration: Case 26-62 [1963] ECR.

Forsyth, D.R. 2006. *Group Dynamics. Business Law: Texts and Cases* (Online). https://www.cengagebraino.com.mx/forsyth68220_0534368220_02_01. Accessed 28 July 2015.

Gathii, J.T. 2011. Third World Approaches to International Law: A Brief History of its Origins, its Decentralised Network and a Tentative Bibliography. *Trade, Law and Development* 3 (1): 1–41 [Online]. Available at: http://www.tradelawdevelopment.com/index.php/tld/article/viewFile/3%281%29%20TRADE%20l.%26%20dev.%2026%20%20%282011%29/73. Accessed 29 August 2014.

Guzman, A.T. 2002. A Compliance-Based Theory of International Law. *California Law Review* 90 (6): 1823–1886.

Haas, P.M. 2003. Choosing to Comply. In *Commitment and Compliance: The Role of Non-Binding Norms in the International Legal System*, ed. D. Shelton, 2003. Oxford: Oxford University Press.

Held, D. 2003. The Changing Structure of International Law: Sovereignty Transformed? In *The Global Transformations Reader: An Introduction to the Global Debate*, ed. D. Held and A. McGrew, 162–176. Cambridge: Polity Press.

Henkin, L. 1995. *International law: Politics and Values*. Dordrecht: Martin Nijholf.

Henkin, L. 1968. *How Nations Behave: Law and Foreign Policy*. New York: Columbia University Press.

Higgins, R. 1994. *Problems and Processes: International Law and How We Use It*. Oxford: Clarendon Press.

Hillebrecht, C. 2014. The Domestic Mechanisms of Compliance with International Human Rights Law: Case Studies from the Inter-American Human Rights System. *Human Rights Quarterly* 34 (1): 959–985.

Janis, M.W. 1984. Jeremy Bentham and the Fashioning of International Law. *American Journal of International Law* 78 (2): 405–418.

Jennings, R., and Watts, A. 1992. *Oppenheim's International Law*, 9th ed. Harlow: Longmans.

Keohane, R.O. 1992. Compliance with International Commitments: Politics Within a Framework of Law. *Proceedings of the American Society of International Law* 86: 176–180.

Koh, H.H. 1996. Transnational Legal Process. *Nebraska Law Review*, Faculty Scholarship Series 2096, 75: 181–207.

Koh, H.H. 1997. Why Do Nations Obey International Law? *Yale Law Journal*, Faculty Scholarship Series Paper 2101, 2599–2659.

Koh, H.H. 1999. How Is International Human Rights Law Enforced? *Indiana Law Journal* 74 (4): 1396–1417.

Koh, H.H. 2002. The Spirit of the Laws. *Harvard International Law Journal* 43 (1): 23–39.

Koh, H.H. 2006. Why Transnational Law Matters? *2006 AALS Annual Meeting*. January 4, 2006.

Lake, D. 2003. The New Sovereignty in International Relations. *International Studies Review* 3 (1): 303–323.

Legro, J.W., and A. Moravcsik. 1999. Is Anybody Still a Realist? *International Security* 24 (2): 5–55.

Mayntz, R. 2002. International Organisations in the Globalisation Process. In *Globalisation of Law II: International Organisations and Regulatory Areas*, ed. P. Nahamowitz and R. Voigt. Nomos: Baden-Baden.

McDougal, M. 1994. *International Law, Power and Policy: A Contemporary Conception*. Boston: Brill.

Merriam-Webster.com. Compliance (Online). http://www.meriam-webster.com/dictionary/compliance. Accessed 11 Nov 2015.

Morgenthau, H.J. 1985. *Politics Among Nations: The Struggle for Power and Peace*. New York: McGraw Hill.

Nijman, J.E. 2010. *Non-state Actors and the Rule of Law: Revisiting the Realist Theory of International Legal Personality*. Amsterdam: Centre for International Law.

Nollkaemper, A. 2014. The Duality of Direct Effect of International Law. *European Journal of International Law* 25 (1): 105–125.

Olivier, S.R. 2014. The Evolution of Direct Effect in the European Union: Stocktaking, Problems and Projections. *International Journal of Constitutional Law* 12: 165–188.

Posner, E.A., and J.C. Yoo. 2005. Reply to Hefler and Slaughter. *California Law Review* 93 (3).

Raustiala, K., and A.M. Slaughter. 2002. International Law, International Relations and Compliance. In *Handbook of International Relations*, ed. W. Carlsnaes, T. Risse, and B.A. Simmons, 538–558. London: Sage Publication.

Roberts, A. 1999. NATO's 'Humanitarian War' over Kosovo. *Survival* 41 (3): 102–123.

Shany, Y. 2012. Should the Implementation of International Rules by Domestic Courts be Bolstered? In *Realising Utopia: The Future of International Law*, ed. A. Cassese, 200–210. Oxford: Oxford University Press.

Smith, M.J. 1986. *Realist thought from Weber to Kissinger*. Baton Ronge, LA: Louisiana State University Press.

Tladi, D. 2009. The Right to Diplomatic Protection, the Von Abo Decision and One Big Can of Worms: Eroding the Clarity of Kaunda. *Stellenbosch Law Review* 20 (1): 1–14.

Tyler, T.R. 1997. Compliance and Obedience. In *International Encyclopaedia on the Social and Behavioural Sciences*, ed. N.J. Smelser, and P.B. Baltes, 2001, 2240–2445. Oxford: Elsevier.

Waldron, J. 2009. Are Sovereigns Entitled to the Benefits of the International Rule of Law. *Indiana International Law Journal* 3 (1): 315–343.

Wallace, W., and C. Phillips. 2009. Reassessing the Special Relationship. *International Affairs* 85 (2): 263–284.

Wallace, R.M.M., and Ortega, O.M. 2009. *International Law*, 6th ed. Pretoria: Juta.

Weiler, J.H.H. 2014. Van Gend en Loos: The Individual as Subject and Object of International Law and the Dilemma of European legitimacy. 12 (1): 94–103.

Waltz, K. 1979. *Theory of International Politics*. New York: Random House.

Weiss, G. 2007. R2P after 9/11 and the World Summit. *Wisconsin International Law Journal* 24 (3): 741–760 (Online). http://hosted.law.wisc.edu/wordpress/wilj/files/2012/02/weiss.pdf. Accessed 20 July 2013.

Young, O.R. 1992. International Law and International Relations Theory: Building Bridges—Remarks. *Proceedings of the American Society of International Law* 86: 172–175.

Dr. Torque Mude is a lecturer in the Department of Politics and Public Management at Midlands State University in Zimbabwe. He has a Doctor of Literature and Philosophy in International Politics from University of South Africa. In the thesis, he examined the potency of the direct effect of international law on human rights enforcement in the domestic courts of Zimbabwe and South Africa. His areas of research interest are international politics, peace and security and international law. He teach international law, international politics, peace and security studies at both undergraduate and postgraduate levels.

Chapter 6
Getting Beyond the Somalia Syndrome? Revisiting the United States' Intervention in Liberia 15 Years Later

Raymond Kwun Sun Lau

Abstract The 2003 US intervention in Liberia was the first time since the Somalia debacle in 1992 that Washington became involved again in military intervention with humanitarian purposes in Africa. While the 'Mogadishu factor' might explain the minimal and limited American involvement in Liberia's second civil war, it does not adequately explain what has motivated the US government to re-engage in Liberia and West Africa since 2003. This chapter seeks to make a contribution to the debate on the use of military force in US foreign policy in arguing that US intervention in Liberia is situated in the broader context of American foreign policy towards Africa after 9/11. The principal argument here is that Washington's partial rehabilitation from the 'Somalia syndrome' and gradual re-engagement with Liberia and the West Africa region is largely motivated by two major factors: the global war on terror and subsequent militarisation of US Africa policy, and the desire to enhance US energy security by shifting America's foreign oil dependency away from the Middle East. The article concludes by examining the implication of US intervention in Liberia for future military interventions that comprise human protection purposes in Africa.

Keywords Mogadishu factor/Somalia syndrome · Rwanda effect · New interventionism · Military intervention for humanitarian purposes · Responsibility to Protect (R2P) · Bush doctrine · Global War on Terrorism

Introduction

While US President George W. Bush made a historic speech from the flight deck of the USS Lincoln on 1 May 2003, which declared the end of major combat operations in Iraq, the second civil war was escalating in Liberia since the eruption of the country's first civil war in 1989. Two bouts of brutal civil wars in 1989–1996 and 1999–2003 left the country impoverished and devastated, making it one of the most

R. K. S. Lau (✉)
Department of History, Hong Kong Baptist University, 15 Hong Kong Baptist University Road, Baptist University Road Campus, Kowloon Tong, Kowloon, Hong Kong
e-mail: raymondlauks@hkbu.edu.hk

© Springer Nature Switzerland AG 2020
E. Benyera (ed.), *Reimagining Justice, Human Rights and Leadership in Africa*, Advances in African Economic, Social and Political Development,
https://doi.org/10.1007/978-3-030-25143-7_6

violent conflicts in Modern Africa. Along with half a million people being internally displaced, an estimated 250,000 out of the country's population of 3.1 million were killed (United Nations Secretary-General 2003). On 28 June 2003, the United Nations (UN) Secretary-General Kofi Annan urged for a deployment of multinational forces and requested the US to consider 'spearheading the deployment of that force' (United Nations Secretary-General 2003: 3) In response, President Bush directed the Secretary of Defense to position 'appropriate military capabilities' off the coast of Liberia to help support the deployment of West African peacekeeping forces (USA Today 2003).

Subsequently, almost one month after Bush's first official trip to Africa in July 2003, his administration positioned some 2300 US Marines off the coast of Liberia and sent some 200 Marines into Monrovia, the Liberian capital in August 2003 (Weiner 2003). The immediate mission of the Marines was to provide logistical support to the Economic Community of West African States (ECOWAS) forces 'in order to mitigate a humanitarian crisis' (Ross 2005: 61). In the aftermath of the 1992 debacle in Somalia where 18 US soldiers were killed, US military involvement in Liberia's second civil war was the first time in a decade that America became involved again in military intervention with humanitarian purposes in Africa. According to J. L. Holzgrefe, humanitarian military intervention is:

> The threat or use of force across state borders by a state, or group of states, aimed at preventing or ending widespread and grave violations of the fundamental human rights of individuals other than its own citizens, without the permission of the state within whose territory force is applied (Holzgrefe 2003: 18).

Yet, the Bush administration's decision to commit troops to Liberia highlighted divergent views on US–Liberia relations. For some policymakers, like the National Security Advisor Condoleezza Rice, the historically close relationship between the US and Liberia obligated Washington to take the special responsibility of preventing 'humanitarian disasters' in Liberia (Talbot 2003). Some other policymakers, conversely, argued that the country was no longer of major strategic importance for US foreign policy interests, thus America had no special responsibility and should not have been involved in the internal affairs of Liberia.

Indeed, the controversy over whether the US government should have intervened to halt the humanitarian crisis in Liberia was closely related to Liberia's historical ties with America. Given that Liberia is one of Africa's oldest republics and considering its unique history among African states, the purpose of this chapter is to consider the motivation of the Bush administration's troop deployment to Liberia in 2003 and the implications of military intervention for humanitarian purposes. Yet, notwithstanding the context of Liberia's distinctive origins, this chapter suggests that US intervention in Liberia needs to be situated in the broader context of American foreign policy towards Africa after 9/11. Rather than averting a humanitarian crisis, America's gradual re-engagement with Liberia and West Africa during the Bush administration was largely motivated by two major factors: the global war on terror and subsequent militarisation of US Africa policy, and the desire to enhance US energy security by shifting America's foreign oil dependency away from the Middle East.

This chapter begins by providing a brief overview of the special relationship between the US and Liberia. It is followed by the analysis of the evolution of American foreign policy towards Liberia from its founding in the mid-nineteenth century to the outbreak of the country's first civil war in 1990. The chapter then considers how the failed intervention in Somalia impacted on US Africa policy in the 1990s, as well as America's re-engagement with Liberia and West Africa since 2003. The development of a new norm of military intervention for humanitarian purposes and the Responsibility to Protect (R2P) principle is also discussed. The chapter concludes by examining the implication of US intervention in Liberia for military intervention for humanitarian purposes in the future.

US, Liberia and That 'Special Relationship'

By and large, it is no exaggeration to state that the special relationship between the US and Liberia can be described as a kind of brotherly affection. American influences on Liberia were clearly visible on numerous occasions. Its constitution was written at Harvard Law School, the Capitol building was a 'facsimile edition' of the US Capitol and Liberia's flag bears a single star and eleven stripes. Monrovia has the distinction of being the only capital in the world named from a leader of another country, the US President James Monroe. At its origin, Liberia was founded as a new homeland for freed black American slaves by the American Colonization Society (ACS).[1] This 'back-to-Africa experiment' (Oyebade and Falola 2008: 20) formally started in 1822 when the US Congress appropriated an initial $100,000 to the ACS to buy the land for the purpose of establishing the Liberian state (Hyman 2003: 3). Some 10,000 African-Americans and several thousand Africans from interdicted slave ships were resettled by the ACS between 1821 and 1867 (US Department of State 2003a). The descendants of these freed American slaves were referred as Americo-Liberians. Most tellingly, after becoming an independent republic from ACS in 1947, the Liberian Declaration of Independence began, 'We, the people of the Republic of Liberia were originally the inhabitants of the United States of North America (Liberia 1848)'.

With such a strong external influence on the country's creation, it is not surprising that politics throughout Liberia's history has been subjected to ongoing American influence (Dunn 1999: 91). The US–Liberia bilateral relations had largely been asymmetrical: With the country being under the control of the Americo-Liberians (representing only 5% of the population) through the True Whig Party (TWP), Liberia was virtually a one-party state for some 133 years.[2] It was not until 1980 when Sergeant

---

[1] The organisation was established in 1816 by the Reverend Robert Finley, a Presbyterian clergyman from Basking Ridge, New Jersey. It is a political project formulated by the ACS for the sake of repatriating Africans and African Americans to West Africa. See *Library of Congress Exhibition* (2010).

[2] The 158-year male-dominant rule was broken when Ellen Johnson-Sirleaf was inaugurated as Africa's first democratically-elected female head of State in Liberia on 16 January 2006.

Samuel Doe, purportedly representing the indigenous people, perpetrated a bloody military coup d'état to overthrow the last Americo-Liberian President William R. Tolbert Jr. after the rice riots on the 14th April 1979 in Monrovia (Hyman 2003: 10, 21). Thus, 133 years of minority Americo-Liberian quasi-colonial rule as well as the relative peace in Liberia ended and were followed by the reign of terror under Samuel Doe and his People's Redemption Council (PRC).

This disparity between the Americo-Liberians and the indigenous people[3] was apparent during the first 133 years of Liberia's history and triggered, though indirectly, the country's first civil war in December 1989. Notwithstanding its popularity among the indigenous majority, the brutal military rule, election-rigging and rampant human rights abuses of the Doe regime combined with the country's economic collapse precipitated the outbreak of the first Liberian civil war. Moreover, the Doe regime's practice of ethnic cleansing of tribes other than his own Krahn tribe to get rid of opposing forces created serious ethnic tension between the dominant Krahns and other ethnic groups in the republic (Hyman 2003: 26–27). It was against this background that Charles Taylor, leader of a rebel group called National Patriotic Front of Liberia (NPFL), invaded Liberia from the neighbouring country Côte d'Ivoire on the 24th December 1989 and ousted the government of President Samuel Doe. The war, with at least seven warring factions involved, lasted until 1996 when a peace accord was signed, and Taylor became the president the following year.

The purpose of understanding the 'special relationship' between Liberia and the US, however, is neither to analyse the underlying cause nor provide a solution for the Liberian civil war. Instead, it should be treated as a point of departure for examining American foreign policy towards Liberia and US–Liberia relations because it is helpful to understand the motivating factors for US engagement with the oldest republic in Africa, and the wider West Africa region.

US Policy Towards Liberia (and West Africa) in Historical Perspective

The African continent hardly featured in the mindset of foreign policymakers in Washington since Africa had little to offer the US (Copson 2007: 5–6). However, the outbreak of the World War II prompted a shift in America's strategic planning in Africa militarily and economically. West Africa, particularly Liberia, played a key role in US Africa policy during the war. The natural resources of Liberia (the country has the largest rubber plantation in the world), alongside strategic raw materials, agricultural and minerals of West Africa, were instrumental in helping America and its Allies to achieve victory in the World War II. As a key ally of the US during the World War II, Liberia's strategic importance to America was underscored by

---

[3] There are officially 16 ethnic groups residing in Liberia, making up 95% of the country's indigenous African population: Kpelle, the largest group; Bassa, Gio, Kru; Grebo, Mandingo; Mano, Krahn, Gola, Gbandi, Loma, Kissi, Vai, Belleh, Mende and Dey.

President Franklin D. Roosevelt's visit to the country in 1943, on his way back from the Casablanca conference in Morocco. During the height of the Cold War, the country hosted one of the largest Voice of America relay stations in the world. A mutual defence pact was also signed between Liberia and the US in 1959. This resulted in the establishment of military bases and sophisticated communications facilities by the US in Liberia (Westcott 2003), thereby consolidating the special relationship between the two nations.

America's special relations with Liberia during and after the World War II demonstrated one of the key features of US foreign policy since 1945: to prevent the spread of Soviet-style communism in the African continent. Yet, the disappearance of the Soviet Union as the major patron in the proxy war with the US following the end of Cold War inevitably meant that US Africa policy lost focus domestically. The fact that a number of US client states, including Siad Barre in Somalia, Mobutu Sese Seko in Zaire (now Democratic Republic of Congo) and Samuel Doe in Liberia, gradually lost power in the 1990s highlighted Washington's reluctance to provide material and military assistance to prop up its African beneficiaries because of the diminishing strategic importance of the continent. Contrary to the active engagement in the Cold War, US Africa policy after the Cold War can be described as of *permissiveness*—'marginal involvement through making sizable contributions to humanitarian assistance, but otherwise leaving the initiative for action to others' (Dunn 1999: 91).

The first Liberian civil war erupted at a time when foreign policymakers in Washington were preoccupied with the Iraqi invasion of Kuwait. This, as Amos Sirleaf argued, made the Liberian war being 'marginalised' by the Gulf War because of the crucial importance of the Persian Gulf to US national interest in terms of oil supplies (Sirleaf 2000: 84). Yet, perhaps more importantly, the timing of the political upheavals in Liberia coincided with the end of Cold War when the US was no longer preoccupied with the pressing problem of containing Communism in Africa. Accordingly, America's response to the country's first civil war in December 1989 was a testimony to Washington's post-Cold War policy of distancing itself from conflicts in Africa in which America has no vital interests at stake (Oyebade and Falola 2008: 20). When Charles Taylor's NPFL forces were reaching Monrovia, 245 US Marines arrived in warships on 4 and 5 June 1990 to fortify the US Embassy and to rescue and evacuate American personnel (Sirleaf 2000: 84). Notwithstanding the country's historical connection with Washington, the American forces did nothing to help the Liberian people. Washington's lukewarm attitude towards Monrovia is illustrated by the position taken by Robert Gates, the Deputy National Security Adviser and Assistant to President George H. W. Bush, that 'we were not responsible for solving the Liberian problem, no matter what the Africans or anyone else expected' because there is not 'any special US responsibility for Liberia's crisis on the basis of historical ties' (Hyman 2003: 31).

While the waning of strategic importance of the African continent after the end of the Cold War resulted in the decline of US interests and motives in intervening in Africa, humanitarian issues played a historically unprecedented role in international politics since the 1990s (Roberts 1999). The post-Cold War era, particularly during the period 1991–2000, witnessed a revitalisation of the UN Security Council (UNSC) and of its role in the maintenance of international peace and security (Boutros-Ghali 1992: 7; 28). In northern Iraq (1991), Bosnia and Herzegovina (1992–5), Somalia (1992–4), Rwanda (1994), Haiti (1994), Albania (1997), Sierra Leone (1997–2000), Kosovo (1999), and East Timor (1999–2000), there were humanitarian military intervention of some kind by explicit UN authorisation, whether by a UN member state or coalition, or by UN peacekeeping forces, or both (Roberts 2006: 83–84). Given this background, the next section will focus on whether (and how) the context of renewed UNSC activism impacts on the US government to carry out humanitarian military intervention to alleviate human suffering in Africa.

New Interventionism in the 1990s and Post-cold War US Africa Policy

The above-mentioned nine cases, while indicating an increased willingness of the UN Security Council to define any serious humanitarian crisis as a potential threat to international peace and security' (Kundsen 1997: 155), marked the arrival of 'new interventionism' during the 1990s (Stedman 1993: 1–2). The emphasis, according to advocates of human rights, is that state sovereignty is now being placed on the moral obligation of the international community and the eagerness of a revitalised UN to intervene in domestic conflicts throughout the world (Stedman 1993: 1–2). As such, the nine cases between 1991 and 2000 support the 'developing international norm' to forcibly protect civilians threatened by genocide, mass killing and ethnic cleansing' (Annan 1999). Accordingly, military intervention for humanitarian purposes is permissible, provided that it is authorised by the UN or some other formal organisation' (Wheeler 2000: 8).

A dominant feature of this emerging norm to protect civilians since the 1990s is that it is an act 'wholly or primarily guided by the sentiment of humanity, compassion or fellow-feeling, and in that sense disinterested' (Parekh 1997: 54). Indeed, the case that best illustrates this emerging norm and its humanitarian character is Somalia. The US and UN intervention in Somalia was the first time that a peace enforcement operation was being authorised by the UN Security Council under Chapter VII of the Charter for purely humanitarian reasons.[4] The humanitarian crisis in Somalia was triggered by the overthrow of the Siad Barre regime in January 1991, a long time US ally during the Cold War. After the fall of the regime, Somalia descended into clan-based civil war as the country's agricultural and livestock production was utterly devastated. Compounded by drought and famine, the eruption of the full-scale civil war has resulted in some 300,000 to 350,000 Somalis deaths, leaving the country as a 'failed state' without any form of a functioning central government (Lewis and Mayall 2007: 120).

---

[4]On 3 December, the Security Council adopted, unanimously, its resolution 794 (1992), authorising the use of 'all necessary means to establish as soon as possible a secure environment for humanitarian relief operations in Somalia'.

Through a close reading of the conflict, it can be argued that the US mission in Somalia was Washington's bold attempt to adopt the emerging norm of military intervention for humanitarian purposes. The decision to send US military force for alleviating human suffering in Somalia was largely attributed to President George H. W. Bush himself (Wheeler 2000: 123). Importantly, Bush Sr.'s decision to authorise the dispatch of American troops to assist with UN's famine relief efforts in December 1992 came after the President lost his re-election bid, in which his room for manoeuvre was less constrained by electoral politics. This US-led intervention, code-named 'Operation Restore Hope', as Martha Finnemore pointed out, was 'perhaps the clearest example of military action undertaken in a state of little or no strategic or economic importance to the principal intervener' (Finnemore 1996: 154).

After achieving initial success, however, the mission to capture a notorious Mogadishu warlord Mohamed Farah Aidid on 3 October 1993 ended in dramatic casualties of American soldiers, resulting in 18 dead and 84 wounded. Some of the US soldiers' corpses were filmed being dragged around the capital city by Aidid's men. The scale of loss of life suffered by the US military in the now famous 'Black Hawk down' incident was not seen since Vietnam (Pflanz 2011a). This debacle provoked such outrage among American people that President Bill Clinton, who succeeded Bush Sr., had to announce the withdrawal of US troops. New and stringent guidelines regarding the participation of US military in future multinational peace operations, known as Presidential Decision Directive 25 (PDD-25) subsequently constituted an integral part of post-Cold War US–Africa policy (US Department of State 1996). Accordingly, US involvement in UN peacekeeping operations would only be possible if America's national interests were at stake and a clear exit strategy was included (Ero et al. 2001).

Indeed, the lesson learned from the Somalia debacle for foreign policymakers in Washington is that US commitment to military intervention out of humanitarian impulse proves to be unsustainable: a moral mission to halt famine could easily turn into a military disaster (Pflanz 2011b). As Michael Mandelbaum argued, helping distant strangers 'in the fashion of Mother Theresa' or treating 'foreign policy as social work' was not conducive to safeguarding US national interests because diplomats should not act as noble social workers (Mandelbaum 1996). The 'Black Hawk down' incident fundamentally changed America's perception of its role in intractable African conflicts. Since then, this 'Mogadishu factor' has been a locus of US foreign policy concern subsequently (Baumann et al. 2004: 1–8).

America's attitude towards the first Liberian civil war in 1989 suggests that Africa was only of secondary importance in the eyes of foreign policymakers in Washington. Yet in a similar manner, while the end of superpower rivalry in the post-Cold War era has made military intervention for humanitarian purposes more permissible, the Somalia debacle associated with President Clinton's Presidential Decision Directive 25 (PDD-25) had all but virtually ruled out US involvement in similar operations abroad in the future. In other words, despite the UN Security Council's increased willingness to authorise intervention for humanitarian purpose in the era of 'new interventionism', it does not necessarily impact on the US post-Cold War foreign policy making in Africa.

Furthermore, in an unfortunate coincidence of timing, an estimated 800,000 Tutsis and moderate Hutus, roughly 10% of Rwanda's population, were slaughtered by majority Hutu militias, known as the Interahamwe, between April and June 1994 throughout all regions of the country. The scale and speed of the killing—an estimated rate of 333 murders per hour or 5.5 lives per minute in the space of merely 100 days—was arguably the fastest genocide in history (Moghalu 2005: 17). This campaign to exterminate all minority Tutsis and their Hutu sympathisers was closely paralleled with the Nazi Holocaust, as if it was designed as the 'final solution' to the 'Tutsi problem' (Moghalu 2005: 9–24).

However, along with ignoring evidence of an imminent genocide, the UN and its Security Council members simply refused to authorise the deployment of a robust peacekeeping mission and, at the height of the genocide, arguably abandoned the Rwandan people. The UN's failure in Rwanda to prevent or halt the genocide, as described by the 1999 Report of the Independent Inquiry, was because 'there was a persistent lack of political will by Member States to act, or to act with enough assertiveness' (United Nations 1999). Washington's lack of will to commit US troops to support the UN's mandate for halting the 1994 genocide in Rwanda, in this context, might be a 'tragic coincidence of history' since it happened one week after the 'Black Hawk down' incident (Bellamy 2015: 52–53). Yet, as will be explored in the next section, it was the international community's inadequate response to the 1994 Rwandan genocide that provided the catalyst for the emergence of the responsibility to protect (R2P) principle in 2001.

Intervention to Stop Mass Atrocities: The Responsibility to Protect (R2P) Principle

As argued above, the Somalia debacle prompted a shift in US attitudes towards humanitarian military intervention in the post-Cold War era. Yet, and perhaps more fundamentally, US inaction during the Rwandan genocide further exposed the limitation of this emerging norm of military intervention on humanitarian grounds: 'permissibility alone does not necessarily generate an obligation' (Tan 2006: 89). This reveals an indisputable fact that 'the eagerness of the rival superpowers to intervene in countries for the purpose of extending their spheres of influence during the Cold War was replaced by a reluctance on the part of the remaining superpower and its allies to commit their military in regions where there are no perceived national security interests, even when human rights violations in these regions acquire genocidal proportions' (Tan 2006: 85).

Nonetheless, evidence of changing expectations in the post-genocide era since Rwanda were showing up in concerns about how to respond to genocide and mass atrocities in a more effective and consistent manner. The then UN Secretary-General Kofi Annan, in his address to the General Assembly in 1999, argued that 'the core challenge to the Security Council and to the United Nations as a whole in the next century' is 'to forge unity behind the principle that massive and systematic violations of human rights—wherever they take place—should not be allowed to stand' (UN Press Release 1999). Then, in an attempt to move the sovereignty-intervention debate forward, the Secretary-General posed a potentially explosive question to the UN Millennium Summit:

> If humanitarian intervention is, indeed, an unacceptable assault on sovereignty, how should we respond to a Rwanda, to a Srebrenica—to gross and systematic violations of human rights that offend every precept of our common humanity? (UN Secretary-General 2000: 35)

In response to Kofi Annan's challenge, the Canadian government announced the establishment of an International Commission on Intervention and State Sovereignty (ICISS) in September 2000 (ICISS 2001). The ICISS was organised around a central question:

> … when, if ever, it is appropriate for states to take coercive—and in particular military—actions against another state for the purpose of protecting people at risk in that other state?'
> The Commission's answer was the phrase 'responsibility to protect. (ICISS 2001)

The Commission argued that states are entrusted with the primary responsibility for the protection of its people from actual or apprehended large-scale loss of life (with or without genocidal intent) or large-scale 'ethnic cleansing', but the principle of non-intervention in the internal affairs of other states yields to the international responsibility to protect when a state is unwilling or unable to fulfil that protection responsibility.

Since then, the R2P was unanimously endorsed by all UN member states at the 2005 World Summit (United Nations General Assembly 2005) and further elaborated by the new UN Secretary-General Ban Ki-Moon as a 'three-pillar strategy' in his 2009 report (United Nations General Assembly 2009). Crucially, this emerging R2P principle is based on a dual responsibility: a state's primary responsibility to protect its own population from mass atrocities and the responsibility of the international community, at the UN Security Council level, to act in cases of a state's incapacity or unwillingness to discharge this protection responsibility. Annan's rallying cry and the endorsement of R2P principle by all UN member states have, therefore, contributed to a subtle change in the terms of international debate on humanitarian intervention. Instead of generating the debate from the perspective of interveners, there is more awareness that the focus should primarily be on 'the requirements of those who need to seek assistance' (ICISS 2001: 16). Given that the international community's inadequate response to the Rwandan genocide has such a profound impact on the development and endorsement of the R2P principle, Jennifer Welsh frames these changing expectations as the 'Rwanda Effect' (Welsh 2009).

But, perhaps more importantly, the issue at stake is whether the 'Rwanda effect' and the development of the R2P principle served as two major driving forces for the evolution of US foreign policy towards Africa in the aftermath of the 1992 Somalia debacle. The probable impact of the 'Rwanda effect' on post-Cold War US foreign policy towards Africa is reflected in President Clinton's public apology for US inaction in Rwanda during his state visit to the country in 1998 (Wertheim 2010:

158–161). Washington's changing position on the use of force for the protection of civilians was further reinforced by Clinton's statement in June 1999 to the North Atlantic Treaty Organisation (NATO) troops in Macedonia that 'whether you live in Africa or central Europe or any other place, if somebody comes after innocent civilians and tries to kill and it's within our power to stop it, we will stop it' (Clinton 1999). In regard to R2P's capacity to shape American foreign policy behaviour in Africa, it is of paramount importance that it is explored through studying US military intervention in Liberia's second civil war in 2003 and is the focus of the next section of this chapter.

America's Gradual Re-engagement with Liberia and West Africa Since 2003

The US decision to intervene militarily in Liberia's second civil war in 2003 was arguably the first big test for the 'Rwanda effect' and the R2P principle since its birth in 2001. According to Donald Nuechterlein, the US had committed its troops to combat overseas on ten occasions during the period from 1989 to 2003 (Nuechterlein 2005: 135–136).[5] Yet it is worth noting that President Bush's decision to use military force in response to the Liberian conflict was the first time since the 1992 Somalia debacle that America became involved again in military intervention with humanitarian purposes in Africa. What is often referred as 'the siege of Monrovia' (Barrett 1992) happened in July 2003 when President Taylor faced two rebel groups pinning his government into the capital: the Liberians United for Reconciliation and Democracy (LURD) from the north and the Movement for Democracy in Liberia (MODEL) from the east (Kuperman 2009). The eruption of renewed violence resulted in the death of 1000 civilians and displacement of nearly one-third of the country's population (Watchlist on Children and Armed Conflict 2004).

At the height of the siege of Monrovia, President Bush committed his troops to conduct stability operations and support operations (SOSO) by establishing the Joint Task Force Liberia (JTF) (Ross 2005: 60). Furthermore, in a bid to support the Nigerian-led ECOWAS peacekeeping forces, America deployed 320 of its Marine Amphibious Ready Group (MARG) troops ashore, as a quick reaction force (QRF) including 150 Marines to Roberts International Airport and 80 to the Freeport on Bushrod Island on the 14th of August 2003 (Ross 2005: 60). Washington's success in pressurising President Taylor to resign had eventually prompted the rebel leader of LURD to declare the end of the war (The Guardian 2003). In October of the same year, the US withdrew its MARG troops from Liberia, ahead of the arrival of the UN peacekeeping force. In stark contrast to the previous US military operation in 1990, the JTF's capacity to save many lives with relatively small military force deployments

---

[5]These US-led military operations include Panama (1989); Kuwait (1991); Somalia (1992); Haiti (1994); Bosnia (1995); Kosovo (1999); East Timor (1999); Afghanistan (2001); Iraq (2003); and Liberia (2003). See Nuechterlein (2005), pp. 135–136.

was, in Alan Kuperman's words, 'a small intervention with a big payoff' (Kuperman 2009):

> In 1990, the U.S. troops avoided entanglement in Liberia's internal conflict and only conducted a non-combatant evacuation operation (NEO) of foreign nationals. The rebels proceeded to occupy the capital and assassinate the president, triggering 13 years of civil war in Liberia that killed tens of thousands…By contrast, in 2003, the United States deployed 320 troops ashore and coordinated with U.S.-trained African troops—helping to end the civil war, avert a bloodbath, and pave the way for a democratic transition (Kuperman 2009: 153).

This timely and decisive deployment of JTF Liberia by the Bush administration, as the Kuperman suggested, served as an excellent example of humanitarian military intervention in ongoing conflicts (Kuperman 2009: 153). At first blush, President Bush's JTF Liberia deployment decision seems to be a strong endorsement of the 2001 ICISS report, particularly when it was made two years before the world's heads of state unanimously adopted the R2P principle at the 2005 UN World Summit. This sparked a debate about R2P's potential capacity to influence US post-Cold War foreign policy behaviour, particularly in Africa.

In relation to the potential impact of R2P on shaping international intervention, France, as a formal colonial power, showed a much greater willingness to intervene in Cote d'Ivoire's civil war in September 2002. When France received the request from Laurent Gbagbo, the President of the former French colony who was facing an attempted coup, to intervene in the Ivorian conflict, it dispatched troops to assist with the evacuation of foreign nationals and provision of logistical support to Gbagbo's government military forces. But perhaps more importantly, Paris's robust military presence had enabled France to take a leading role in the mediation process, thereby paving the way for the subsequent deployment of ECOWAS Mission in the Cote d'Ivoire (ECOMICI) (Boyer 2008). Efforts by France, ECOWAS and the UN in carrying out forceful intervention in Cote d'Ivoire proved effective in resolving the Ivorian conflict. Given France's favourite position on humanitarian intervention (Allen and Stvan 2000), R2P seemed to be at play in pushing the international community to take timely and decisive action to protect populations at risk of mass atrocities crimes.

In stark contrast to France's swift and affirmative response, a close reading of US intervention in Liberia, however, suggests that the international debate about R2P was not associated with the American foreign policy decision-making process. There are three explanations for this puzzle: first; the Bush administration was concerned with the possibility that humanitarian intervention or extended peacekeeping mission may undermine America's readiness for carrying out traditional combat missions in the Persian Gulf and other distant trouble spots (Gordon 2000). The real danger of reconceptualising sovereignty as responsibility under the R2P framework was that Washington would find its hands tied by the need and resulting commitment of 'saving strangers' (Wheeler 2000). While being cautious of R2P's potential to ripen into a general legal obligation to intervene, the Bush administration would not allow itself to be hamstrung by foreign commitments when it comes to protecting American sovereignty and maintaining its freedom to act. Applying this standard, military intervention for humanitarian purposes had to be carried out as an *option* without compromising US 'decision-making sovereignty' (Luck 2009). The lure of America's historical tie to Liberia (and Washington's moral responsibility to Monrovia thereafter) had proved irrelevant to the Bush administration.

Second, the 'Mogadishu factor' continued to define and shape foreign policy-makers in Washington on the use of military force abroad. Rather than carrying out direct military intervention in Liberia, President Bush just ordered its troops to position 'a limited US military force off the coast of Liberia' for the purpose of 'supporting the deployment of Nigerian-led ECOWAS forces into Liberia' (Murphy 2006: 108). After securing President Taylor's forced resignation in August 2003, the Bush administration decided to dispatch only a 'US military assessment team' whose function was to begin 'gauging humanitarian needs and possibly to lay the groundwork for a deployment of US peacekeeping troops' (CNN 2003b). Bush's policy of minimal and limited engagement stands uncomfortably with the fact that a majority of American public (over 60%) favoured the use of US ground troops in an international peacekeeping force in Liberia (Carlson 2003). The Bush administration's reluctance to carry out direct military intervention for saving strangers like the Liberians, therefore, can only be attributed to the impact of the 'Mogadishu factor': 'states intervening from humanitarian motives refused to risk the lives of their own soldiers to make that intervention effective' (Robertson 2012: 71).

The third explanation for the lack of explicit reference to R2P in American foreign policy is that the global war on terror[6] since the terrorist attacks on 11 September 2001 assumed higher importance during the first Bush administration. Eliminating transnational terrorism and dismantling terrorist networks have generated a new sense of urgency to develop adequate means to prevent such occurrences. This situation led to the development of a more assertive and unilateral foreign policy known as the Bush doctrine: Washington preserves the right to use pre-emptive military force against any state for combating perceived threats to US national security (Singh 2006: 12–22). The subsequent invasion and occupation of Afghanistan and Iraq bore testimony to the militarisation of American foreign policy.

This increased militarisation of US foreign policy following the 9/11 attacks was closely associated with the neoconservative agenda, whose objective was to reassert America's global dominance and to promote US ideals of democracy and freedom—forcefully if necessary. The neoconservatives tend to believe in the importance of advancing US security interests through pushing democratic transformation in the Middle East. America—as the only superpower in the world—has the power and willingness to use its military strength to transform global politics.

While promoting democracy in the Middle East emerged as the predominant foreign policy concern of the Bush administration, it is worth noting that the 9/11 attacks have fundamentally changed Washington's perception of Africa's strategic significance. In the context of the global war on terror, Africa has resonance for American foreign policy. The 2002 US National Security Strategy (NSS) underscored the

---

[6]The Bush administration has published three documents in a bid to coordinate US response to 9/11: *National Security Strategy of the United States*, the *US National Strategy for Combating Terrorism* and the *US National Strategy to Combat Weapons of Mass Destruction*.

links between Africa's fragile states and their vulnerability to transnational terrorism (White House 2002). This stood a stark contrast to the remarks made by Bush during the 2000 Presidential campaign, when the Republican candidate once suggested that Africa was important but 'not a priority' in comparison with his 'four top priorities' once assuming presidency: Middle East, Europe, the Far East and North America.[7] Then, what would the ever-increasing centrality of Africa mean for US–Liberia relations after 9/11? The final part of this article will discuss the Bush administration's re-engagement with Liberia and the wider West Africa region since 2003 with respect to its motives.

US Re-engagement with West Africa: Stated Objectives and Ulterior Motives

As mentioned previously, it appeared that the US has attached great importance to developing its relations with Africa during the first Bush administration. For instance, Bush's initiative to commit $15 billion in five years (fiscal years 2004–2008) for support HIV/AIDS prevention, care and treatment programmes in Africa, being known as the President's Emergency Programme for AIDS Relief (PEPFAR), was the largest commitment ever to a global health initiative dedicated to a single disease (Centre for Global Development). President Bush's first official trip to Africa in July 2003 (CNN 2003a) and his JTF Liberia deployment decision following his trip, in this context, was indicative of America's re-engagement with Africa as a whole, including West Africa.

With Africa gradually emerging as prominent US foreign policy concerns since 9/11, what are the motivating factors for US re-engagement with the continent under the Bush administration? First, Africa's newfound strategic importance after 9/11 was largely consolidated by President Bush's inauguration of the global war on terror. Indeed, even before 9/11, the 1998 bombing of the American embassies in Nairobi (Kenya) and Dar es Salaam (Tanzania) by Al Qaeda was a wake-up call for Washington since the continent would turn into a potential 'breeding ground' for terrorists and a safe haven for Al Qaeda (Prestholdt 2013: 127). This situation provided an impetus for the Bush administration to implement the militarisation of US foreign policy in Africa: the creation of Combined Joint Task Force-Horn of Africa (CJTF-HOA) in October 2002[8] and, ultimately, the US–Africa Command (AFRICOM) in 2007.

---

[7]See 'Africa's important but not a priority; no nation-building', Presidential Debate at Wake Forest University 11 October 2000. http://www.debates.org/index.php?page=october-11-2000-debate-transcript (Accessed 30 March 2018).

[8]According to its official website, the CJTF-HOA was aimed to "assist[s] its East African partners with countering violent extremist organisations in the region to prevent them from threatening US, or East African people or interests".

Yet, while Liberia played a crucial role in American Cold War strategy, it is no longer the case that the country assumed the same degree of importance in President Bush's global campaign to eliminate terrorism. In contrast, the Charles Taylor administration was a constant target of criticism from Washington: the warlord-turned-president's entanglement in Sierra Leone's civil war and, more importantly, his strong ties to Al Qaeda (by harbouring its members for operating illegal diamond trades on Liberian soil (Paye-Layleh 2002). As a demonstration of Washington's hostility to Monrovia, the UN Security Council (under pressure from the US), imposed sanctions against Liberia—including arms embargo, travel ban for officials and a prohibition on the import of Liberian diamonds—for three consecutive years from 2001 until Taylor's forced resignation in 2003 (Hyman 2003: 102–109). With Charles Taylor being identified as a potential terrorist threat and a destabilising force in the West Africa region, it was unreasonable for Washington to justify military intervention to save lives in Liberia. Ultimately, the security imperatives of President Bush's global war on terror overruled the concern with protecting civilians in Liberia.

As further evidence that the Taylor Presidency was no longer referred to as an ally of Washington after 9/11, Liberia was not on the itinerary of President Bush's first trip to Africa.[9] But, despite his opposition to President Taylor, there was a compelling need for President Bush, ahead of his historic Africa trip, to 'back up his rhetoric about helping Africa in a concrete way with a commitment to put troops into Liberia' (Gwertzman 2003). In this sense, the President's JTF Liberia deployment decision was necessary, not for the sake of averting humanitarian crisis in Liberia, but for the sake of laying the groundwork for US re-engagement with West Africa: Liberia was just one of the many trees in the West Africa's forest. The remarks of Walter H. Kansteiner, Assistant Secretary of State for African Affairs, on US policy towards Liberia overtly reflected this kind of 'instrumental value':

> A successful political transition leading to a stable Liberia will serve US strategic interests. US follow-through on Liberia will affect our relations with Nigeria and the other 14 countries of ECOWAS…Peace and security in Liberia will have a profound impact in the areas of human rights, good governance, the rule of law, environmental preservation, and opportunities for US investors. (US Department of State 2003b)

Then, along with the global war on terror narrative, a second motivating factor shaping America's re-engagement with West Africa was to look for alternative oil supplies in other areas. Available evidence suggests that the US government has already imported more oil from Africa than Saudi Arabia, as some 40% increase of oil imports from six key suppliers in sub-Saharan Africa (Angola, Cameroon, Chad, Gabon, Nigeria and the Democratic Republic of the Congo) were recorded from 2001 to 2010 (Andreasson 2014). This explains why among the countries included on the itinerary of Bush's first Africa tour was Nigeria, the 13th largest oil producer in the world and America's fifth largest supplier (George 2003). After all, West Africa encompasses the Gulf of Guinea, which has the largest reserves of oil and natural gas on the continent.

---

[9] The five countries included in Bush's first trip to Africa are Senegal, South Africa, Botswana, Uganda, and Nigeria.

In relations to enhancing US energy security, the National Energy Policy Development Group (NEPDG) was created during the Bush administration to examine the energy situation of the country and, most importantly, address the problem of US dependence on imported petroleum (National Energy Policy Development Group 2001). Its first report, formally titled the *National Energy Policy* (*NEP*), was released in May 2001. By suggesting that the 'concentration of world oil production in any one region of the world is a potential contributor to market instability', the *NEP* recommended that the US government to assiduously court potential non-Persian Gulf suppliers around the world so that the sources of its oil imports can be diversified. With the *NEP* highlighting that 'West Africa is expected to be one of the fastest-growing sources of oil and gas for the American market, along with Latin America' (National Energy Policy Development Group 2001:11), it stands to reason that West African oil has played a major role in the implementation of this diversification strategy.

Interestingly, and perhaps ironically, Liberia confirmed that it has discovered substantial crude oil along its Atlantic coast in late 2003 (Hyman 2003: 207). Geological and seismic tests indicated vast untapped oil reserves along the Liberian coastline. As the US State Department noticed the increasing interest of foreign companies in Liberia's offshore oil, the sizeable amount of crude oil along Liberia's Atlantic coast would not be far from Washington's mind. Strategically, this therefore made it imperative for Washington to open up fields off the coast of West Africa so as to reduce dependence on oil from the Middle East.

In a nutshell, the US doctrinal shift from a 'decade of disengagement' (Taylor 2010) in the 1990s to gradual re-engagement in Liberia and West Africa after 9/11 is no coincidence. Cold War politics was hardly applicable, as containment of global communism was no longer the dominant factor in understanding US Africa policy in the post-Cold War era. R2P's potential capacity to shape American foreign policy towards Africa in general and US intervention in Liberia in particular also appears to be minimal. Conversely, the principal reason for America's strategic perception of the continent to undergo fundamental change is arguably the 9/11 terrorist attacks and Bush's global war on terror thereafter. Since then, Washington's eagerness to reduce its foreign oil dependency from the Middle East and its concerns about Africa's potential to become a fertile breeding ground for terrorism have arguably resulted in US re-engagement with the continent.

Conclusion

Few would deny that the Bush administration's JTF Liberia troop deployment decision in 2003, during the height of Liberia's second civil war, had largely stabilised the country through granting support to the ECOWAS forces. Despite Liberia's historical ties with the US, this chapter has sought to demonstrate that the motives behind Washington's gradual re-engagement in Liberia and the West Africa region during the Bush administration have relatively little to do with 'the Rwanda effect' and the emerging norm of military intervention for humanitarian purposes. Instead, it argues that the Bush administration's JTF Liberia troop deployment decision is nothing more than a testimony to the persistent influence of the 'Mogadishu factor': President Bush was only psychologically prepared to provide supplementary logistical support for ECOWAS forces instead of carrying out direct military intervention for saving lives.

The absence of US concerns over humanitarian aims was confirmed by the Bush administration's obsession with national security interests in the context of the global war on terror after 9/11. As identifying (and eliminating) potential terrorist threats had become the primary objective of American foreign policy, the humanitarian crisis in Liberia was hardly on top of the Bush administration's agenda since there was no direct US national security interests at stake. The fact that Liberia is the only African country with official historical ties to America has minimal effect on pushing foreign policymakers in Washington to protect the Liberian people from mass atrocities.

The case of this 2003 US intervention in Liberia, however, demonstrates that military intervention for humanitarian purposes can still be triggered on an ad hoc basis. Yet, the rationale may not be a normative commitment to stop mass atrocities or to save lives but can be considered as more of a strategic approach to tackling transnational terrorism. Given the newfound strategic and economic importance of Africa after 9/11, military intervention for humanitarian purposes has morphed into a terror-centric measure that ad hoc humanitarianism as a means is being used to achieve strategic ends.

References

Allen, Tim, and David Styan. 2000. 'A Right to Interfere? Bernard Kouchner and the New Humanitarianism', *Journal of International Development* 12 (6): 825–842.
Andreasson, Stefan. 2014. 'US Fracking Boom Puts West African Oil Economies at Risk', *The Conversation*, 6 August.
Annan, Kofi. 1999. *The Question of Intervention: Statements by the Secretary-General*. New York: United Nations Department of Public Information.
Barrett, Lindsay. 1992. 'The Siege of Monrovia', *West Africa*, 23–29 November.
Baumann, Robert and Lawrence Yates with Versalle Washington. 2004. *My Clan Against the World: US and Coalition Forces in Somalia 1992–1994*. Fort Leavenworth, Kansas: Combat Studies Institute Press.
Bellamy, Alex J. 2015. *The Responsibility to Protect: A Defense*. Oxford: Oxford University Press.
Boutros-Ghali, Boutros. 1992. *An Agenda for Peace: Preventive Diplomacy, Peacemaking and Peace-Keeping*. New York: United Nations.
Boyer, C.D.R. Timothy E. USN. 2008. 'Cote d'Ivoire: Intervention and Prevention Responses', in Douglas C. Peifer (ed.), *Stopping Mass Killings in Africa: Genocide, Airpower and Intervention*, pp.101–126. Alabama: Air University Press.
Carlson, Darren K. 2003. 'Should the U.S. Keep the Peace in Liberia?', *Gallup Poll Tuesday Briefing*, 5 August.
Centre for Global Development. n.d. Myra Sessions. 'Overview of the President's Emergency Plan for AIDS Relief (PEPFAR)'.

Clinton, Bill. 1999. 'Remarks by the President to the KFOR Troops', Skopje, Macedonia, 22 June, http://clinton2.nara.gov/Africa/19980325-16872.html (accessed 31 March 2018).
CNN. 2003a. 'Bush Trip Evokes Mixed Response', 8 July.
CNN. 2003b. 'Liberia's Taylor Not Ready to Leave'. 7 July.
Copson, Raymond. 2007. *The United States in Africa: Bush Policy and Beyond*. London: Zed Books.
Dunn, D. Elwood. 1999. 'The Civil War in Liberia', in Taisier M. Ali and Robert O. Matthews (eds.), *Civil Wars in Africa: Roots and Resolution*. Montreal & Kingston: McGill-Queen's University Press.
Ero, Comfort, Waheguru Pal Singh Sidhu, and Augustine Toure. 2001. *Toward a Pax West African: Building Peace in a Troubled Sub-Region*. A report on the IPA-ECOWAS, 27–29 September, Abuja Seminar, New York: International Peace Academy.
Finnemore, Martha. 1996. 'Constructing Norms of Humanitarian Intervention', in Peter Katzenstein (ed.), *The Culture of National Security*. New York: Columbia University Press.
George, Liz. 2003. 'Is oil drawing Bush to Nigeria?', *CNN*, 8 July.
Gordon, Michael R. 2000. 'The 2000 Campaign: The Military; Bush Would Stop U.S. Peacekeeping in Balkan Fights', *New York Times*, 21 October.
Gwertzman, Bernard. 2003. 'Lyman: Liberia Issue Dogged Bush's Africa Trip', *Council on Foreign Relations*, 14 July.
Holzgrefe, J.L. 2003. 'Humanitarian Intervention Debate', In J. L. Holzgrefe and O. Keohane Robert (eds.), *Humanitarian Intervention: Ethical, Legal and Political Dilemmas*. Cambridge: Cambridge University Press.
Hyman, Lester. 2003. *United States Policy Towards Liberia: 1822 to 2003: Unintended Consequences?*. Cherry Hill, NJ: Africana Homestead Legacy Publishers.
ICISS (International Commission on Intervention and State Sovereignty). 2001. *The Responsibility to Protect: Report of the International Commission on Intervention and State Sovereignty*. Ottawa: International Development Research Centre.
Ioan, Lewis, and James Mayall. 2007. 'Somalia', in Mats Berdal and Spyros Economides (eds.), *United Nations Interventionism 1991–2004*. Cambridge: Cambridge University Press.
Knudsen, Tonny. 1997. Humanitarian Intervention Revisited: Post-Cold War Responses to Classical Problems. In *The UN, Peace and Force*, ed. Michael Pugh. London: Frank Cass.
Kuperman, Alan. 2009. A Small Intervention: Lessons from Liberia 2003. In *Naval Peacekeeping and Humanitarian Operations: Stability from the Sea*, ed. James J. Wirtz and Jeffrey A. Larsen. New York: Routledge.
Liberia. 1848. *The independent Republic of Liberia: Its Constitution and Declaration of Independence: Address of the Colonists to the Free People of Color in the United States, with Other Documents: Issued Chiefly for the Use of the Free People of Color*. Philadelphia: W.F. Geddes, Printer.
Library of Congress. 2010. 'Colonization: The African-American Mosaic', 23 July. http://www.loc.gov/exhibits/african/afam002.html (accessed at 31 March 2018).
Luck, Edward C. 2009. 'Sovereignty, Choice and the Responsibility to Protect', *Global Responsibility to Protect* 1 (1): 10–21.
Mandelbaum, Michael. 1996. 'Foreign Policy as Social Work'. *Foreign Affairs* Vol. 75, no. 1 (January/February): 16–32.
Moghalu, Kingsley. 2005. *Rwanda's Genocide: The Politics of Global Justice*. London: Palgrave.
Murphy, Sean. 2006. *United States Practice in International Law: Volume 2, 2002–2004*. Cambridge: Cambridge University Press.
National Energy Policy Development Group (NEPDG). 2001. *National Energy Policy*. Washington, DC: The White House, 17 May.
Nuechterlein, Donald Edwin. 2005. *Defiant Superpower: The New American Hegemony*. Washington, DC: Potomac Books.
Oyebade, Adebayo, and Toyin Falola. 2008. 'West Africa and the United States in Historical Perspective', in Alusine Jalloh and Toyin Falola (eds.), *The United States and West Africa: Interactions and Relations*. Rochester, NY: University of Rochester Press.

Parekh, Bhikhu. 1997. 'Rethinking Humanitarian Intervention', *International Political Science Review*, Vol. 18, no. 1: 49–69.
Paye-Layleh, Jonathan. 2002. Liberia Denies Al-Qaeda Link. *BBC News*, 31 December.
Pflanz, Mike. 2011a. US 'should not have left Somalia after Black Hawk Down', sole survivor says. *Telegraph*, 9 August.
Pflanz, Mike. 2011b. 'Black Hawk Down: How a Moral Mission to halt famine became America's worst military disaster in Africa', *Telegraph*, 9 August.
Prestholdt, Jeremy. 2013. 'The United States and Counterterrorism in Eastern Africa', in Everard Meade and William Aceves (eds.), *Lessons and Legacies of the War on Terror: From Moral Panic to Permanent War*. London: Routledge.
Roberts, Adam. 1999. 'The Role of Humanitarian Issues in International Politics in the 1990s', *International Review of the Red Cross*, Vol. 81, no. 833: 19–43.
Roberts, Adam. 2006. 'The United Nations and Humanitarian Intervention', in Jennifer M. Welsh (ed.), *Humanitarian Intervention and International Relations*. Oxford: Oxford University Press.
Robertson, Geoffrey. 2012. *Crimes Against Humanity: The Struggle For Global Justice*. London: Penguin.
Ross Jr., Blair A. 2005. The U.S. Joint Task Force Experience in Liberia. *Military Review* 85: 60–67.
Singh, Robert. 2006. The Bush Doctrine. In *The Bush Doctrine and the War on Terrorism: Global Responses, Global Consequences*, ed. Mary Buckley and Robert Singh. London and New York: Routledge.
Sirleaf, Amos (2000). *The Role of the Economic Community of the West African States (ECOWAS) in the Liberian Civil Conflict 1980–1997: A Case Study of Conflict Management*. Washington DC: Blackology Research and Development Institute.
Stedman, Stephen John 'The New Interventionists'. 1993. *Foreign Affairs* 72 (Winter): 1–16.
Talbot, Chris. 2003 July 7. Bush Administration Divided Over Intervention in Liberia. *World Socialist Web Site*.
Tan, Kok-Chor. 2006. The Duty to Protect. In *Nomos XLVII: Humanitarian Intervention*, ed. Terry Nardin and Melissa Williams. New York: New York University Press.
Taylor, Ian. 2010. *The International Relations of Sub-Saharan Africa*. New York: The Continuum International Publishing Group.
The Guardian. 2003 August 11. Liberian President Taylor Steps Down.
UN Press Release. 1999 'Secretary-General Presents his Annual Report to the General Assembly', SG/SM/7136-GA/9596, 20 September.
United Nations General Assembly. 2005 October 24. '2005 World Summit Outcome', A/RES/60/1.
United Nations General Assembly. 2009 January 12. 'Implementing the responsibility to protect: report of the Secretary-General', A/63/677.
United Nations Secretary-General. 2000 March 30. *We the Peoples: The Role of the United Nations in the 21st Century*. Report of the UN Secretary-General, A/ 54/2000.
United Nations Secretary-General. 2003. 'Report of the Secretary-General to the Security Council on Liberia', S/2003/875, 11 September.
United Nations. 1999. *Report of the Independent Inquiry into the Actions of the United Nations During the 1994 Genocide in Rwanda*, 12 December.
US Department of State (Bureau of International Organizational Affairs). 1996. 'Clinton Administration Policy on Reforming Multilateral Peace Operations' (PDD-25), 22 February.
US Department of State. 2003a. 'Background Note: Liberia', 17 February.
US Department of State. 2003b. 'US Policy Toward Liberia', 2 October.
USA Today. 2003. 'Bush Orders Troops to Liberia', 25 July.
Watchlist on Children and Armed Conflict. 2004. 'Nothing Left to Lose: The Legacy of Armed Conflict and Liberia's Children', 28 June.
Weiner, Tim. 2003. '200 U.S. Marines Land in Liberia to Aid African Force', *New York Times*, 15 August.
Welsh, Jennifer. 2009. 'The Rwanda Effect: Development and Endorsement of the "Responsibility to Protect", in Phil Clark and Zachary Kaufman (eds.), *After Genocide: Transitional Justice,*

Post-Conflict Reconstruction and Reconciliation in Rwanda and Beyond, p. 333–350. New York: Columbia University Press.

Wertheim, Stephen. 2010. 'A Solution from Hell: The United States and the Rise of Humanitarian Interventionism, 1991–2003', *Journal of genocide Research*, Vol. 12, No. 3–4 (September-October): 149–172.

Westcott, Kathryn. 2003. 'Liberia's Historical US Ties', *BBC News*, 26 June.

Wheeler, Nicholas. 2000. *Saving Strangers: Humanitarian Intervention in International Society*. Oxford: Oxford University Press.

White House. 2002. *The National Security Strategy of the United States of America*. Washington, DC: The White House.

Dr. Raymond Kwun-Sun LAU is a lecturer at the History Department, Hong Kong Baptist University. He holds a PhD in Political Science from the University of Queensland, Australia. His doctoral research examined the international response to genocide and mass atrocities in Africa and explored the relationship between the Responsibility to Protect (R2P) principle and the International Criminal Court (ICC). He is the author of "Protection First, Justice Later? Stopping Mass Atrocities in Northern Uganda", a book chapter in the edited volume, Civilian Protection in the Twenty-First Century: Governance and Responsibility in a Fragmented World (Cecilia Jacob and Alistair D.B. Cook, eds.), published by the Oxford University Press in October 2016. His teaching interests include International Relations/Global Politics, history and politics of Africa since Independence and twentieth-century European history.

Chapter 7
NATO's 2011 Invasion of Libya: Colonialism Repackaged?

Chidochashe Nyere

Abstract Global coloniality privileges the Euro-North American-centric form of humanity, at the expense of diminishing, dismissing and obliterating anything else other than the Euro-North American-centric civilisation, in the process making Euro-North American-centric modernity a global empire. The politics of empire are problematic because they set precedence, justify and perpetuate global coloniality. This is the conundrum that confronted and enveloped Libya in 2011 with the NATO-led invasion and which continues to entangle and disenfranchise the Libyan polity today, hence the need for a decolonial epistemic approach that seeks to re-humanise and affirm all forms of humanity. The current socio-economic-politico world order is a creation and direct result of modern European thought and civilisation (modernity) and European colonialism. In turn, colonialism produced global coloniality. The turning point is that global coloniality entraps humanity to a predetermined reality modelled on Euro-North American-centric modernity. Thus, coloniality is limiting to and eliminates 'other' epistemological creativity; it hinders 'other' ontological expressions of what humanity is and could be other than the predetermined Euro-North American-centric form of being and knowledge. Modernity negates, forcibly condemns forms of humanity found in the peripheries of Euro-North American civilisation, to non-humanity. Non-human beings are of less ontological value than beings of Euro-North American ancestry.

Keywords NATO · Libya · Invasion · Coloniality · Euro-North American modernity · Humanity

---

C. Nyere (✉)
Department of Political Science, Faculty of Humanities, University of Pretoria, Office 24, 7th Floor Theo van Wijk Building, UNISA Main Campus, Pretoria 0003, South Africa
e-mail: chidonyere@gmail.com

© Springer Nature Switzerland AG 2020
E. Benyera (ed.), *Reimagining Justice, Human Rights and Leadership in Africa*,
Advances in African Economic, Social and Political Development,
https://doi.org/10.1007/978-3-030-25143-7_7

Introduction

Global coloniality privileges a Euro-North American-centric form of humanity, at the expense of diminishing, dismissing and obliterating anything else other than the Euro-North American-centric civilisation, in the process making Euro-North American-centric modernity a global empire. The politics of empire are problematic because they set precedence and justify and perpetuate global coloniality. This is the conundrum that confronted and enveloped Libya in 2011 with the North Atlantic Treaty Organisation (NATO)-led invasion and which continues to entangle and disenfranchise the Libyan polity today (2019), hence the need for a decolonial epistemic approach that seeks to re-humanise and affirm *all* forms of humanity. This chapter seeks to disentangle and strips bare the asymmetrical global power structural configurations that the current world order rests upon and which are camouflaged in the so-called objectivity of science and the skewed universality of knowledge. The current socio-economic-politico world order is a creation and direct result of modern European thought and civilisation (modernity). It was scattered across the world through the violence of colonialism. In turn, colonialism produced global coloniality. The turning point is that global coloniality entraps humanity to a predetermined reality modelled on Euro-North American-centric modernity. Thus, coloniality is limiting to and eliminates 'other' epistemological creativities; it hinders 'other' ontological expressions of what humanity is and could be 'other' than the predetermined Euro-North American-centric form of being and knowledge.

This logic results in the social, political, economic and epistemic creation and definition of the human and the non-human by 'other' human beings. Modernity negates, forcibly condemns forms of humanity found in the peripheries of Euro-North American civilisation, to non-humanity. Non-human beings are considered beings of a lesser ontological value than humans of Euro-North American ancestry. Because there is no humanity in the peripheries of the Euro-North American-centric world, any enterprise or innovation from the zone of non-being cannot be good enough (Fanon). Libya could have not been successful, it could not have been an example of a decolonial state, hence it had to fail because it threatened the established Eurocentric world order.

Coloniality of Power and the Global Power Structural Configuration: Unmasking the Politics and Philosophy of Empire

Epistemologically, this chapter seeks to unmask the fault lines of the philosophy of the European-centric empire as implicated in the generation of problems epitomised by the invasion of Libya in 2011 by NATO forces. It seeks to do so, by exposing some myths that informed, fueled and continue to precipitate global coloniality in the absence of physical colonialism. Current international relations (IR) theories have proven to be limited and unable to solve and eradicate this epistemic challenge, partly because dominant and traditional IR theories are located in the very European modernity that they disguise and camouflage in the purported objectivity of science. The philosophy of the Eurocentric empire universalised these particular theories of IR by force (violence of colonialism) as they are part of the modernity project of colonisation (Howe 1990: 677). The chapter further aims to demonstrate the deficiency and bankruptcy that foregrounds traditional IR theories' assumptions, assertions and proclamations particularly that Western-centric IR theories are scientific, objective and universally applicable or replicable. Such proclamations overlook the fact that these IR theories are located in particular ecologies of Europe and therefore, are subjective. All knowledge is particular and subjective to its ecology or locality.

Since 1919, the official initial academic inquiry of IR as a discipline, IR theories have not adequately addressed what the discipline initially set out to do—to curb and liquidate international conflict. This suggests that the epistemologies (particular epistemic ecologies and localities) that have informed IR theories to date are inadequate and have reached some sort of cul-de-sac, or a dead-end. These epistemologies beg the question and engage in circular reasoning. This necessitates an alternative frame of reference. Contingent upon Albert Einstein's idea that insanity is doing the same thing over and over again and expecting a different result each time, this chapter opts to engage a non-conventional theory in the discipline of IR. As such, this work advances the decolonial perspective as a possible solution to problems caused by epistemologies located in the ecologies and localities of Western, Euro-North American-centric modernity that purport themselves as objective, scientific and universal. The chapter will unmask the inadequacies of Euro-North American-centric modernity in the face of mounting and current global problems, particularly those played out in the field of international relations.

IR as an academic discipline started in 1919 at Aberystwyth, University of Wales (now Aberystwyth University), a year after the end of World War I (Ziegler 1987). This, however, as Nyere (2014: 18) argues, "does not mean that intellectual origins of political realism and liberalism only started in 1919". The main objective and aim of IR theorising was solely to find peaceful solutions to international disputes and therefore avert a similar conflict to World War I. IR failed in that regard because just barely after a decade, World War II started. Like the predecessor of the United Nations, the League of Nations, IR as an academic discipline has failed in achieving what it set out to do in the first place. Since 1945, the end of World War II and the signing of the United Nations Charter in San Francisco, USA, there has not been a single decade that the world has not witnessed an international conflict or war (Bennet 1998: 7).

Rational theories in the discipline of IR, such as realism, liberalism, feminism, Marxism and constructivism, are expressive of ideas, concepts and views located in modernity. The ideas expressed in IR rational theories are embodied by scholars that are mainly located in modernity, particularly from the Global North and reflect the rationale of European modernity. The major problem of modernity is the inexplicable discrepancy and inconsistency between its rhetoric and its lived reality, its illusion vis-à-vis its essence, particularly from the experience of people of the Global South in general, but by Africans in particular. As such, this chapter intends to unmask the inadequacy of mainstream theories and lenses in explaining the ghosts and blind-spots of empire because these ghosts and blind-spots are born within the empire. The European-centric empire is not sufficiently able to be reflexive on its theories and to see beyond its assumptions and assertions. As such, this chapter suggests the need to explore outside the lenses of established theory.

The Masquerade of Colonialism in the Peripheries of the Eurocentric World

Throughout history, there have been different colonial establishments, for example the Spanish colonial order of Latin America (Grosfoguel 2000: 355); the Islamic colonial order of Africa (North Africa particularly), Asia and the USA (Kissinger 2014: 5), and the British colonial order of the whole world (Quijano 2000: 533; Grosfoguel 2000: 360). As far back as the seventeenth century, the Islamic civilisation and the European (Western) civilisation competed for dominance and each sought to define itself and the other, around itself. The two civilisations each thought of itself as a legitimate standard of ordering human society. Each civilisation imagined that all it knew and was conscious of, was all of humanity; imagining that by ordering its immediate locality, it was governing the entire world (Kissinger 2014: 4). In relation to these civilisations (Islamic and European) and their conceived or established orders of the world, Africa was afflicted and assailed by the European order of the world the most, which arguably has affected the whole world. Hence, the European colonisation of Africa is the most immediate one in the African experience. As such, colonialism, in this work, is to be understood as phenomena that affected Africa specifically. Physical colonialism in relation to Africa refers to the invasion and occupation of spaces and places in Africa, among other spaces/places, by European imperial powers that included, but were not limited to, Belgium, Britain, France, Germany, Italy and Portugal; from the 1800s (Pakenham 1992), to their departure from the late-1950s to the mid-1990s (Chamberlain 2010). European colonialism of Africa centred Europe to Africa's psyche, being, epistemology, religion, spirituality, the arts and imagination. The self-imposed centring of Europe in Africa through the violence of colonialism, and by extension, Europe's central positioning of itself to the whole world, reveals the attitude of Eurocentrism. Eurocentrism perceives itself as superior and therefore, has a right to order, control and name everything around it.

Eurocentrism

European modernity and empire tended to centre itself as a measure and standard with which everything else is judged. It centred itself as the focal point of all inquiry as well as the centre that contains all knowledge. By doing this, it negated the fact that it was just one among other civilisations and orders of the world. European modernity pathologised anything else other than itself, or anything else that was different to it (Pillay 2018: 33). This resulted in Eurocentrism. Eurocentrism, in this sense, became the attitude of superiority of being, epistemology and the standard therefore, of being and epistemology. Hence, Eurocentrism in its epistemic enquiry, centred itself as a doyen of scientific enquiry and knowledge, thereby dismissing any other form of knowledge as opinion or perspective, but not knowledge, and therefore, as inferior. Eurocentric scientific enquiry gave rise to epistemological enterprises that produced current IR theories that centre Europe and its standards. Current IR theories cannot stand without Europe at the centre of their enquiry. This limits the lenses through which IR could be conceived and conducted and renders IR theories limited.

Theory and International Relations Theories

The very idea of theory is Eurocentric and compels some attention. Theorising and epistemic enterprises that emanated from the European civilisation regarded themselves as the standard and measure with which every other theorising or epistemic enterprising ought to refer to. This further entrenched Eurocentrism. Consequently, Eurocentrism justified and gave rise to European colonisation. If Europe was the standard with which all being and knowledge was to be modelled on, this then justified, and suggested to Europeans, that they ought to control and order the whole world. This was the onset of colonialism. Kissinger notes that the contemporary world order, which is Eurocentric and a creation of modernity, has attempted to circumscribe the anarchical structure in which international relations are conducted. It does so through international relations theories and international legal networks (international law), international organisational structures (chief among them is the United Nations), international financial systems such as the International Monetary Fund (IMF) and the World Bank Group (WBG), these two endorse and sustain capitalism, and through establishing conflict/dispute-resolution mechanisms as well as codifying the conduct in war of warring parties, should war occur (Kissinger 2014: 7). In other words, there is an acceptance of the status quo in relation to the current world order, such that it is codified, legislated and institutionalised. But, why not abolish wars in the first place or stop the domination of one civilisation by another civilisation? The paradigm that presents war as an acceptable means of dispute-resolution is problematic because the solution to this paradigm is violence. One wonders therefore that, is the UN perpetuating coloniality of power in itself, or is the UN used as an instrument to perpetuate coloniality of power by the Euro-North American-centric modernity that has captured this institution for its own agenda of domination? Worse still, was there ever a time when the UN was not captured by the Euro-North American-centric modernity?

Colonialism

Colonialism resulted in the establishment of the European empire. Although one could also argue that empire actually invented or created colonialism. For the purposes of this argument, it suffices to note that the two are mutually defining and therefore could very well be the proverbial case of 'egg and chicken'. Valentine Mudimbe, an African scholar, born and raised in the then Zaire, now the Democratic Republic of Congo, wrote a book, *The Invention of Africa*. In it, he submits that the term colonialism is derived from the Latin word *colere* which means to "cultivate or to design" (Mudimbe 1987: 1). Mudimbe notes that despite the noble meaning of the word *colere*, the experience of European colonialism in Africa is far from the semantics of the word. The lived experiences of colonialism by the colonised populations in general, but by Africans particularly, were dehumanising and often violent experiences. The experiences and encounters of colonialism in Africa, specifically in the perspectives and views of Africans, were of a condescending and imposed monolithic European culture and civilisation. This points to the ambivalent character of modernity contained in colonialism; its rhetoric means one thing and its lived reality, quiet another, as evinced by Gould (2010: 112).

To better clarify this point, Mudimbe highlights two major myths about Africa by drawing the readers' attention to Hodgkin (1957: 174–175), who identified the first myth as the Hobbesian picture which is informed by the writings and imagination of the English philosopher, Thomas Hobbes. The myth speaks of an Africa prior to European encounters, where "there was no account of Time; no Arts; no Letters; no Society; and which is worst of all, continued fear, and danger of violent death" (Quoted in Mudimbe 1987: 1). To Hodgkin's credit, it could be argued that he was right as evidenced by reflections and thoughts of a Lord Macaulay, a British explorer and Member of Parliament who once visited India in the 1800s and made some very condescending remarks that nonetheless disproved this myth. While it can be argued that what Lord Macaulay stated was in relation to India, it is the attitude that Europeans embodied that is of merit in this case and is relatable to the European settlers' attitudes in Africa. Lord Macaulay stated the following observations, while addressing the British Parliament on 2 February 1835:

> I have travelled across the length and breadth of India and I have not seen one person who is a beggar, who is a thief, such wealth I have seen in this country, such high moral values, people of such calibre, that I do not think we could ever conquer this country, unless we break the very backbone of this nation, which is **her** spiritual and cultural heritage and therefore I propose that we replace **her** old and ancient education system, **her** culture, for if the Indians think that all that is foreign and English is good and greater than their own, they will lose their esteem, their Native culture and they will become what we want them, a truly dominated nation. (Ghosh 2016: 64)

Lord Macaulay's statement speaks of an organised civilisation that existed in India prior to its encounters with European civilisation. Yet, European literature and discourse want to portray spaces and places it colonised as though they were tabula rasa, empty slates that got discovered and civilised by European modernity. Without doubt, Lord Macaulay's observations expose the first myth of a civilisation

7 NATO's 2011 Invasion of Libya: Colonialism Repackaged?

without any form of account of time and organisation or order. Further, his address reveals vacancy, ignorance, arrogance and misogyny of patriarchy that is located in the European-centric worldview, by referring to India as a gendered place. This work notes that Lord Macaulay used the pronoun her while referring to India, by that he demonstrated the inherent patriarchisation of the world by European civilisation and thought. His speech, to the British parliament, reveals how European thinking has always been geared towards the ascribing of the female gender to that which it considered inferior or weak, to the superior or strong male, such as India and Africa were, and still are, regarded by Europe. In protest to, and combat of, the patriarchisation of the world by the Euro-North American-centric civilisation's worldview, this chapter asserts that India and Africa particularly are places and spaces without gender; they should be referred to as "it" respectively (McFadden 2016).

The second myth that Hodgkin (1957: 174–75) draws the reader's attention to is the "Rousseauian picture", named after Jean Jacques Rousseau, the French philosopher. The Rousseauian picture speaks "of an African golden age of perfect liberty, equality and fraternity" (Quoted in Mudimbe 1987: 1). Lord Macaulay's address to the British Parliament again exposes the second myth. His beautiful and wonderful experience of India paints a picture of a golden age in a space undisturbed by European colonial encounters. His experience of India in the 1830s cannot have been representative of all of the experiences of India's localities of the time. If anything, it was Lord Macaulay's particular experience of India, and therefore cannot be equated to all of Indians' experiences of their localities. Meaning his reading or perception of India, glorious and flattering as it sounded, was limited to a particular local space or place in India. Yet he universalised and absolutised his experience of a particular locality of India, Bengali specifically, to represent all of India. So, deducing from Lord Macaulay's reading of India as a singular country, and not a continent, what is revealed by that assertion is the attitude of naming, and thus controlling the named, that is located in the Eurocentric civilisation. In relation to Africa, therefore, the point that Mudimbe succinctly makes is a call to exercise caution by avoiding an over-romanticising of experiences of African ecologies and localities before colonial encounters with Europe and also challenging and correcting the idea that Europe discovered Africa and that Africa was devoid of civilisation. Put differently, the second myth is that of thinking that Africa lived in harmony and perfect liberty before European colonial encounters. There may very well been places in Africa that lived in harmony, but that cannot have been true of all of Africa at that time.

Mudimbe goes further to note that colonialists in Africa "tended to organise and transform non-European areas into fundamentally European constructs" (Mudimbe 1987: 1). Africa, as a non-European area, suffered the same fate of being forcefully transformed into a resemblance of Europe. It is also important to note that the two philosophers that Mudimbe draws the readers' attention to are Europeans; an English man and a French man. Both men had no lived experience of any ecology or locality of Africa, neither had they had any contact or encounters with Africans and yet they pronounced on Africa as authorities on Africa. This reveals the Eurocentric nature of epistemology and theory. African scholars such as Mudimbe have to make reference to Europe and its epistemology for them to make a point of to be understood, almost as if to appeal for validation and approval. European colonialism entailed the "domination of physical space, the reformation of Native's minds, and the integration of local economic histories into the Western perspective" (Mudimbe 1987: 2). This phenomenon is what Mudimbe identified and called the "organising structure" of European colonialism and domination (ibid.). The idea of the organising structure is what this work identifies as representative of coloniality. In other words, Mudimbe identifies that Eurocentrism tended to re-order and re-organise spaces and places they invaded to suite their European order. Eurocentrism negated the local orders of spaces and places they imposed themselves on.

Similarly, Ngugi wa Thiongó, in his book, *Decolonising the Mind: The Politics of Language in African Literature* (1981), speaks of what he called the "organising principle" that European literature taught in African schools and universities in Africa in general, but in particular Kenya—wa Thiongó's Native birth place. European literature, the likes of Shakespear, was used in Kenyan universities, as a standard with which all writings on experiences of Kenyan ecologies and localities were judged (wa Thiongó 1981: 94). European literature spoke of experiences located in the ecologies and localities of Europe and thus it made sense to Europeans. This imposition of European literature on Kenya meant that Natives were made to imbibe values, information and education that was foreign to them and often unrelatable to their experiences. In that process, their minds and psyche, as Natives of Africa, were captured by the minds and psyche of Natives of Europe. This Western-centred education taught Africans to order their lives, thoughts and subsequently, action around European thought and action (wa Thiongó 1981: 94). This intones coloniality and control of knowledge produced in African ecologies by foreign forces, in this case, European.

The organising principle that wa Thiongó speaks of is that of methods of inquiry, organisation and presentation of Kenyan literature according to European standards and ideals. This idea of the organising principle is what this work isolates as representative of coloniality. Whereas wa Thiongó's idea of organising principle relates to literature, what is of value to this work is the very idea of transplanting theory that is particular to European reality to Africa and trying to get Africa to conform to European theory and standards. The centring of Europe in Africa is the gist of colonialism and, as such, problematic. This is one of the fault lines of European theorising in general, but equally a fault line of IR theorising as well, that it seeks to control all knowledge by centring itself in the enquiry. This produces no new knowledge or information; what Eurocentrism does is that it simply galvanises what could have been new knowledge to what it already knows.

Colonially Established Relationships

The other myth that came with colonisation is the natural acceptance of the hierarchical order of colonially established race relationships. If to colonise is to design as revealed in Mudimbe (1987: 1), then there must exist a designer, and by extension the designed. Eurocentrism ascribes itself the position of designer, and it designs everything and everyone else around it. Europe claims to have discovered the world and therefore entitles itself to naming its discoveries. The discoverer implies the discovered. The designer is European, and the discoverer is European; this narrative reinforces Eurocentrism. The centring of Europe in the world is the beginning of coloniality.

The idea of coloniality, i.e. the rationale and ultimately, the reinforcement of colonialism, can be traced as far back as 1492; the year it is claimed Christopher Columbus discovered America (Otfinoski 2011: 2). Mamdani argues that the year 1492 signalled the beginning of European Renaissance and the nativity of political modernity (2004: 4). Columbus, an Italian explorer, was headed west on route to the West Indies, Asia for mercantile pursuits, that included gold and oriental spices, when he got lost and landed in the present-day vast area of the islands of Trinidad and Tobago, Porta Rico and Dominican Republic, in the territory under South America (Cohen 1969: 7). Columbus sailed for the "New World" as an emissary of the King, Ferdinand and Queen, Isabella, the conquerors of the City-State of Granada, which was perceived as the last Muslim citadel in the Western-centric Christian stronghold (Mamdani 2004: 4). When Columbus landed in America on 3 August 1492, he thought he had landed in the Indies (India), hence the erroneous ascribed reference of Native Americans as Indians (Cohen 1969: 9). One can deduce the arrogance that accompanies Columbus' positionality. This same arrogant tendency accompanied many European voyagers and explorers who purported to discover the already existing ecologies and localities outside of Europe's consciousness. For example, David Livingstone, a British explorer, maintained that he discovered the Victoria Falls between 1852 and 1865, one of the eight natural wonders of the world (Udeze 2009: 604). Natives of that ecology, located in present-day Zimbabwe, were aware of the gorge and called it *Mosi oa Tunya*, meaning the "smoke that thunders" referring to the mist and showers created as the water gushed down the more than 100-m-deep falls, for example (Udeze 2009: 604). Eurocentrism negates the existence of local orders and imposes itself in other spaces and places. This suggests that Eurocentric modernity cannot live with other civilisations in one and the same space/place at the same time. Competition is inherent in this civilisation. Hence, annihilation of the other is seen as progress, control and influence.

The very idea of discovering an already existing ecology or locality suggests the very problem of coloniality and, by extension, European modernity. This idea of discovering something centres the discoverer as the agency of consciousness over the discovered. One can only discover what is hidden, or one can discover what is not in one's consciousness. Columbus' position of discovering America negates the ontological being, agency and consciousness of the Natives of America who already were occupying that space when Columbus discovered it. That position totally negates and pathologises the existence of people in that so-called discovered space.

The colonisation of the Americas resulted in the colonised Natives assuming an inferior position to that of the White colonisers of British descent. This domination of Native Americans signalled the beginning of "legitimising the already old ideas and practices of relations of superiority/inferiority between dominant and dominated"

(Quijano 2000: 535). This relationship of the conquered and the conquerors produced social relations that were based on race and subsequently, class. The conquering race apportioned itself a superior status to that of the conquered. The Natives of America who were erroneously referred to as Indians occupied the bottom position in the hierarchy of the new world order. It is argued, therefore, that modernity ordered human society in a hierarchy where the White race occupies the top position in the hierarchy. The Europeans who had conquered the Natives of America—Indians—naturally assumed a position of subservience to Portuguese, Hispanics or Spanish and other white-looking races. Modernity is also credited for the creation of the capitalist system. The conquering race structured a new world order in such a manner that they controlled the means of production. The conquered race, Indians and *Mestizos* (children born of Spanish men and Indian women), were made to work as labour for the conquering race. From the onset of the colonisation of America, "Europeans associated non-paid or non-waged labour with the dominated races because they were 'inferior' races" (Quijano 2000: 538). Europe was centrally located to the sites of mercantile activity and hence Europe became the "central site of the commodification of the labour force" (ibid.).

Grosfoguel (2000: 349) submits that in Latin America, following the nineteenth-century revolutions of independence, White elites "maintained after independence racial hierarchy where Indians, Blacks, *Mestizos, Mulattoes* and other racially oppressed groups were located at the bottom". Grosfoguel points the reader to Quijano (1993) who called this hierarchisation of races "coloniality of power" (2000: 349), and it is this hierarchical ordering of humanity that is of relevance to this chapter.

Partitioning of Africa: European Modernity's Double-Standards

Another myth that festers and perpetuates modernity is the idea of accepting present-day Africa as an organic and natural occurrence. Europe is organised mainly along kinship ties, one speaks of the French who are located in France, the English or British who are located in England and or Britain, the Germans who are located in Germany, the Swedish who are located in Sweden and so forth. European modernity saw the value of maintaining kinship ties, and they formed states organically. Yet, Europe denied Africa the same kinship and organic structures by partitioned Africa according to European interests. The contemptuous partitioning of Africa by imperial powers (1885/6), followed by the "unjust wars of colonisation" of Africa, particularly (1890s onwards), disposed Africans—the rightful owners—of their land (Ramose 2003: 2). These two injustices—the distribution of Africa to European imperial powers and the colonial violent takeover of Africa by Europeans—were in direct contrast to the principles of sovereignty that Europe had recognised and adopted in 1648. Imperial conquests over Africa meant the loss of sovereignty of Africans, thereby institutionalising European empire in Africa. What this also reveals is that sovereignty and universal human rights, including property rights, were never meant for the beneficiation of Africans. When these so-called principles were crafted and designed, they did not have in mind the African, as a part of humanity.

There is a consistent inconsistency of European modernity; at one point, it says one thing [state sovereignty that presumes equality of states, 1648] and at another point, it does the opposite [Africa is Europe's property and can be divided according to Europe's whims, 1885/6]. In other words, the rhetoric of European modernity is seemingly consistent; it is the reality or lived experience of modernity that is unequivocally inconsistent. For example, while Europe ascribed universal human rights including property rights to all of humanity, it by the same token denied those rights to non-Europeans and in particular, the Black African race. The dispossession of Africans of their land by Europeans signalled the expansion of European empire. Kissinger speaks of European expansion that came with the "blueprint of their [Europe's] international order" (Kissinger 2014: 6). What is of interest is the very idea of European expansion. The concept of expansion reveals the problematic nature of European domination of other civilisations. How does Europe expand, and into what? Expansion speaks of matter and space; how could Europe possibly expand? It is this expansion that controlled where Europe expanded into, how it expanded and subsequently how it sustained the expansion that resonates with the concept of coloniality. This is Eurocentrism par excellence.

Universal Human Rights

The other myth that is at the foundation of Eurocentrism and European modernity is the veneer of universal human rights. The so-called human rights are applicable and ascribed to everyone when it suites European modernity. The rights can be easily denied other races particularly the Black race when it is convenient for Europe. This epitomises Eurocentrism. Europe seemingly is the only civilisation that dictates what goes and for who it goes. In convergence with this notion, Ramose (2003: 2) speaks of an intrinsic link between land and human life. Life exists and is located somewhere; the attachment and location of human life to land are unquestionable. In other words, life is geographically located. The colonisation of Africa—"losing land to the conqueror"—therefore, was tantamount to losing a "vital source of life" for the Africans (Ramose 2003: 2). Hence, European colonial conquests not only entrenched its domination in foreign spaces and places, it literally killed and murdered other civilisations that occupied those spaces and places it invaded and conquered. So far, this work has noted the inconsistency of the lived experience and reality of European prescription of modernity to other civilisations. The inconsistency lies in that the rhetoric speaks of ideals presumably ascribed for, and on, everybody. The reality proves the rhetoric to be untrue.

The United Nations was created in 1945 following the so-called World War II, formed to liquidate and obliterate "international wars" (UN 2018). The irony is that when the UN was formed, colonialism was at its peak in Africa. The formation of the UN, therefore, did not include Africa because it was just Europe's extension, if not property. In other words, Africa was forcibly incorporated into the international system without its involvement, consultation, consent and ascent. Not only was Africa forcibly incorporated into the international system, it was also forcibly incorporated into the capitalist market system (Ndlovu-Gatsheni 2015: 485). Ramose concurs with Ndlovu-Gatsheni's view and submits that Africa's loss of sovereignty meant that:

> [T]he African was compelled to enter into the money economy. Having been thus rendered poor by the stroke of the pen backed by the use of armed force, the African was compelled to find money to assure not only individual survival but also to pay tax for owning a hut, for example. In this way, the African's right to life—the inalienable right to subsistence—was violated. (Ramose 2003: 2)

The assumption of sovereign equality bequeathed on all states in the 1648 Westphalian Treaty, and the de-recognition of Africa as a sovereign space and place in 1886 by European imperial powers, and the re-incorporation of Africa in 1945 into the European international system, proves the consistent inconsistency and the absurdity of European modernity. Ramose (2003: 2) asserts that human rights "revolve around the recognition, protection and respect of the right to life". As such, the continual violation of human rights by the current world order is problematic and unjust, which renders the rhetoric of human rights meaningless to Africans. If the rhetoric about human rights is to arouse or evoke any meaning in Africans' experiences and consciousness, it must reinstate and rehabilitate materially and bestow recognition of, and uphold Africa's "inalienable right to subsistence" (Ramose 2003: 2).

The UN, a perceived global authority that seeks to champion universal human rights by some states and actors, and if at all well-meaning, should it not then seek to revisit the colonial question for redress especially to victims of the greatest crime against humanity—colonialism? It cannot be that Africa's human rights continue to be trampled on and left unchallenged. Kissinger (2014: 7) draws the readers' attention to the current "world community" modelled on the European Concert of State which was formed as a result of the Westphalian Treaty of 1648. The modelling of the entire world on the European Concert of State is representative of Eurocentrism and the idea of coloniality.

In August 2001, the United Nations held a Conference on Racism in Durban, South Africa. At that Conference, the USA withdrew its delegation together with Israel, in protest of demands put by Africans that the rights of Africans particularly be recognised and that crimes against humanity committed by colonial masters be accounted for and recognised for what they are. Ramose observed that:

> The majority of the Western countries present at the conference insisted that the prevailing inhumanity of the global structural violence and poverty should be maintained. This they did by ensuring that the conference would adopt resolutions that would absolve them from both the moral and the legal guilt of the violence of colonisation and the inhumanity of racism. (2003: 3)

Accounting for colonial injustices would mean acknowledging the dispossession of Black people of their land, among other elements; a thorny issue that capitalism cannot admit to, seeing that the dispossession was covered up by property rights—a fundamental principle of capitalism—and contained in a façade of legal documents including international law and National Constitutions of various countries. Colonialism and capitalism are thus protected by law, particularly the Roman Law and the Roman–Dutch Law. Needless to note that the Roman Law and the Dutch Law are European and naturally seek to entrench Eurocentrism.

Modernity and the Global Power Structural Configuration

A study of European history, especially the histories of Britain, France and Germany, reveals that the seventeenth-century Reformation, the Enlightenment period and the French Revolution are commensurate with what has come to be known as the beginning of the modern era (Escobar 2007: 181; Grosfoguel 2000: 348; Mamdani 2004: 4). In the words of Escobar (2007: 181), "historically modernity has identifiable temporal and spatial origins in seventeenth-century Northern Europe". Modernity is the corollary of colonialism because the former was scattered across the world through the latter. Hence, a discussion of one necessitates the interrogation of the other. The problem with colonialism is that, while it could be argued that, in Africa, it ended when European countries embarked on decolonisation in the 1960s, it was survived by coloniality. In the same fashion as modernity outlived the modern era, coloniality outlived colonialism as it produced, among other things, patterns of thought, being, culture, epistemology and consciousness modelled on European thought and standard. As such, Ndlovu-Gatsheni correctly argues that:

> [T]he problem is not colonialism, [today], but coloniality, which emerged from colonialism and has assumed global proportions to the extent of being best understood as global coloniality. This global coloniality is a leitmotif of the current existing empire, that of the United States of America. (Ndlovu-Gatsheni 2013: viii)

This chapter acknowledges Ndlovu-Gatsheni's position that noted that coloniality emerged from colonialism. However, this chapter makes further observations and departs from that position, and advances the argument that coloniality preceded colonialism. In other words, this work asserts that, it is coloniality that produced colonialism. Colonialism was informed by some rationale—coloniality. What Ndlovu-Gatsheni's position reveals is that had it not been for colonialism, anyone outside the positionality of Euro-North America-centric modernity, would have not been aware of coloniality. Borrowing from Nyere (2015: 95), an analogy can help put this point across succinctly. If one is in a house or room, one cannot see the car parked outside unless they look through the window. Yet the car would be there in spite of one who is not aware of its presence. Put differently, the glass window (colonialism) allows one who is in the house (peripheries of modernity) to see the parked car outside (coloniality).

According to Quijano (2000: 533), modernity can be specifically traced to the constitution of America. America was constitutionally founded on 4 July 1776, by a Europe-based religious order, the Puritan Order who are known as the "Founding Fathers" of America. America's founding was based on Christian principles. So, Britain was an instrumental signatory to the US Declaration of Independence of July, signalling the beginning of the colonisation of America (Lambert 2003: 2). What is noteworthy is that America, unlike Africa, was colonised by negotiation. The founding (a fancy word meaning colonisation) of America by Europeans resulted in the current global power structural configuration. Quijano avers that "America was constituted as the first space/time of a new model of power of global vocation, and both in this way and by it became the first identity of modernity" (Quijano 2000: 533). Grosfoguel concurs and submits that by the nineteenth century, Great Britain had positioned itself as the central power and the prototype of 'modern' civilisation. He argues that in "the nineteenth century, Great Britain had become the new core power and new model of civilisation" (Grosfoguel 2000: 349). Kissinger equally evinces the centrality of Europe to modernity and submits that "Europe loomed as a geographic designation, as an expression of Christianity, … centre of enlightenment of a community of the educated and of modernity" (Kissinger 2014: 11). Hence, Europe purports itself as the centre of civilisation, knowledge and geopolitical power.

Modernity is clouded with, and equally credited for, the nineteenth and twentieth centuries' wars and violence. Mamdani (2004: 3) argues that the "world wars and colonial conquests; civil wars, revolutions and counterrevolutions" attest to that. Modernity is violent and is tolerant of violence because it sees violence as a necessary means to progress. Mamdani (2004: 4) observes that "the modern sensibility is not horrified by pervasive violence". Implying that, modernity is accepting of violence and it reinforces it in its operationalisation of the developmentalist agenda.

The modern era's conception evolved and resulted in the production of patterns and soft-structures that predetermine, control and regulate being and epistemology modelled on European thought and standards. Those patterns and soft-structures that continue and perpetuate the dictates of seventeenth-century European culture and thought are what identifies modernity. The main idea that came with modernity is an implied "idea that everything new is necessarily good and desirable" (Grosfoguel 2000: 348). This idea of esteeming anything new was mistakenly believed to represent progress and development.

Escobar further defines modernity from a sociological perspective and asserts that modernity is "credited with the creation of modern institutions such as the nation-state and basic features such as self-reflexivity" (Escobar 2007: 182). The concept of nation-state is modelled on the European Concert of State, which is still the prototype of statehood to date. Habermas (1973; 1987 quoted in Ndlovu-Gatsheni 2013: vii) avers that from a cultural perspective, modernity is accredited for the "substitution of folk-knowledge by expert and techno-scientific knowledge". To its credit, modernity valued literature—the written word—and the advantage of that is it is better kept and preserved, almost in its original state. Of course, the written word can always be interpreted and re-interpreted. The problem with modernity is that in its quest for 'scientific knowledge', it negated orature—the spoken word—a value and practice that is ancient and sacred in African ecologies and localities. Modernity substituted orature for literature in African ecologies and localities particularly, and relegated orature to 'folklore' or 'folk-knowledge' (Zondi 2017). Modernity is further accredited with the creation of the "Cartesian subject as the fountain of all knowledge about the world" from a philosophical perspective (Ndlovu-Gatsheni 2013: vii).

In affirmation of the aforementioned views, Biakolo (2003: 14) advances the argument that "Western civilisation owes its origin to writing". The invention of the alphabet by the Greeks proved to be an unprecedented catalyst to the organising and storage of information and subsequently knowledge production. The point that Biakolo makes is that the archival and retrieval of information in Western civilisation meant that access to knowledge and information was unrestricted, save for those that were illiterate perhaps, whereas in oral traditions such as most cultures in Africa, "the poets, sages, and thinkers depend on poetic rhythm and narrative structure to ensure the remembrance of past utterances" (Biakolo 2003: 15). Admittedly, memory may not always accurately preserve the details of phenomena as it happened and this could be correctly argued to have been somewhat cumbersome. Information and knowledge storage and retrieval that depended on memory was not always accurate in the oral traditions and so remembering alone sets the limitation to knowledge production in oral cultures. The inscribing of information and knowledge on manuscripts—the art of writing—made for easier "storage and retrieval of knowledge" (Havelock 1963 quoted in Biakolo 2003: 14–15). Kissinger converges with Biakolo's (2003) assertions and notes that, fifteenth-century Europe saw the "invention of movable type printing … [which] made it possible to share knowledge on a hitherto – unimaginable scale" (Kissinger 2014: 19). This speaks to the lever of control of knowledge and subjectivity that the industrialisation of knowledge production came with, mass printing that allowed the dissemination of accounts and views from a Eurocentric perspective (ibid.).

Biakolo (2003) evinces Kissinger's (2014) view, while noting that the change in the presentation of knowledge, that is, the mass printing of writings and accounts, resulted in the "dominance of discourses that were more and more definitional, descriptive, and analytical" (Biakolo 2003: 15). What remains is that, whatever description or qualifier that the accounts were ascribed, they were written from the perspectives of their writers, which essentially were European. Hence the Eurocentric domination in literature, and "the origin of Western science and philosophy" (ibid.). Havelock (1991: 24 quoted in Biakolo 2003: 15) argues that "without modern literacy, which means Greek literacy, we would not have science, philosophy, written law, nor the automobile or the airplane". Havelock's view is problematic because it assumes that if something is not written down, it does not exist or will never exist. Yet, writing down ideas presumes their existence in the first place.

Biakolo (2003: 15) is of the view that the cultural invention of print media by Europe became its currency of its domination of literature. He argues that "the transformation of the mode of codification and structuration of knowledge led to a cultural regimen which placed greater premium on innovativeness, inventiveness, and objectivity" (ibid.). Biakolo further highlights that the narratives that came from this cultural regimen of literature tended to be "analytic, syllogistic, and definitional, and their immediate context of production is generally privatist", whereas oral cultures took the form of a traditionalist and conservative outlook (Biakolo 2003: 15). The accumulation of knowledge in the oral cultures entailed a participatory and pragmatic realm where its members interiorised communal knowledge (ibid.). This is arguably the bone of contention between ontology and epistemology; the Western civilisation tended to separate the episteme from the ontology of the knowing subject. This does not give the literature tradition superiority over the oral African ecologies and localities that valued the participatory and practical accumulation of communal knowledge. Communal knowledge is valued in African ecologies and localities, and the Western civilisation espoused a privatist episteme. It is a matter of difference of modes of accumulating knowledge and information, rather than superiority and inferiority of one mode over another.

The knowledge that is valued by modernity is that which it considers scientific—abstract, objective, rational, logical and syllogistic. As evinced by Grosfoguel (2000: 348), modernity valued scientific knowledge over religious knowledge, thereby peripherising religion and its values and virtues. Grosfoguel's observation highlights an implied attitude by Western 'scientific' knowledge's conception. It implies that if knowledge is primitive, it is illogical, irrational and unscientific. Western knowledge, therefore, puts itself as the standard by which all other forms of knowledge are judged. It gives the illusion that only it is valid and true. However, Biakolo (2003) reveals that, despite what Western modern knowledge wants to purports, it is only just but a façade. He argues that the so-called primitive thought is at worst "rational but illogical and not scientific", or at best primitive thought is "rational and logical and scientific within its own cultural context" (Biakolo 2003: 18). What Biakolo manages to succinctly reveal is that Western knowledge purports itself as objective, yet in actual fact, it is subjective to its own cultural context.

Therefore, from the subaltern perspective, what Western modern science calls 'primitive thought' is in fact rational and logical in the oral traditions' view; very much in the same fashion as 'science' is to the literary traditions. If Western modern 'scientific' thought seeks order, unity, regularity underneath the seeming diversity, and simplicity, the African oral traditional thought "also seeks this through the structure of the pantheon and the categorial relations of its spiritual forces" (Biakolo 2003: 18). This means that, just as Western modern scientific methods, the African oral traditions seek to explain causal connections between phenomena, for example between "dis-ease states and social conduct" (ibid.). Western modernity expressly names one thing and ascribes particularly meaning to the named thing; and by the same token implies the opposite to that which it views as opposite to the named thing. For example, the description of one society as civilised implies that the opposite is savagery; or, framing an argument or writing as logical implies the illogical of the other. Now, in relation to Africa particularly, the written tradition's opposite is oral, and the scientific's opposite is magical (Biakolo 2003: 20). In the conception of Western modernity, one cannot live or survive as one and the other, it is always an either, or, scenario. Modernity always distinguishes between being and non-being and never being together with 'non-being'. This is yet another of modernity's myths.

The Irrationality of Modernity's 'Rationality'

The Enlightenment period (eighteenth-century Europe) emphasised rationality. Aristotle argued that "man (*sic*) is a rational animal" (Quoted in Ramose 2001: 2). In the words of Ramose, this means that "those animals whose being or nature includes reason as their distinctive characteristic fall within his definition" (ibid.). Rationality, therefore, sets apart man (*sic*) from animal. Suffice to note that this definition of "man (*sic*)" as a 'rational animal' is proffered by a Greek, and therefore White European man who, unwittingly, entrenches Eurocentrism. Ramose interprets Aristotle's definition of man (*sic*) to mean that "any other animal which might look like a human being but be without reason does not qualify as a human being" (Ramose 2001: 2). Non-human beings are defined by lack and therefore precast as victims of the human beings because they are disadvantaged and without reason. Ramose highlights that the demarcation between reason and unreason "established the nature of the relationship between those inside and those outside the line of reason" (Ramose 2001: 2). This is similar to the "Abysmal lines" that Maldonado-Torres (2002: 998) speaks about. They are imaginary lines such as the line of Capricorn or the Equator. They represent false demarcations that are socially constructed and are only a reality to those conscious of them. Eurocentrism thrives on imaginary lines that do not really exist ontologically.

Aristotle's legacy or tradition is what informed European conquerors of Africa, this European-centric definition of humanity excluded animals without reason (Ramose 2001: 2). The definition of man (*sic*) as a rational animal proffered by Aristotle excluded the African, among others. The conundrum of this definition lies in that the conqueror applied it religiously when they came into contact with the "African, the Amerindian and the Australasian" (Ramose 2001: 2). This speaks of a Eurocentric definition of humanity that is limited to a geographical location of the Northern Hemisphere; any other human being not located in the geography of Europe is deemed to be with "unreason" or without reason (ibid.). This is a myth that is based on imaginary lines that demarcates humanity from non-humanity. Geography then becomes manipulated to make believe that the imaginary demarcations of humanity from non-humanity are actually real. The manipulation of imaginary demarcation lines is aimed at furthering the myth that Europe embodies humanity and that anything else that exists outside Europe is of a lesser ontological value and could be used and manipulated by humanity located in Europe.

The exclusion of the African, and other non-European races, in Aristotle's definition of man (*sic*) as a rational animal, gave grounding for treating the African "only as an animal" (Ramose 2001: 2). This definition provided justification, therefore, for the enslavement and subjugation of Africans among other non-European races, as it was in the African's nature to be without reason. If unreason defined the African, what would be the reason to not conquer the African? In this line of thought, it was "necessary and proper" for the conqueror to subjugate the African; after all, this was contingent upon the practical application of Descartes' "I think therefore, I exist", only it practically meant "I think therefore, I conquer" (Ramose 2001: 3). This is the very problematic fabric of thought that justified, and continues to perpetuate, coloniality of power. Ramose quips therefore that it is of no surprise that European conquests of Africa, and the slave trade particularly, are conspicuous features that defined the asymmetrical relationship between the conquering Europeans from the West and Africans, but specifically Africans from sub-Saharan Africa (Ramose 2001: 2–3). Even the imaginary demarcation of sub-Saharan Africa exists only in mind and not in reality. Material power is then used to perpetuate the framing of conditions that exist in the so-called sub-Saharan Africa.

In the European conquerors' framework, civilisation was possible only in so far as the agent of progress, or the recipient of progress, was capable of rationality. Since Africans were equated to animals without reason, they were deemed incapable of progress. The incapability to progress meant that Africans could not attain civilisation to the European standard or to the satisfaction of the European. Ramose adds that "this line between civilisation and barbarism was an extension of the boundary between reason and unreason" (Ramose 2001: 3). Europeans' self-claim to the exclusive possession of civilisation was contingent upon a belief that they were superior or possessed superior civilisation to that of the African or any other non-European civilisation. As such, they encountered non-Europeans, particularly Africans, with a predetermined attitude that negated, belittled and inferiorised non-Europeans. Hence, the European conqueror thought of himself and herself as civilised and the African as barbaric, with the latter's rights, competences and obligations predetermined by the former (Ramose 2001: 3).

The European conqueror thus determined and established a gulf between civility of the self and barbarity of the other, and thus, between superiority in the self and inferiority in the other. The othering of others was thus established and secured. This imaginary chasm meant that the relationship between the European conqueror and the conquered African was devoid of reciprocity. It was a unilateral relationship where "the African had only obligations towards the conqueror but no rights" (Ramose 2001: 3). This could be argued as the genesis of hierarchisation of human beings according to race, reason and civilisation according to a particular European-centric standard projected as universal in Africa. This is the crux of coloniality of power, the ordering and organising of all civilisations according to a particular, Eurocentric standard. The very idea of centring Europe in the development of every civilisation speaks of Europe's insatiable thirst of controlling humanity.

The Façade of Modernity

America was the first space to have been colonised by Britain and turned out to be the prototype of modernity and the new world order. It follows then that Britain, located in Europe, has become the centre of the world; hence, this chapter's assertion that the current world order reflects a Euro-North American-centric conception. Kissinger submits that America idealises and projects itself as a "city on a hill"; America thinks of itself as an ideal possessing values that are universally applicable and relevant (Kissinger 2014: 16). To evince this observation, in 1961 the then American President Harry S. Truman in response to Kissinger's question on "what in his presidency had made him most proud", quipped, how Americans had entirely annihilated their nemeses and in turn brought their former enemies to the "community of states" (Kissinger 2014: 1). American Presidents have over the years urged other governments to accept the conservation and consolidation of universal human rights (Kissinger 2014: 2). Yet, while making that call to the world, the USA at that time was simultaneously embarking on what it called the "role back strategy" that was meant to fester destruction in the Soviet system. Does it mean then the so-called universal human rights were not applicable to the Soviet Union? This reveals the double-standards embedded in the Euro-North American-centric civilisation and modernity. This further reveals the centrality of Europe to humanity. Eurocentrism perpetuates the myth that only in Europe is located humanity and therefore, human rights apply to where humanity is located, Europe.

The destruction of the Soviet system was to compel the Soviet Union to renegotiate a settlement on America's terms (Chomsky 2011: 10). America had the upper hand in the negotiation. Besides the unmatched economic and military power of America, it enjoyed a perceived legitimacy in the negotiation owing to the mass media and propaganda machinery that propped America up as a legitimate party to the negotiations. At the time of the end of World War II, 1945, America had 50% of the world's wealth, yet its population was a mere 6.3% of the world's population (Chomsky 2011: 11). This statistic speaks of an uneven and asymmetric economic and power balance when America is compared to the rest of the world. Making America an empire as such, and will do anything to maintain that status quo as evinced by this declaration from the National Security Council (henceforward NSC) Document 68 attributed to an US Planner of post-world war strategy, George Kennan, 1948:

> Our real task in the coming period is to devise a pattern of relationships which will permit us to maintain this position of disparity…We should cease to talk about vague and unreal objectives such as human rights, the raising of the living standards and democratisation…The day is not far when we are going to deal in straight power concepts. The less we are then hampered by idealist slogans, the better. (Chomsky 2011: 12)

The problematic nature of Euro-North American-centric modernity is that it condemns one thing, in this instance, and does the same thing, in the next. For example, the Central Intelligence Agency's (CIA) core objective is to conduct secret activities that are not in line with legal norms for the US' executive branch. The executive does not want these secret activities to be known, as they are potentially disastrous to their reputation, popularity and acceptance from the general public. What this reveals is that, contrary to populist propaganda of the USA, within its government machinery, the USA notably goes against democratic principles (Chomsky 2011: 162).

At the height of the Cold War, America was devising a plan that sought to dominate what was to be a 'new world order'. The plan was called the "Grand Arena" (Chomsky 2011: 13). The Grand Arena plan included:

> [T]he Western Hemisphere, Western Europe, the Far East, the former British Empire (which was being dismantled [through Britain's decolonisation]), the incomparable energy resources

of the Middle East (which were then passing into American hands as we pushed out our rivals France and Britain), the rest of the Third World and, if possible, the entire globe. These plans were implemented as, as opportunities allowed (ibid.).

The Grand Arena entailed that every part of the world, meaning every geo-locale in the new world order, was allocated a particular purpose. The industrialised or developed countries—developed on the basis of unpaid labour provided by the Black race particularly, but by non-European races generally—were to be led by Germany and Japan, the so-called great workshops (Chomsky 2011: 13). Germany and Japan were revered as the great workshops following their show of military superiority during the Cold War, this bearing testimony to the Euro-North American-centric civilisation's esteem of war; violence is used as a tool that brings honour and prestige. The two great workshops were to work "under US supervision" (ibid.).

The Northern and Western Hemisphere were placed at the apex of the hierarchy of this new world order, with the rest of the world—labelled as "the Third World", at the very bottom and peripheries of the Euro-North American-centric civilisation's world order. The periphery was meant to meet its primary function of providing labour, raw materials and the consumer market of finished products. The periphery was meant to be "exploited" to the benefit of Europe and Japan (Kennan quoted in Chomsky 2011: 13). Kennan worked as a US State Department Official in 1949, and is credited to have drafted the memo that exposed the US's plans (ibid.). It can be deduced from Chomsky's analysis that the USA, as the architect of the "Grand Arena", determined and controlled who did what, when and how, the 'why' rested with the USA itself. This speaks to coloniality of power at a global level; hence, this chapter's assertion that the Euro-North America-centric modernity continuously pursues global coloniality. Anything or anyone that stands antithetical to this new world order becomes a threat that is violently dealt with. Saddam Hussein of Iraq, Thomas Sankara of Burkina Faso, Patrice Lumumba of the Congo, and Muammar Gaddafi of Libya are cases in point. The common element that the aforementioned figures shared is their locality in the peripheries of the Euro-North American-centric civilisation.

Modernity's Creation of Zone of Being and Zone of Non-being

In the Euro-North America-centric worldview, the accident of geography is esteemed more than the essence of humanity. There is more value placed on the geography of where human beings originate from, than the actual humanity. This worldview perceives two distinct zones; zone of being and the zone of non-being based on the exclusion that emanates from geography and subsequently, race. Kissinger highlights the fact that, despite the global power structural configuration that was created and is perpetuated by the Euro-North American-centric global domination, it is in fact a European accident that was realised and now purports itself as an essence;

the realisation was, and is, maintained by force and aggression. He argues that the "international relations" of the 1490s were a mere European regional undertaking which was to be globalised through the violence of colonialism (Kissinger 2014: 18).

The Euro-North American-centric new world order was born out of imagination. The socially constructed borders of what determined humanity and non-humanity were realised by force and are consistently consolidated by either the use of aggression or the threat thereof. The demarcation is not only imaginary, it was materialised. Ramose (2001: 5) submits that the "amity lines" that enveloped the Euro-North American-centric civilisation while isolating the rest of the "overseas zone" were geographically located "along the equator or the Tropic of Cancer in the South, along a degree of longitude drawn in the Atlantic Ocean through the Canary Islands or the Azores in the west, or a combination of both". This demarcation, that separated the Western Meridian from the Azores, was to not be shifted under whatsoever circumstances.

In other words, this Western Meridian separated the Western Hemisphere and the overseas zone signalling the end of Europe and the geography that existed beyond the "amity line" signalled the beginning of the "New World" (Ramose 2001: 5). The overseas zone was not governed by Europe and hence no law applied there, except for the "laws of the stronger"; this meant civility was curtailed to exist only in the Western Meridian, beyond that lay a territory of barbarity. Kissinger (2014: 18) quips that as far back as 1550–1551, King Charles the V, a Christian, summoned a council of theologians for deliberations and that council concluded that "people living in the Western Hemisphere were human beings with souls—hence eligible for salvation". That pronouncement implied that people who lived beyond the Western Hemisphere where therefore, non-human beings and without souls. In fact, that conclusion justified "conquest and conversion" (Kissinger 2014: 19). This then speaks to the audacity with which Europeans imposed their religion, even forcefully at times, on people in spaces and places they colonised and conquered. Coloniality of power was henceforth geographically and asymmetrically constituted in favour of the Western Hemisphere. This was the creation of the European-centric "zone of being" and the "hellish zone of non-being" for non-Europeans, but Africans particularly.

What is noteworthy of the amity lines is that, unlike the "*Rayas*" lines, they represented a zone that was subject to conflicting interests arising between a duo of "contractual parties" that sought to seize land and commandeer the inhabitants of that land. The conflicting parties only shared consensus on the "freedom of the open spaces that began beyond the line" (Ramose 2001: 5). This speaks of the condescending attitude that engulfs the Euro-North American-centric civilisation. It ascribes humanity to itself and, beyond the geography of what it knows and the proximity to it, denies *other* humans of their humanity. The interaction between the conflicting parties in the zone of being are amicably resolved through a contract, and beyond the zone of being, the barrel of the gun, aggression and violence become the order of the day—the "hellish zone of non-being".

In the 'hellish zone of non-being', "force could be used freely and ruthlessly" because there existed no humanity in those spaces and places (Ramose 2001: 5). This meant that anything that happened outside the Euro-North American-centric world did not have legal merit nor consequence and had no moral or political merit. Hence, John Tully's observation that "there is no sin beyond the equator" (2011: 85). Sins and transgression are only committed in the zone of being, where civility, legality, morality and reciprocity are located and enforceable. In the hellish zone of non-being, chaos, pandemonium and disorder are the norm. To this effect, Mamdani (2004: 4) argues that "when violence does not cross the boundary between 'the west' and the rest—it is called 'communal conflict', as in South Asia, or 'ethnic conflict', as in Africa" (Mamdani 2004: 4).

Chossudovsky (2015) evinces what he terms the "hegemonic project" of the "globalisation of war" by the USA. He submits that there are major US-sponsored military and undercover intelligence operations that are run concurrently in regions such as, but not limited to, the Middle East, sub-Saharan Africa, Eastern Europe, the Far East and Central Asia. These covert operations are designed to destabilise sovereign states, particularly those states that defy the global power structural configuration of the Euro-North American-centric world view. The USA and its allies, Western Europe, do this to consolidate its grip on the control of the 'new world order', and by so doing, continuously defines and sustains global coloniality through the control of colonial power matrices—coloniality of power.

Coloniality as a Framework for Theorising Africa

Ndlovu-Gatsheni (2013: 7) defines coloniality as the "dark side of modernity" that has been consistently packaged to camouflage the inconsistency and discrepancy between the rhetoric of modernity and the lived experience thereof. While modernity esteems values of democracy, human rights, progress and development, the implementation of these values is often violent and disastrous when outside the Western Hemisphere— the Euro-North American-centric space and geography. One wonders if this rhetoric of the universal human rights covers spaces and places outside Europe and North America—the epitome of the Western world.

Coloniality is therefore the rationale that gives rise and justifies colonialism. Coloniality is the software of colonialism; the latter being the physical and violent conquering of a people/civilisation by another, arising from the former. Coloniality could also be understood as the after-effects of colonialism; it refers to "long-standing patterns of power that emerged as a result of colonialism" (Ndlovu-Gatsheni 2015: 487).

The concept of coloniality of power is a particular strand that lies within the broader decolonial theory; it is informed and attributed to Peruvian national and Professor of Sociology Anibal Quijano who identified four levers of coloniality. The first is "control of the economy". The second is "control of authority". The third is "control of gender and sexuality". The fourth is "control of knowledge and subjectivity" (quoted in Ndlovu-Gatsheni 2015: 487). Mignolo (2001: 424) submits that, it is the "colonial experiences" that "outlived decolonisation" and thereby continue to provide a template of thought and action that reproduces colonial-like forms that is problematic; and these patterns or structures constitute coloniality of power. The patterns that emerged as a result of colonialism and continue to fester and consolidate modern empire and its operations are constitutive of coloniality of power.

At the centre of control is power, hence the concept of coloniality of power. "As the centre of global capitalism, Europe not only had control of the world market, but it was also able to impose its colonial dominance over all the regions and populations of the planet, incorporating them into its world-system and its specific model of power" (Mignolo 2001: 424). It is this concept of coloniality of power that this study will appropriate in analysing the application of Right to Protect (R2P) in the NATO invasion of Libya in 2011 mindful that this study seeks to establish and determine whether or not, the Libyan invasion was linked to the dynamics of coloniality of power. According to Quijano (quoted in Grosfoguel 2000: 368), coloniality of power is the classification of people through "historical process of colonial/racial domination".

Coloniality of power is manifested especially after the independence of former colonised countries in the form of the continuation of "control of economic, cultural, and political structures of society" (Quijano 1993 quoted in Grosfoguel 2000: 368). Grosfoguel adds that the continuation of "power relations from colonial to postcolonial times allowed the white elites to classify populations and to exclude people of colour from categories of full citizenship in the imagined community called the 'nation'" (2000: 368). Civil liberties, rights and privileges of citizenship were never truly extended to colonial subjects such as Blacks, Indians, *Mulattoes* and *Mestizos*. The control of the internal grouping of populations by colonialism is the perpetuation of colonialism in *abstentia*. This is the essence of coloniality of power.

Kissinger (2014: 2-3) echoes what Mignolo (2001) observed that coloniality of power is represented by the long-standing patterns that emerged as a result of colonialism; he argues that "what passes for order in our time was devised in Western Europe nearly four centuries ago, at a peace conference in the German region of Westphalia, conducted without the involvement or even the awareness of most other continents or civilisations", such as Africa. Yet, the so-called world wars involved Africans as foot soldiers who were used as proxies of the global powers. They required of Africa cheap (military) labour for the industrialised and capitalist world. South Africa, under the apartheid regime, sent its contingent comprising of more than 600 Black men who were to perish at sea when their ship, the *SS Mendi* sunk on route to participating in World War I on 21 February 1918, yet South Africa, as part of Africa,[1] had nothing to do with World War I, for example (South African Navy 2014).

Europe is unquestionably the originator and epicentre of the crafting of colonial conditions that were to be "approximated" globally to what is now understood as the contemporary world order. In other words, a particular, subjective, shallow

---

[1] Admittedly, South Africa under the apartheid regime did not identify with Africa's quest for decolonisation and political freedom of the Black race particularly; this could very well explain its participation in World War I and its insistence of sending Black men to war for its self-serving interests probably as sacrificial lambs.

and narrow perspective, and to use Kissinger's words, "an accident" of Europe's imagination of order "became the hallmarks of a new system of international order" (Kissinger 2014: 3). This is essentially where coloniality of power lies, in Europe's accident that "shaped and prefigured the modern" times of Europe into a universally pertinent structure (ibid.: 4). It is this universally/globally appurtenant structure that determines the global power structural configuration. It is prefigured and can only be re-configured by the originator—Europe and its allies, particularly the USA and much of the Western world. Europe's allies often endorse and never are opposed to this global power structural configuration that is inherently asymmetrical in favour of the Euro-North American-centric alliance' perspective. Anyone/entity that dare oppose the global power structural configuration is dealt with violently, including death, as was President Muammar Gaddafi. This makes Europe an empire. In other words, Europe's accident was scattered across the globe in an intentional and malicious manner that sought to expand Europe's influence and territory.

Contemporary global society is ordered around the patterns that emerged from British colonialism of America and the rest of the world. America, hence, became the prototype of a colonial state. Kissinger (2014: 6) points out that "in time, the US would become the indispensable defender of the order Europe designed". The USA will defend the system that Europe designed because it was included in the prefiguring of the global power structural configuration based on the imagined superiority of race, and hence races were ordered hierarchically with the White race occupying the apex of the hierarchy. The influence that Britain and America have in the contemporary world order is unparalleled. The Euro-North American-centric orientation is thus monolithic and imposing. Today's society is dominated by Europe and North America as the two protagonists of the current world order or the global power structural configuration.

Kissinger further reveals that "in the American view of world order, peace and balance would occur naturally, and ancient enmities would be set aside – once other nations were given the same principles say in their own governance that Americans had in theirs" (Kissinger 2014: 6). But, who are 'they' that give other nations those so-called American principles? What Kissinger reveals here is that America sees itself as part of the design team of the global world order. It too, is above the world system as it is the designer of the current world order. The Euro-North American-centric modernity hence is supra the global power structural configuration because it prefigured it. It cannot be that the designer of a thing will be governed by the same rules that govern the designed thing.

In 1648, the doctrine of sovereignty was officially codified and conferred sovereign rights and autonomy to all states. All states were to be treated as equal in authority as sovereigns in their domains and in relation to other sovereigns, regardless of economic stature or arsenal power. Yet in 1815–1886, this sovereignty was denied to Africa. Kissinger intones the double-standards of Europe in the haphazard and spurious application of the principle of sovereignty; he argues that "they [Europeans] often neglected to apply concepts of sovereignty to the colonies and colonised peoples" (Kissinger 2014: 6). Since the current global power structural configuration was an idea of Europe, it is only the Euro-North American-centric modernity that can reconfigure the design because this modernity is outside the design. To evince this assertion, it is argued that "Europe has set out to depart from the state-system itself designed and to transcend it through a concept of pooled sovereignty" (Kissinger 2014:7). The European Union (EU) is the case in point; ironically, Gaddafi was calling for a United Africa (UA) at the time of his assassination.

Admittedly, the utility value of these institutions (EU, AU, UN, etc.) lies in that they have potency to provide an even-handed and impartial framework for the engagement of a diverse community of states, if handled fairly, justly and with symmetrical influence of the involved parties (Kissinger 2014: 7). The current global power structural configuration was an invention of Europe, and as the architect of this system of world governance, Europe championed the "balance of power concept" with itself as the author and adjudicator of that system (Kissinger 2004: 7). This reveals the genesis of the asymmetrical power configuration in this 'new world order' system. This means that the rationale of colonialism is coloniality. Coloniality propelled the Europeans to conquer other civilisations in order to impose their sense of order on every 'other' civilisation.

The Westphalian Peace Treaty was signed in 1648, indicating the official codification of the doctrine of state sovereignty. The Berlin West Africa Conference, known for the slogan 'Scramble for Africa' occurred in 1885–1887 (Iliffe 1979; Pakenham 1992; Chamberlain 2010). The Versailles Treaty was signed in 1919 signalling the end of World War I (Kissinger 2014: 24) demonstrating the European double-standards and asymmetrical power relations. This also speaks of the inconsistencies of European modernity. The double-standards applied by Europe in its interactions with the rest of the world are conspicuous. Another example of this is that the same European-centric worldview developed international law. International law entailed that "if a state would accept these basic requirements, it could be recognised as an international citizen able to maintain its own culture, politics, religion and internal policies, shielded by the international system from outside intervention" (Kissinger 2014: 27).

Europe as the self-appointed architect, arbiter and adjudicator of states' behaviours considered international law "as an expandable body of agreed doctrine aimed at the cultivation of harmony, with the Westphalian treaties themselves at its heart" (Kissinger 2014: 27). It can be deduced, therefore, that international law was designed for Europe and had only Europe at the centre of its creation and intended application, which then explains why international law was not upheld at the Berlin West Africa Conference, Africa was partitioned to the whims of European imperial powers without any consequence. This renders international law whim some as it is selectively applied, revealing the impunity of international law.

International law speaks of recognition as the precondition for the acceptance of a state in the fold of the international community of states. It consequently speaks of being shielded and protected from external intervention. Recognised by who? Shielded from who? This is problematic for the African polity. How can an imposed order maintain a culture, politics and internal processes of African ecologies and localities, when an outside imposition has already been put? If a state does not accept or conform, it is not protected from outside intervention. Is this not coloniality of power at its highest expression? Europe is the recogniser of states and therefore the guarantor of political independence of states; Europe is the power that recognises states, protects states and policies states into conformity and order. The European civilisation is the ordering state, from which all order is derived. Such is the control that Europe has on the current global power structural configuration. This undoubtedly makes Europe an Empire.

A British Statesman, Lord Palmaston, once quipped that "our interests are eternal and perpetual, and those interests it is our duty to follow" (quoted in Kissinger 2014: 29–30). Europe prescribes what order is and what it is not, if a state conforms to the prescribed order it is insulated from Europe's wrath, but a deviant state is meted with violence. The problem with the order of Europe is that it is foible and it varies and changes depending on whom is in question. The Euro-North American-centric modernity is not even apologetic about this matter. Kissinger evinces the rationale behind this arrogance; he notes, "we mean to do what may seem to be best, upon each occasion as it arises, making the interests of our country one's guiding principle" (Kissinger 2014: 30). This, in fact, is not a principle because it is whim some, always depending on circumstances; should a principle not be mandible depending on circumstance(s)?

Coloniality and Control of Africa's Economies

European colonialism and the capitalist 'market system' are intrinsically linked. The definition of one is constituted in the other, thereby making colonialism and capitalism mutually defining. Capitalism was a result of the colonial system to control labour; and it maximised profits of Whites at the expense of non-Whites' labour force. Capitalism is an instrument of colonial domination of other races by Europeans. As expounded by Quijano (2000:539), "capital's specific social configuration was geographically and socially concentrated in Europe, and above all, among Europeans in the whole world of capitalism". The Black labour force was imported from Africa to Europe for unwaged or non-paid labour. Arguably, this move signalled the beginning and legitimatising of slavery and subjugation of the Black race as "slavery was assigned exclusively to the 'black' population brought from Africa" (Quijano 2000: 539). The conceptual link of colonisation, racism and slavery can be traced to capitalism; Ramose (2003:3) avers that capitalism provides a "conceptual link between colonisation, racism, and slavery". In the grand scheme of things, Africa's only utility value was to provide unpaid and unwaged labour for the Eurocentric world.

Therefore, cheap labour in the view of the Euro-North American-centric colonial project is a necessary component of the organisation and control of the labour market. Put differently, capitalism is by design meant to consolidate the modern system of power distribution and maintaining and preserving the social structures of the dominated and the dominant; the conquered and the conquerors. Capitalism is embedded in, and sustains, coloniality which safeguards the perpetuation of colonialism, in the physical absence of the conquerors and colonisers. Quijano (1993 quoted in Grosfoguel 2000: 368) argues that modernity is responsible for the social and historical construction of classifications of "labour and capital; ... between Europeans and non-Europeans". These classifications perpetuate the colonial order. In other words, the global power configuration is such that capital resides with Europeans, and labour with non-Europeans. This asymmetry is a construction of the European-centric capitalist system. This epitomises coloniality of power through the means of the economy, means of production and financial resources. The Brenton Woods Institutions such as the World Bank Group (WBG) and the International Monetary Fund (IMF) are vanguards of European modernity that control and regulate the global economy today.

Since the colonisation of the Americas, European colonisation was expanded to the rest of the world from the eighteenth century and progressively controlled what has been the world order since (Quijano 2000: 536). Essentially, and because of the capitalist configuration, "Europeans were enabled to increase their wealth" at the expense of non-European civilisations but particularly the unwaged and enslaved Black race (Kissinger 2014:19). The start of capitalism was never on a just basis, this was the beginning of asymmetrical economic relations, and capitalism enabled economic superiority of European, the beginning of control of the economy. Hence this study's position on combative ontology, in combat of the monolithic Euro-North American-centric civilisation.

The Power to Control Other Countries

Authority speaks of legitimacy, whereas legitimacy speaks of the rightfulness of that which is said to be legitimate (Ramose 2003: 3). The Euro-North American-centric modernity claims universal legitimacy to existence, and it further claims legitimacy to ordering other existences modelled on its own. The authority of the Euro-North American-centric modernity is geographically derived from the Western Hemisphere. It is specifically derived from five European countries, namely Britain, France, Germany, Italy and Greece. In all 'classic' European writings, one finds that they either are informed by the thoughts and works of writers that include, inter alia, Aristotle, Plato, Locke, Hobbes, Kant, Giddens, Rousseau, Machiavelli and Marx, or they make reference to authors that are located in the five aforementioned European countries.

It is this citation of these so-called authority figures in various academic disciplines, especially the humanities and social sciences, that is an appeal to the European 'authority' for the endorsement of individuals' research, knowledge production or opinion pieces for that matter. While this could be viewed as coloniality of knowledge, it is equally coloniality of authority as the Euro-North American-centric modernity views itself as the only legitimate authority of knowledge and truth, and hence the only legitimate authority to produce knowledge and order 'other' civilisations (Ramose 2003: 5).

European modernity is also responsible for creating institutionalism as a way of controlling global affairs. Institutions such as state, citizenship and democracy are products of European modernity. Institutionalism, both as a theory and practice, emanates from the Euro-North American-centric discourse and rhetoric of accountability that seek legitimacy. On the international level, institutions such as the United Nations (UN), the World Health Organisation WHO), International Law (IL), the International Criminal Court (ICC) and the North Atlantic Treaty Organization (NATO) are used to camouflage coloniality of power by the Euro-North American-centric civilisation, which makes these institutions nothing more than representatives of coloniality of authority.

Control of Gender and Sexuality

Coloniality of gender and sexuality speak to the broader concept of coloniality of being. It has to do with the role geography plays in sustaining coloniality. It speaks to the actual and physical space, time and the subjection that these aspects impose on human beings, particularly colonial subjects. It further speaks of the objectification of beings in the colonised spaces and places. In turn, the objectification of the colonial subject results in the self-objectification of the colonial subjects themselves, hence coloniality of being. Humanity is divided into the zone of being, which is located in Europe and North America, and the zone of non-being which is all of the Global South. Being is apportioned to Europe and North America and anything that is non-European and non-North American has no ontological density in the framework of coloniality.

In most African localities and ecologies, the colonial 'order' established colonial societies that were based on the illusory 'superiority' of the male gender over the illusory 'inferiority' of the female gender, modelled on European male chauvinistic and bigoted society. Europe transplanted its society to colonial places and spaces, and Africa was not spared. Europe imported its hierarchised and patriarchised society and infiltrated the fabric of African societies. Men provided labour in colonial settlers' towns and more often than not, would leave their families in their natural localities and migrate to settler towns hence there was a creation of townships (Turino 2008: 28). Before colonialism, there was no concept of township in African localities and ecologies. Colonial establishments forcibly evicted Black people from their homes and forcibly relocated them to "townships" and "ghettos" (Desai and Vahed 2013: 14). What the colonial establishment did in the psyche of the conquered and colonialised Africans is that it taught African men particularly to treat their women with disregard. Men, as labourers and latter earners of a merge income, became breadwinners in a fast-changing world were labour replaced subsistence farming due to the loss of land of the Africans to colonial settlers. The colonial establishment taught the African what it was to be a man or a woman in the colonial order. It hierarchised race and gender, with Whites as 'superior', to the 'inferior' Black, and male as 'superior' to the 'inferior' female. The 'inferiority' of the female probably emanated from the fact that men were stronger physically and could provide the commodified labour much better than women.

Control of Knowledge and Subjectivity

Ramose (2003) argues that the rationale that European colonialism operated on was an unsubstantiated belief that Africans, among other non-European races, were not rational beings hence, they were not entitled to what rational beings claimed as their entitlement and rights. He argues that:

> One of the bases of colonisation was that the belief 'man is a rational animal' was not spoken of the African, the Amerindian, and the Australasian. Aristotle's definition of man was deeply inscribed in the social ethos of those communities and societies that undertook the so-called voyages of discovery—apparently driven by innocent curiosity. But it is well known that these voyages changed into violent colonial incursions. It seems then that the entire process of decolonisation has, among others, upheld and not jettisoned the questionable belief that 'man is a rational animal' excludes the African, the Amerindian, and the Australasian. (Ramose 2003: 1)

What Ramose manages to reveal is that the imaginary right and exclusive claim to rationality by Europe(ans) is only realised because of material power fashioned to guard and preserve the myth that Africa is unable to rationally construct knowledge. The power of the gun is what Europe used to scatter its patterns, templates, designs and standards across the globe. Power in European terms is tantamount to instruments of control emitted by violence. This imaginary exclusive right to rationality by Europe(ans) has wide-ranging and extensive implications for knowledge production about Africa by Africans. This is meant to cast doubt and reinforce the modern bias on Africa and other non-European races; it is also meant to make the non-European doubt themselves as to their capacity to rationalise, think and philosophise. European imagination, and hence modernity, "is doubtful [that] Africans are wholly and truly human beings" and it questions the Africans' capacity to philosophise (Ramose 2003: 5). The pattern that European imagination implanted in the mind of the African is to doubt herself and himself. This pattern is relatable to what Mudimbe (1987: 2) called the "organising structure" and what wa Thiongó (1981: 94) called the "organising principle". This chapter adds the 'ordering structure' to the long-standing patterns of control that European civilisation subjected Africa to. The self-doubting African cannot and is not meant to know or produce knowledge about herself and himself, let alone her/his surroundings and localities.

Europeans, as are self-acclaimed exclusive recipients of rationality, have thus put themselves on a pedestal of knowledge production, and at the apex of correct and therefore truthful knowledge. There is an underlying attitude that exudes itself as though Europeans were the only race and civilisation that holds and embodies the truth. As a result, an African's right to knowledge is contingent upon a "passive as well as uncritical assimilation" of the knowledge produced in Europe for Europeans and the whole world (Ramose 2003: 2). Africans are then supposed to faithfully implement the knowledge that is constructed, defined and designed "outside Africa" (ibid.). Coloniality of knowledge therefore refers to the Euro-North American intellectual thought as the referral point upon which all other epistemologies and knowledges are judged against. As an epistemological movement, "it has always been overshadowed by hegemonic Euro-north American-centric intellectual thought and social theories" (Ramose 2003: 2). Knowledge production, and the capacity to think and generate is a preserve of Euro-North American-centric modernity resulting in the creation of "border thinking" (Arturo Escobar in Mignolo 2001: 179). The thinking is located in the Euro-North American civilisation, beyond that geography, there exist no rationality. Such is the thinking of Euro-North American-centric civilisation.

Contextualising Coloniality of Power

To control is to induce/evoke in another a reaction/response, or take a course of action that they would not otherwise willingly choose. As such, control is the essential and primary currency of empire. Coloniality of power is a unit of analysis that unmasks the control patterns and of modernity. The architects of modernity and colonialism had in mind, control of the world, for the survival of their colonial project. The coloniser and the colonised are by design unequal. An inherent asymmetrical power relationship exists between the two. The design cannot be greater than the designer, neither a creation greater than the creator. A creator cannot be part of the creation or created. The creation is a product of the creator, so is the design a product of the designer. What (cause) limits and regulates (control) the design is the designer (agency). As such, the rules that apply to the design may not be applicable to the designer. The creator is above and beyond the creation. This scenario places the creator in an asymmetrical power relation with its creation, the two are incomparable.

What are the implications of the asymmetrical power relations? The Euro-North American-centric civilisation is outside the global power structural configuration. It created this configuration, and it is the force that does the configuration. All other civilisations are the ones to be configured. Any deviant civilisation or perspective to the established 'global order' becomes a threat to the functioning of this global imperial design. In this paradigm, there can never exist more than one centre of power; the Euro-North American-centric civilisation views itself as the only legitimate seat of power and control.

The designer regulates and controls the design. The design could have not existed without the designer. This is the bone of contention; since the design could have not been without the designer, how then can the same rules that regulate the design be applied to the designer? As such, coloniality of power perpetuates the patterns and designs of Euro-North American-centric modernity. The perpetuation of modernity's designs, patterns and structures is the essence of coloniality. Coloniality is the vehicle that transports and transplants modernity. Coloniality of power is the vehicle that transports and transplants control of institutions of authority, the markets, sexuality and gender as well as what is acceptable as knowledge, from Europe to the rest of the world.

What would be of value to the analysis that this chapter embarks on is the four levers of control that Quijano identified as core to understanding and unpacking the concept of coloniality of power. In analysing and assessing the events that occasioned the NATO invasion of Libya in 2011, this chapter will analyse how Libya was a threat to the current global power structural configuration on four levels—control of authority, control of knowledge and subjectivity, control of the economy and control of gender and sexuality.

Going forward, this chapter will analyse how Libya's stance on, and call to, forming a United Africa, as evinced by Koenig (2017: Online), went against the authority component of the current global power structural configuration. This work will also go on to demonstrate how Libya's proposal for African countries to develop and adopt their own monetary currency that was to be backed by gold reserves, as submitted by Koenig (2017: Online), went against the economy and markets component of the Euro-North American-centric power structural configuration. Libya's quest to develop a communication satellite that was to improve communication technologies in Africa, as averred by Bowen (2006: 14), went against the knowledge and subjectivity component of the global power structural configuration. At the time of Gaddafi's demise, Libya was increasingly beginning to be seen as a good example of a decolonial state, as opined by Bowen (2006: 15), and that was a threat to the gender and sexuality component of the global power structural configuration. It is therefore conceivable that the NATO-led UNSC acted to consolidate the global power structural configuration. As such, this work will now go on to demonstrate and evince these assertions and convictions in the subsequent chapters.

Conclusion

This chapter demonstrated the conundrum of European colonialism to today's society, particularly in the view of African ecologies, localities and civilisations. It also evinced how modernity has continued to perpetuate colonial orders, particularly in African societies and localities. This chapter discussed the concept of coloniality of power and demonstrated how coloniality of power particularly has thwarted African ontology and epistemology and keeps Africa at the bottom of the hierarchy that was socially constructed by European architects of modernity. The chapter highlighted how modernity favours the male gender over the female and privileges masculinity over femininity, and the White race over the Black race and other non-White races; thereby modernity presented itself as superior to and all other civilisations as inferior.

This chapter also highlighted how the Euro-North American-centric modernity convolutes appearance and essence; it deliberately presents an attractive appearance of universal human rights, sovereign equality and yet the essence of implementing those universal human rights is marred by violence, inequality, impunity, underdevelopment and barbarity. This chapter also evinced how capitalism is intrinsically linked to modernity and coloniality of the global power structural configuration. At the centre of the control of global socio-economic-politico affairs is the Euro-North American civilisation that has potency to act unilaterally to pursue its own agendas that are particular and subjective, but purported as universal and objective.

Bibliography

Achebe, C. 1994. In Williams, J. *Chinua Achebe and the 'bravery of lions'*. [Online]. Available https://artsbeat.blogs.nytimes.com/2013/03/22/chinua-achebe-and-the-bravery-of-lions/. Accessed 15 March 2018.
Bennet, C. 1998. *Maritime Defence in South Africa*. Cape Town: South African Maritime Interest CC.
Biakolo, E. 2003. Categories of Cross-Cultural Cognition and the African Condition. In *The African Philosophy Reader*, 2nd ed, ed. P.H. Coetzee and A.P.J. Roux, 9–21. New York: Routledge.
Boron, A.B. 2005. *Empire and Imperialism: A Critical Reading of Michael Hardt and Antonio Negri*. London and New York: Zed Books.
Bowen, W.Q. 2006. *Libya and Nuclear Proliferation: Stepping Back from the Brink*. London: Routledge.
Chamberlain, M.V. 2010. *The Scramble for Africa*. New York: Longman.
Chomsky, N. 2011. *How the World Works*. New York: Soft Skull Press.
Chossudovsky, M. 2015. *The Globalization of War: America's "Long War" Against Humanity*. Montreal: Global Research Publishers.
Coetzee, P.H., and A.P.J. Roux (eds.). 2003. *The African Philosophy Reader*, 2nd ed. New York: Routledge.
Cohen, J.M. (ed.). 1969. *The Four Voyages of Christopher Columbus*. London: Penguin Books.
Comaroff, J. 2002. Governmentality, Materiality, Legality, Modernity: On the Colonial State in Africa. In *African Modernities: Entangled Meanings in Current Debate*, ed. J.G.D.P. Probst and H. Schmidt, 107–134. Oxford: James Carrey.
Comaroff, J.L., and J. Comaroff. 1997. *Of revelation and Revolution: The Dialectics of Modernity on a South African Frontier*, vol. 2. Chicago, IL: University of Chicago Press.
Desai, A., and G.H. Vahed. 2013. *Chatsworth: The Making of a South African Township*. Durban: University of Kwa-Zulu Natal Press.
Diop, C.A. *The African Origin of Civilization: Myth or Reality?* New York: Lawrence Hill & Company.
Escobar, A. 2007. Worlds and Knowledges Otherwise. *Cultural Studies* 21 (2–3): 179–210.
Ghosh, S. 2016. *Transitions and Civics*. New Delhi: Madhubun, Vikas Publishing House, Private Ltd.
Gould, E.H. 2010. Liberty and Modernity: The American Revolution and the Making of Parliament's Imperial History. In *Exclusionary Empire: English Liberty Overseas, 1600–1900*, ed. J.P. Greene, 112–131. Cambridge: Cambridge University Press.
Grosfoguel, R. 2000. Developmentalism, Modernity, and Dependency Theory in Latin America. *Nepantla: Views from South* 1 (2): 347–374.
Grosfoguel, R. 2007. The Epistemic Decolonial Turn: Beyond Political Economy Paradigms. *Cultural Studies* 21 (2–3): 211–223.
Hardt, M., and A. Negri. 2000. *Empire*. Cambridge, MA: Harvard University Press.
Howe, G. 1990. Sovereignty and interdependence: Britain's place in the world. *International affairs (Royal Institute of International Affairs 1944)* 66 (4): 675–695.
Iliffe, J. 1979. *A Modern History of Tanganyika*. New York: Cambridge University Press.
Kissinger, H. 2004. *Ending the Vietnam War: A History of America's Involvement in and Extrication from the Vietnam War*. New York: Simon & Schuster.

Kissinger, H. 2014. *World Order: Reflections on the Character of Nations and Course of History*. New York: Penguin Books.

Koenig, P. 2017. *Let's Never Forget Why Muammar Gaddafi Was Killed*. [Online]. Available: https://www.pambazuka.org/pan-africanism/let%E2%80%99s-never-forget-why-muammar-gaddafi-was-killed?utm_campaign=shareaholic&utm_medium=email_this&utm_source=email. Accessed 15 November 2017.

Lambert, F. 2003. *The Founding Fathers and the Place of Religion in America*. New Jersey: Princeton University Press.

Maldonado-Torres, N. 2007. On the Coloniality of Being. *Cultural Studies* 21 (2–3): 240–270.

Mamdani, M. 2004. *Good Muslim, Bad Muslim*. New York: Jacana Media (Pvt) Ltd.

McFadden, P. 2016. *Inaugural Alumnae Conference*. Thabo Mbeki African Leadership Institute. [Online]. Available: https://www.youtube.com/watch?v=A8uAhUkRD7k. Accessed 9 February 2018.

McKeown, G. 2014. *Essentialism: The Disciplined Pursuit of Less*. Croydon: The Random House Group.

Mignolo, W. 2000. *Local Histories/Global Designs*. New Jersey: Princeton University Press.

Mudimbe, V.Y. 1987. *The Invention of Africa*. [Online]. Available: https://libcom.org/files/zz_v._y._mudimbe_the_invention_of_africa_gnosis_pbook4you_1.pdf. Accessed 26 November 2018.

Ndlovu-Gatsheni, S.J. 2013. *Empire, Global Coloniality and African Subjectivity*. New York and Oxford: Berghahn.

Ndlovu-Gatsheni, S.J. 2015. Decoloniality as the Future of Africa. *History Compass* 13 (10): 485–496.

Nyere, C. 2014. *Sovereignty in International Politics: An Assessment of Zimbabwe's Operation Murambatsvina, May 2005*. Master's Dissertation. Pretoria: University of South Africa. [Online]. Available: http://uir.unisa.ac.za/bitstream/handle/10500/18531/dissertation_nyere_c.pdf?sequence=1&isAllowed=y. Accessed 11 July 2019.

Nyere, C. 2015. The Continuum of Political Violence in Zimbabwe. *Journal of Social Science* 48 (1,2): 94–107.

Otfinoski, S. 2011. *The Voyages of Christopher Columbus*. New York: Benchmark Education Company.

Pakenham, T. 1992. *Scramble for Africa*. New York: Harper Collins.

Pillay, K. 2018. The 'Indian' Question: Examining Autochthony, Citizenship and Belonging in South Africa. In *Relating Worlds of Racism: Dehumanisation, Belonging and the Normative of European Whiteness*, ed. P. Essed, K. Farquharson, K. Pillay, and E.J. White, 63–88. Palgrave McMillan [eBook]. [Online]. Available: https://books.google.co.za/books?id=ml5qDwAAQBAJ&printsec=frontcover&dq=Pillay+2018&hl=en&sa=X&ved=0ahUKEwjC6fHsyqzjAhVsRxUIHVeQCPM4ChDoAQhHMAY#v=onepage&q=Pillay%202018&f=false. Accessed: 5 March 2019.

Quijano, A. 1993. Modernity, Identity and Utopia in Latin America. *Bounday 2: An International Journal of Literature and Culture* 20 (3): 140–155.

Quijano, A. 2000. Power, Eurocentrism, and Latin America. *Nepantla: Views from South* 1 (3): 533–580.

Ramose, M.B. 2001. An African Perspective on Justice and Race. *Polylog: Forum for Intercultural Philosophy* 3.

Ramose, M.B. 2003. The Struggle for Reason in Africa. In *The African Philosophy Reader*, 2nd ed, ed. P.H. Coetzee and A.P.J. Roux, 1–9. New York: Routledge.

Schmitt, C. 1996. The Land Appropriation and the New World. *Telos* 109: 36–37.

South African Navy. 2014. *The SS Mendi: A Historical Background*. [Online]. Available: http://www.navy.mil.za/newnavy/mendi_history/mendi_hist.htm. Accessed 7 March 2018.

Tully, J. 2011. *The Devils' Milk: A Social History of Rubber*. New York: Monthly Review Press.

Turino, T. 2008. *Music as Social Life: The Politics of Participation*. Chicago and London: University of Chicago Press.

Udeze, B. 2009. *Why Africa? A Continent in a Dilemma of Unanswered Questions*. New York: Xlibris Corporation.
United Nations (UN). 2018. *Overview*. [Online]. Available: https://www.un.org/en/sections/about-un/overview/index.html. Accessed 16 June 2018.
Wa Thiongó, N. 1981. *Decolonising the Mind: The Politics of Language in African Literature*. [Online]. Available: https://www.uibk.ac.at/anglistik/staff/davis/decolonising-the-mind.pdf. Accessed 26 November 2018.
Ziegler, D.W. 1987. *War, Peace and International Politics*, 4th ed. Boston: Little, Brown and Company.
Zondi, S. 2017. *Pointers on Shifting the Geography of Reason in the Classroom: A Decolonial Turn in Pedagogy*. South African Association of Political Science First Limpopo/Gauteng Regional Colloquium, 13 August 2018.

Part IV
Leadership

Chapter 8
When Mandela Meets Rousseau: An Exploration of South Africa's Civil Religion

Ahmed Haroon Jazbhay

Abstract This chapter grapples with the existence of civil religion in South Africa using Jean Jacques Rousseau's notions of patriotism, good citizenship, a good lawgiver, separation of powers and an elective aristocracy. After outlining Rousseau's thoughts on civil religion, it investigates the existence of a Mandela-mythology phenomenon built on the persona of Nelson Mandela by focusing on the importance of events and performative displays in his life, *inter alia*; the Rivonia Trial, his imprisonment on Robben Island, his release from prison, his presidential inauguration and the Rugby World Cup in 1995, as well as the proliferation of statues, roads and movies in his honour. Thereafter, using Rousseau's civil religion ideas, the chapter explores whether these events and displays constitute a civil religion a lá Rousseau. The chapter concludes that there indeed exists such a civil religion embodied in a set of beliefs, rituals and symbols as laid out by Rousseau with the purpose being used for political gain by the ruling ANC government.

Keywords Mandela · Mandela-mythology · Rousseau · Machiavelli · Civil religion

Introduction

The modern secular state has undergone constant evolution both in terms of its form as well as philosophical interpretations. South Africa is no exception to this, having evolved from a divisive colonial and apartheid setting to one that now broadly encompasses the principles of liberal democracy. This, however, has not meant that debate over the status, applicability and influence of religion has now been settled. Bellah (1967) and Cristi (2001), for example, contend that the constitutionally enshrined separation of church and state does not mean that a religious dimension cannot exist

---

A. H. Jazbhay (✉)
Department of Political Sciences, University of South Africa,
Office 26, 7th Floor Theo van Wijk Building, UNISA Main Campus,
Pretoria 0003, South Africa
e-mail: jazbhah@unisa.ac.za

in the political sphere. Sacred authority, in their opinion, remains a central political attribute of modern states.

This debate has its roots in the thoughts of Jean Jacques Rousseau. Rousseau believed that the quest of modern states for legitimation and social solidarity could be achieved through the creation of a national civil religion capable of binding all individuals to the state (Cristi 1997: 31). Much has been theorised about Rousseau's civil religion ideas. There is, however, very little on the potential impact and application of his accounts on post-1994 South Africa. This chapter is a contribution to this ongoing debate and situates a religious facet to the South African context. It argues that Nelson Mandela's political persona has come to embody a mythology which resonates with Rousseau's ideas on civil religion. Rousseau's ideas on civil religion will be used as the theoretical lens through which to analyse whether Mandela's political ideas and the institutionalised beliefs, rituals and symbols that accompany it have evolved into a state-sponsored civil religion in post-apartheid South Africa.

Although research is abound on Mandela's unifying influence and the 'rainbow nation' phenomenon as a civil religion in South Africa, no scholar to date has attempted to comprehend the personality of Mandela as a unifying civil religion for South Africans. This civil religion, it will be argued, is distinct from Christianity but is not militantly secular. It feeds on the persona of a political figure that members of all religious, ethnic and racial communities can relate to. The mainstream media contributed to the narrative by propagating the values of reconciliation, unity and non-racialism. For the most part, Mandela was judged by his contribution to constructing this miracle nation narrative. The infatuation with Mandela centres on the fact that his leadership style was moulded by historical experiences. Any serious study of Mandela must take cognisance of this fact. Mandela was able to seize the moral high ground in the immediate aftermath of the post-1994 South African landscape and was thus able to shoulder the burden of national expectation.

I propose a novel interpretation of the Mandela mythology and aim to position it as interrogating and interrupting the linear narrative of the Mandela story. It is an attempt to provide a unique understanding of the "shape-shifting" (Barnard 2014: 9) quality of Mandela which allowed him to bridge the gap and appeal to the different worlds he inhabited. Building up towards the main argument consists of three parts. First, Rousseau's thoughts on civil religion will be analysed which effectively entails a relationship whereby the secular state is administered by a religion encompassing civil principles. Second, the chapter provides an account of the ever-developing Mandela mythology from his birth in Qunu in 1918 up until his passing in December 2013. Here, I undertake a pointed discussion on the significance of his political thought and performative displays. The third part then situates the Mandela mythology within the contemporary debate on civil religion in South Africa.

Rousseau's Thoughts on Civil Religion

Rousseau's civil religion thoughts are the theoretical pillar upon which this chapter rests. In the *Social Contract*, Rousseau sets out to explore whether human beings can achieve an unbiased and impartial secular state administered by a religion incorporating civil principles. Rousseau places immense importance on civil religion in attaining political unity and argues that without it, "no state or government will ever be well constituted" (Rousseau 1997 [1762]: 146). There are two basic assumptions of Rousseau's civil religion. First, every state needs a religious foundation, and second, Christianity is the antithesis to a state's well-being. Simply understood, Rousseau assumes that religion is "politically indispensable for it is the base on which the state is legitimately anchored" (Cristi 2001: 21).

To avoid the problem of Christianity's incompatibility and the Machiavellian solution of returning to Roman paganism, Rousseau envisaged crafting a religion that creates and fosters civic creed. It was not "intended as a kind of surrogate religion, but one that concerns itself with moral and civic duties to other individuals" (Cristi 2001: 23). He based his vision for a civil religion where society was anchored on the principals of patriotism, good citizenship, a good lawgiver, separation of powers and an elective aristocracy all directed by a shared understanding of the general will. Central to this is the belief in God. Rousseau (1997 [1762]: 150–151) defines civil religion as the "existence of a powerful, intelligent, beneficent, prescient, and provident divinity (God), the life to come, the happiness of the just, the punishment of the wicked, the sanctity of the Social Contract and the laws".

For civil religion to succeed, Rousseau believed that it needed to be reinforced in some way. Citizenship and patriotism are the reinforcing elements that will assist inhabitants in making the duty to their fatherland their primary business. According to Barnard (1984: 251), citizenship is the "work of rational will, in which instrumental reasoning of one sort or another plays a decisive role. The purpose of what we say or do lies beyond the action itself. It is the instrumental reasoning that mediates agreement, the source and justification, indeed the authorisation of human association within a state" (Barnard 1984: 251). Patriotism, on the other hand, is based on intrinsic reasoning of sentiment and requires no justification based on reason in a similar way that loving a mistress cannot be argued to be reasonable.

Despite having the same end in sight, Barnard (1984: 253) argues that patriotism and citizenship differ substantially in their respective origins and provides an appropriate understanding of their difference. He writes that,

> a citizen, unlike a patriot, may entertain whatever private thoughts and beliefs he happens to hold; what vitally determines the quality of citizenship, or what indeed characterises the will of the citizen, is his readiness to match public utterances with public deeds. Without such coherence or consistency, Rousseau emphatically maintains, there can be no social order, for it would lack trust to sustain it (Barnard 1984: 253).

This points to the superiority of citizenship over patriotism and, subsequently, the important role citizenship plays in the achievement of order in society. Social order is important for civil religion; thus, citizenship performs this function effectively because it is based on discursive reasoning. However, Rousseau believes that discursive reasoning alone cannot make individuals love their fatherland and hence puts forward the possibility of citizenship and patriotism coinciding. Although patriotism may make citizenship stronger, it does not constitute it. Patriotism is the unreasoned love for one's fatherland, whilst citizenship is rational agreement on the common objective and the will to stick to that agreement. It is imperative that citizens have this common collective outlook.

In short, citizens need to be interdependent beings as opposed to working with one another as if they are still independent beings (driven by *amour-de-soi*—self-preservation). To elucidate this, citizenship makes inhabitants think that their continued existence lies in them working together as opposed to for themselves (motivated by *amour-propre*). *Amour-propre* is a heightened consciousness of, and regard for, an individual in relation to others around him. The transformation from *amour-de-soi* to *amour-propre* is necessary for the sustained success of the civil religion.

Rousseau's civil religion also necessitates a superior being (lawgiver) to regulate laws, to have the necessary foresight and to declare them in the appropriate instance. He places tremendous emphasis on the lawgiver's wisdom to pursue the aforementioned tasks. Gourevitch (1997: xxii) believes that Rousseau conceived of the lawgiver as someone able to convince individuals to forsake their adherence to particular wills and focus on attaining a general will. Riley (2001: 125) claims that Rousseau's general will allows the lawgiver the best possible tool to achieve the civic goals of the social contract since the notion of the general will allows the lawgiver's civil knowledge to be enlightened and correct.

In analysing the most suitable traits that a lawgiver should possess and the tasks he should undertake, Rousseau writes that he should be able,

> to discover the best rules of society suited to each nation [this] would require a superior intelligence who saw all of man's passions and experienced none of them, who had no relation to our nature yet knew it thoroughly, whose happiness was independent of us and who was nevertheless willing to care for ours; finally, one who, preparing his distant glory in the progress of times, could work in one century and enjoy reward in another. It would require Gods to make laws (Rousseau [1762] 1997: 68–69).

The mission of the lawgiver is to "attach the citizens to the fatherland" and this is done through a civil religion. He (the lawgiver) should "resort to the intervention of heaven and to honour the Gods with their own wisdom" and make the people realise that "he proclaims himself their interpreter" (Rousseau [1782] 1997: 71). The lawgiver should aim to entrench fundamental patriotic habits, tastes and dispositions of the populace by placing emphasis on the religion, morals and unique lifestyles of citizens. It is evident that Rousseau regards a lawgiver as a rare person who is "an authoritative person who is neither authoritarian nor personal, who generalises will while leaving it voluntary" (Riley 2001: 142). Rousseau further argues that a lawgiver should be capable of transforming the nature of people from being individuals from being in a state of *amour-de-soi* to one of *amour-propre*.

Civil religion also necessitates the doctrine of separation of powers to ensure that there is no abuse of power by the lawgiver and the sovereign, thereby ensuring that the civil religion prospers. Rousseau wrote that the people who make the laws should not execute them since this would confuse public and private interest. Rousseau talks about the dangers of uniting the legislative and the sovereign authority, citing Rome as an example. Those who enact laws should play no part in the legislative. He writes:

> Rome in its finest period witnessed the rebirth of all crimes of tyranny in its midst, and found itself on the verge of perishing, for having united the legislative authority and the sovereign power in the same hands (Rousseau [1762] 1997: 70).

The sovereign cannot implement laws because its purpose is to attend to matters of general concern and not laws that are of particular importance. It cannot allow one part of the sovereign to implement laws since Rousseau argues that the sovereign is inalienable. As soon as the sovereign tends towards a particular will (in effect having two sovereigns), the body politic dissolves. This is because the particular will tends towards partiality and the general will towards equality. Partiality endangers the transformation from independent to interdependent beings thereby jeopardising the civil religion.

In terms of governance, Rousseau argues that this needs to be entrusted to those who could devote all their time and energies to it and this would only be possible through an elective aristocracy. Ordinary citizens, however, would be represented through popular assemblies. Assemblies, Rousseau argued,

> ...are more easily convened, business is discussed better, and dispatched in a more orderly and diligent fashion, the state's prestige is better upheld abroad by venerable senators than by an unknown and despised multitude (Rousseau [1762] 1997: 93).

Rousseau is critical of aristocracies to a certain extent, arguing that they require virtues such as "moderation amongst the rich and contentment among the poor", something inconceivable in practice (Rousseau [1762] 1997: 94). Rousseau nevertheless argues that the inequality in wealth is a small price to pay in exchange for governance by those who can devote all their time and energy to it. Rousseau is not concerned with utopia but rather a form of administration that is legitimate in different forms of society (Masters 1968: 303). Gourevitch believes that the elective aristocracy "seeks to combine and reconcile popular sovereignty with wisdom" (1997: xxv). Popular assemblies are the manner in which he believed popular sovereignty could best be constituted.

For the above components to be effective, Rousseau desired to make religion important to the state and the individual. In, *the Social Contract*, Rousseau occupied himself with the political sphere of religion since it makes obligatory an individual's responsibility as a member of the state. In the *Letter to Montaigne*, Rousseau argues that his civil religion arguments are to do with "those aspects of religion which concern public welfare and social morality, the duties of man and the citizen, which came under the jurisdiction of government" (cited in Cobban 1934: 83). By placing these issues under the jurisdiction of the state, Cobban argues that Rousseau is not referring to the executive but rather the superiority of the body politic acting through the general will (1934: 83).

The civil principles that comprise Rousseau's civil religion hold glaring similarities and serve a comparable function with the principles that characterise modern liberal democracies, that is, they help protect and enhance political power. They, however, do not need to be the same but merely serve a similar function. I intend to probe this further later on to extract its contemporary philosophical relevance. It is envisaged that Rousseau's thoughts will assist in conceptualising the Mandela mythology as a civil religion aimed at binding citizens to the post-1994 South African state. First, it is necessary to discuss the Mandela-mythology phenomenon.

The Making of the Mandela-Mythology Phenomenon in South Africa

Solani (2000) contends that historical narratives and myths fulfil psychological and social needs rather than scientific demands. During the liberation struggle, many myths were created from struggle icons in order to boost the people's morale, none more so than that of Mandela. I postulate that the Mandela-mythology phenomenon comprises three distinct yet interrelated narratives: first, from his birth in Qunu in 1918 until his release from incarceration in 1990 (dominant narrative), second, the narrative that emerged after his release from prison until 1999 (extension of the dominant narrative) and third, the construction of the Mandela-mania phenomenon (official narrative). The first two phases form the basis of the third phase.

The first phase is primarily constructed through Mandela's dominant roles as co-founder of the African National Congress Youth League (ANCYL), volunteer-in-chief of the Defiance Campaign, his role in the Freedom Charter, his life as The Black Pimpernel, supreme courtroom performer in the Treason and Rivonia trials, founder of uMkhonto we Sizwe (MK) and his incarceration on Robben Island.

Of these, his performative displays at the Rivonia Trial and his incarceration on Robben Island played the most important part. Deliberately refusing to testify, Mandela delivered a four-hour-long principled political speech even though he knew it carried less weight than evidence provided through rigorous cross-examination. This iconic statement is probably the defining moment in the Mandela mythology's creation since it signalled the beginning of his status and image as a universal hero. Mathebe (2012: 318) agrees and states that "the folklore of South African history [is] rich with the stories of the hero's mystical qualities [and is] traceable to the Rivonia Trial of the sixties where the former president made recourse to the universalism of the Enlightenment era". Mandela ended his statement with the now iconic words,

> During my lifetime I have dedicated myself to this struggle of the African people. I have fought against white domination, and I have fought against black domination. I have cherished the ideal of a democratic and free society in which all persons live together in harmony and with equal opportunities. It is an ideal which I hope to live for and to achieve. But if needs be, it is an ideal for which I am prepared to die (Mandela 1964 [1994]: 181).

This speech won widespread approval since it epitomised the ideals of dignity and freedom and propelled him to saint-like status. It was "principled, defiant, uncompromising, lofty and dignified revealing Mandela's own great integrity and spirit of self-sacrifice" (Maylam 2009: 26).

Mandela's incarceration on Robben Island is an irony of history since the regime thought they were securing apartheid by imprisoning him. Rather, twenty-seven years of incarceration saw Mandela mythology's further development since it "lent a powerful historical resonance, integrating [him]—initially, at least—into an extended historical narrative of political oppression and martyrdom" (Van Heerden 2012: 36).

Robben Island was the place at which Mandela underwent a maturing of his political views and ultimately his view of a democratic South Africa. Thus, Robben Island is not only symbolic of tyranny, oppression and martyrdom but also of reconciliation, transformation and nation-building. Mandela became the theoretical, rhetorical and visual signifier of the liberation struggle. Although incarceration suppressed his physical freedom, it tremendously enhanced his status as a hero and the mystique that surrounded him. Mandela had "gained mythical status—the lost leader whom the world yearned to see again" (Meredith 2010: xv). Lodge (2006: 192–193) believes that "the imprisonment and isolation from public view kept the narrative and the images that accompanied it pristine, invested with the glamour of martyrdom, but reinforced by apocalyptic possibilities of second coming". It served to enhance his legitimacy as the most famous liberation fighter.

Stage two of the Mandela mythology from 1990 to 1999 bears some similarities with the rainbow nation civil religion since it comprised important events such as his release from prison in 1990, his inauguration in 1994 and the Rugby World Cup in 1995. I posit that these performative displays were calculated political moves as opposed to an inherent societal component and were characterised by a reconciliatory-centred political philosophy which helped consolidate the dominant narrative of the first stage.

Television stations were constantly bracing South Africans for change in the lead up to Mandela's release. He was the "central ceremonial figure" of this historic media event and is described by Dayan and Katz (2009: 181) as "a messiah figure, a mediator of extreme oppositions, a realistic dreamer, both utopian and practical, shrewd and imaginative". Attributing messianic and saint-like qualities to Mandela were part of a number of religious metaphors utilised by both religious and secular scholars to describe the relatively peaceful transition to democracy when arguably the entire world expected a civil war (Suttner 2007).

Mandela's presidential inauguration became another media spectacle and the ANC utilised this opportunity to help cement its nation-building ideology which would serve to improve the country's poor global image. The live television event helped create the impression of diverse citizens united behind the new South Africa. It facilitated the promotion of nation-building through reconciliation by merging symbols of Afrikaner nationalism with new national symbols. The new national anthem, for example, consisted of both *Die Stem* as well as *Nkosi Sikelel iAfrica*, whilst the crowd was awash with the new South African flag. The inauguration symbolised the transfer of political authority to the majority through military and legal authority.

Mandela was sworn in by a white Chief Justice whilst being flanked by white apartheid-era military officers. The inauguration was ended with a military salute to military planes flying overhead and which released smoke in the new flag's colours. This was complemented by the release of white doves symbolising the dawn of a new peaceful era in South African history. The inauguration occurred at the Union Buildings in Pretoria, the traditional seat of white supremacy. Mandela stated that it now represented a rainbow nation gathered for the inauguration of the country's first non-racial and democratic government. Evans (2010: 316–317) postulates that the inauguration was a "merger of discordant symbols" but which was harmonised through the "official adoption of the miracle discourse" through Mandela's speech.

Sport formed an integral part of Mandela's performative displays of reconciliation and nation-building. Mandela, acutely aware of this, remarked that sports "speaks a language which reaches areas where a president and politician cannot" (Evans 2014: 177). It was not until the 1995 Rugby World Cup final, however, that Mandela won over the hearts of white South Africans by donning the Springbok jersey during the trophy handover ceremony.

This carefully choreographed performance was significant since Rugby was traditionally seen as an Afrikaner preserve. Van Heerden (2012: 125) comments that Mandela managed to centre a "new conception of nationhood on a traditional site of division and cultural specificity, and by appropriating a sport which had been the subject of ANC-lobbied sanctions during apartheid". For Russell (2009: 33), the ever-astute politician in Mandela sensed an "opening into the Afrikaner soul and [also] another way of ensuring stability".

Despite this, the aftermath of the post-Mandela presidency was still characterised by apprehension from Blacks and Whites. The ANC attempted to allay these fears by fostering and enhancing the Mandela mythology through the creation of the Mandela-mania phenomenon which started after Mandela left office in 1999 and continues even after his death. It entails a plethora of rituals, beliefs and symbols that have been and continue to be constructed around Mandela and include the wilful government construction of, inter alia, Mandela's image on South Africa's official currency, Mandela gold coin and five-rand coin collections, an annual philanthropic Mandela Day, names of roads, bridges, stadiums and a municipality.

These beliefs, symbols and rituals are not exhaustive and most were instituted after he left office in 1999 which provides credence to the point that the Mandela mythology gained traction after his presidency in order to cement his legacy and narrative. Though many of these components, such as the 46664 clothing range and the House of Mandela range of wines are not government endeavours, they did nothing to stop it presumably because of the benefit it brings to the country. These components consolidate the dominant narrative of the first two phases and become the official Mandela-mythology narrative. This arises out of the belief that "great men and women can attain the status of symbols, legends and myths" (O'Toole 2003: xl).

Together, these three phases provide an epiphenomenal description of the Mandela mythology since it is at odds with the intuitive conception of Mandela as an autonomous agent in the mythology's construction. I contend that the construction of the Mandela mythology was anything but an accident of history. It was a conscious construction of historical, political and personal influence that resulted in Mandela being referred to in messianic and saint-like terms.

Mathebe (2012: xi) posits that the avoidance of conflict is infused with the values of national reconciliation, unity and non-racialism. These values controlled the discourse of post-apartheid history and created a kind of "national consensus" around a leader—Mandela. This was an important aspect of the making of the saint-like image (Meredith 2010). It was also a major performative act of post-1994 South Africa, which saw the dominant Mandela narrative of the past being consolidated, whilst a new narrative of him as a reconciliator and nation-builder was emerging (Van Heerden 2012).

This helped exculpate him from the most critical reflections on his political and personal life. An extension to the mythology's exculpatory ability is its immense resistance to any one particular definition. It has constantly evolved before it obtained the status of "hero", "saint", "saviour" "reconciler", "messiah", etc., which has allowed the public to view him as possessing angelic qualities. These are also noticeably religious terms and I will argue that, together with the myth's exculpatory ability, is the beginning of a religious argument to the Mandela mythology in the Rousseauian sense. This points to an inherently Christian logic to the Mandela narrative of not trying to damn him but merely to unearth his human shortcomings.

Mandela was ultimately "a physical and biological man and a myth or symbol" (Van Heerden 2012: 128). Whilst the former has passed on, the latter undoubtedly remains. The Mandela mythology was constructed, I will argue below, to create a national civil religion along Rousseauian lines. Before then, its positionality within the contemporary civil religion debate must be ironed out.

Situating the Mandela Mythology in Contemporary Civil Religion Debate

Two different traditions encompass the contemporary civil religion debate—the Durkheimian sociological tradition and the Rousseauian political/ideological conceptualisation. The former views the phenomenon as an inherent component of social life and is based on "shared beliefs, rituals and symbols that express its most fundamental values" (Cristi 2001: 7). Purdy (1982), Swindler (1986), Wilson (1971) and Wuthnow (1988) argue that it serves an integrating function and allows for order and stability of society. Most contemporary analyses follow this route and simply begin by making passing references to Rousseau as the intellectual father.

Chief amongst them is Robert Bellah who, in 1967, conceived of American civil religion. For Bellah, the civil religion's primary role is to build, affirm and celebrate a common national heritage. He states that, in civil religion, the presidential inauguration is an essential ceremonial event. "It affirms", he believes, "the religious dimension of the highest political authority" (Bellah 1967: 4). Bellah claims that the references to God in presidential inaugural speeches, the Declaration of Independence and the Constitution, Fourth of July celebrations, Memorial Day and Thanksgiving holiday provide the annual ritual for the American civil religion.

Bellah's thesis continues to provoke widespread debate but is difficult to transfer into the understanding of other civil religions because of its sociological conceptualisation. We may circumvent this problem by understanding civil religion in a political/ideological sense (Cristi 2001). The latter encompasses a broader understanding and allows for its applicability in different contexts. Civil religion may thus be understood as a phenomenon expressing an implicit culture or as a political resource used to support an existing political regime. Understood in this way allows it to be distinguished conceptually but not in reality (Cristi 2001).

The Rousseauian understanding views civil religion as a premeditated political ideology constructed by a state's political leaders. This tends to place emphasis on, and "sacralise[,] certain aspects of civic life by means of public rituals and collective ceremonies" (Cristi 2001: 3). Civil religion can therefore be understood as a "political resource at the service of the state" (Cristi 2001: 4–5).

Cristi is effectively calling for a greater political dimension to the civil religion debate since this allows behaviours and beliefs to acquire a religious dimension. "As such, civil religion may be considered a belief system or, a surrogate religion that expresses the self-identity of a collectivity" (Cristi 2001: 3). I utilise this understanding to advance the idea that the Mandela-mythology phenomenon is a political resource which the post-apartheid South African state uses to serve as the primary unifying factor in achieving reconciliation, nation-building, social cohesion and political stability.

Mandela Mythology as a Civil Religion in South Africa

In calling for an analysis of the "inclusion of the ideological side of civil religion, its inherent political nature and its profound political significance" (Cristi 2001: 122), we open up the space for investigating the existence of a Rousseauian civil religion in South Africa which postulates that religion, although an undesirable feature of society, can have constructive political effects. It follows that we should consider the important role played by those in power who purposefully create, disseminate and diffuse the civil religion as a tool for social cohesion and political stability (Cristi 2001). Posel (2014: 74) believes that leaders within ANC ranks were "party to Mandela's symbolic choreography, not least in accommodating the salient role assigned to him by his jailers" since he was unanimously assumed to be best suited to unite South Africans. Posel (2014: 74) further contends that, "perhaps the most striking, and distinguishing, feature of the national and international consensus that went into his making: [is] the shared recognition of the desirability of the myth, as well as key elements of its content, across racial lines and political divisions". Even the apartheid regime realised that there could no peace without Mandela playing a leading role in the process.

Although South Africa does not privilege any one religion's God, the country's constitution does make references to God. The preamble to the constitution, for example, states that "may God protect our people" and "God bless South Africa"

(Constitution of the Republic of South Africa Act 1996: 1243). The latter is echoed in the opening verse of the national anthem.

Additionally, the oath of office of the President, cabinet ministers, Parliamentarians, etc., all culminate with the words "So help me God" (Constitution of the Republic of South Africa Act 1996: 1243). Post-apartheid South Africa's various presidents, although advocating that religious belief is a matter of an individual's inward concern, have mentioned God in many speeches. Mandela, for example, remarked that "to lose faith in fellow humans is, as the Archbishop would correctly point out, to lose faith in God" (Mandela 2003 [1994]: 320). These specific references to God may indicate that it serves a mostly ceremonial function intended to pacify the majority of citizens to whom religion is still important. Critics argue that religion is frequently used as an electioneering tool. As Bellah (1967: 2) states, a "semblance of piety is merely one of the unwritten qualifications for the office".

Besides the constitutional and other rhetorical references to God, the Mandela leadership was frequently referred to as a gift from God. Mandela was viewed as God's hand on earth chaperoning the bloody democratic transition (Posel 2014). Such rhetoric resonated deeply amongst a citizenry, Posel (2014: 86) argued, "long accustomed to a religious metaphysics of social and political life and a version of political leadership as divinely ordained". Simply dismissing religion or the belief in God as somewhat ceremonial or ritualistic will be counterproductive since what people say on "solemn occasions need not be taken at face value, but it is often indicative of deep-seated values and commitments that are not made explicit in the course of everyday life" (Bellah 1967: 2). Notably, just as in the American civil religion, the Mandela-mythology civil religion only makes references to God's existence and not to any specific religion thus preserving its secular nature.

To entrench the civil religion, Rousseau believed individuals needed to prioritise the duty to their fatherland. This entails abandoning their devotion to their particular wills in favour of society's general will. I argue that the Mandela-mythology phenomenon is the civil religion's lawgiver since it creates "pride and self-esteem together with their vigour and strength in spectacles which by reminding them (citizens) of the history of their ancestors, their misfortunes, their virtues, their victories, stirred their hearts, fired them with a lively spirit of emulation" and strongly attaches "them to the fatherland with which they were being kept constantly occupied" (Rousseau 1997 [1782]: 181).

The lawgiver should take away from people's natural inclinations and help them develop new ones that assist them in making their citizenry duties their primary business. The Mandela-mythology civil religion fulfils Rousseau's purpose for the lawgiver since it helps "elicit feelings of civic membership and enforce the duties of citizenship in national communities no longer bounded by traditional religious links" (Cristi 2001: 16). Whilst this integrative component is crucial, it should not be assumed that these are a cultural given. Rather, political elites may construct these to further political agendas. This conceptualisation contends that it is necessary for rulers to be cognisant of realpolitik. The Mandela-mythology civil religion is "uniquely situated to fulfil this requirement, not only through visual self-display, but essentially by scripting a narrative to anchor and naturalise his different representations" (Roux 2014: 212). South Africa's civil religion has resulted in the creation of group identity and the legitimation of the existing political order by injecting a religious gloss over it. This allows individuals to feel a sense of connection to the national community, and this consequently fuels social unity across time and space (Engel 2005).

The lawgiver would need to enact laws and create artificial institutions that take into account man's innate nature and make them act according to the general will. The lawgiver should fundamentally transform individuals from a state of *amour-propre* to *amour-de-soi*. I argue that the Mandela-mythology civil religion helps South Africans make this transition by stressing that they are required to be both patriotic and good citizens.

This dual theory of public willing allows citizens to be interdependent beings as opposed to independent beings. Although distinct terms, Rousseau views patriotism as a reinforcing element of citizenship but both as essential for his civil religion. In this respect, I define patriotism as the unreasoned love for one's fatherland whilst citizenship is the rational agreement on the common good and the will to stick to that agreement through discursive reasoning. Patriotism makes the Mandela-mythology civil religion stronger allowing it to become the mode of life. Although citizenship is more desirable since it is based on discursive reasoning, this alone could not make individuals prioritise the state's business and hence patriotism was needed for an effective civil religion.

The Mandela-mythology civil religion achieves patriotic South Africans who espouse good citizenship by instituting public spectacles, festivals and games since these are crucial in directing the attention of citizens towards the common good. The various components of the Mandela-mythology phenomenon can serve as such spectacles. These beliefs, rituals and symbols are used to both maintain and enhance the sense of community that exists amongst adherents. "Collective memories are used to mobilise people" (Dickow et al. 1999: 249). The politics of national sentiment has helped shape the transition of Mandela mythology and its legacy. Mandela himself was a master of performative displays "scripted to meet public expectations, or calculated to shift popular sentiment" (Lodge 2006: ix). Posel (2014) argues that mythology is a modernity of enhancement that manifests itself in many ways from religion to spirituality to the secular magic of the commodity.

The components of the Mandela-mythology civil religion form a "highly articulated self-conscious belief system, the result of conscious political determination" (Swindler 1986: 279). This comprises roughly ninety-five statues and other Mandela artworks in various places around South Africa and the world, South Africa's official currency bearing Mandela's image, gold collector and five-rand collector coins also bear the Mandela image. This is in addition to clothing and wine ranges, an abundance of films, documentaries, songs and approximately eighty-five known streets, roads, buildings, stadiums and bridges named after Mandela. Added to this is the annual philanthropic Mandela Day celebrated on his birthday.

Such fascination with all things Mandela, Gordimer explains, is the country's desperate need to redeem itself from the ghost of apartheid. Gordimer (1990: 4) states that "the white [liberal] population has not merely accepted the return of Mandela but turns to him now as the one—the only one—who can absolve and resolve: absolve the sin of apartheid and resolve the problems of reconciliation and integration". Mandela has been judged as an ethical and cleansing agent and the motivating power behind the new South Africa and is inserted within the dominant Christian paradigm of deliverance from evil. Moulding complex mythology in messianic terms can be seen in light of the implicit Christian inclination to fit everything into Western historiography (Modisane 2014). White (2004: 2) agrees and states that "these notions of revival and rebirth derive, it would seem, from the peculiarly Christian idea that meaningful temporality describes a process of expectation and deliverance".

The 1987 movie *Mandela*, starring Danny Glover and Alfred Woodard as Mandela and Winnie, respectively, epitomises this idea. The film characterises the future in abeyance until Mandela's return. Mandela, the messiah, given the task of ending the apartheid evil and ultimately delivering liberation, thus stood to fulfil his destiny (Modisane 2014). The Christian paradigm continued after 1994 with the words "miracle" and "magic" joining the narrative. This, in essence, signalled hopefulness that transcended race, culture, ethnicity and religion. Blacks viewed Mandela as the magic that saved them from the transition to democracy's horrific political violence. Whites viewed the transition as a miracle since it promised to save them from their feared existential predicament; the fear to be "spared the dreaded brunt of the black rage" (Posel 2014: 76). This provides a structure of belief—a novel way of thinking in the new South Africa. Posel (2014: 84) states that "the idea of a miracle effaces process and renders discussion and analysis thereof unnecessary. A miracle simply is, and is compelling and captivating for that revelatory attitude". The Mandela-mythology civil religion is the new South Africa's novel way of thinking.

Van Robbroek (2014: 247) uses this undercurrent Christian theme to analyse the 1999 *Time Magazine* cover page featuring Mandela. She argues that the black-power salute mirrored the "iconic Christ figure's right hand, which was conventionally raised in benediction". Such depiction of Mandela tells us much about the world's perception of Mandela in messianic terms—as a product of the unfolding of destiny. The endless statues and artworks of Mandela serve to entrench the exemplary status of him in the public's collective consciousness (Van Robbroek 2014).

Rousseau contended that such mobilisation for the civil religion is best achieved in small states governed by an elective aristocracy where citizens may regularly and personally share in its components and hence more easily achieve patriotism and citizenship. Contemporary South Africa is able to bypass this restriction with the advent of film, television, the Internet and social media which allow citizens to instantaneously share the civil religion's articles with millions of their countrymen.

The Mandela-mythology civil religion can thus also be characterised as an imagined community whose patriarch is Mandela. Imagined because even though South Africans will never know most of their fellow citizens, "meet them, or even hear of them", yet in the "minds of each lives the image of their communion" (Anderson 2006: 6). Mathebe (2012: 49) adds that Mandela is the "imagined leader who embodied the great fantasies and moral aspirations of the new nation at the precise moment at which the forces of liberation were seeking to tear down the political authority of the apartheid state".

The civil religion's rituals and symbols serve to mobilise people towards the support of the post-1994 state, and its commitment to unity and reconciliation provides an uncomplicated view of Mandela by reducing extremely complex mythology into a person who simply forgave and forgot and moved on in building the new South Africa. Essentially, rituals and symbols of the Mandela-mythology civil religion are being used for political ends (Dickow et al. 1999).

The ritualistic annual celebration of Mandela Day, for example, has become an occasion for "public indoctrination rather than means of exploring principled public sentiment" (Bennet 1979: 129). Politicians, corporations and celebrities use the occasion to cram as much free publicity as possible into sixty-seven minutes of supposed charitable endeavours. Rousseau was convinced that only passionate patriotism created by such commemorative public rituals can help breathe patriotic citizens who desire to prioritise the general will. Such elicited sentiment, Lodge (2006: 212) argues, may be referred to as "multiracial patriotism" in line with the constitution's vision.

Posel (2014: 72) contends that it is acceptable to proclaim that national politics is "lubricated by sentiment" and that "political mobilisation is never an appeal to the resources of reason alone". To analyse South African politics as such is to draw attention to the country's realpolitik which infuses intellectual ideas, policies and interests with premeditated calculation on the part of the political elite to create a general will. Engel (2005) believes that an ideal state is one in which the general will guides its citizens and if patriotism guides the individual to the general will, then it is consistent with freedom. Patriotism provides support to freedom since without it, citizens will be torn between the particular and general wills.

The utilisation of rituals, beliefs and symbols is moreover meant to create a civil religion that entails "a love of country independent of, but not contrary to, a love of God" (Noone 1980: 145). Such an understanding would satisfy Rousseau's quest for social solidarity and legitimation. It is clear that the Mandela-mythology civil religion is an earthly endeavour distinct from mainstream religions since its goal is to improve the state's well-being. It aims to instil secular and political citizenship that is religiously enforced. It "elevate[s] citizenship to quasi-sacred heights" thus creating a new citizen who prioritises his citizenry duty resulting in a better-functioning state (Cristi 2001: 25).

This integrative role is important, but may also result in conflict, division and tension. It may only appeal to a certain segment of a country's population or may only benefit some groups. Total state appropriation of the civil religion or it descending into totalitarianism usually occurs in weak states with the absence of active civil society formations. This scenario is not foreseen since South Africa has active civil society organisations which, for their part, entrenches the Mandela mythology by positioning him as the unquestionable saviour of the new South Africa. At the global level, Zeleza (2013: 8) argues that Mandela represents "global moral authority, of humanity at its best, the last in the hallowed canon of twentieth-century saintly liberators from Mahatma Gandhi to Martin Luther King".

I nevertheless remain mindful that the Mandela-mythology civil religion "is more likely to produce a 'qualified consensus' rather than total social integration" (Cristi

2001: 9). There are those, for example, who accuse Mandela of abandoning the pursuit of conquering the white-dominated economic kingdom in favour of cementing his personal legacy (Ndlovu-Gatsheni 2014: 918). A Rousseauian-inspired civil religion, however, need not be a national religion. It does not need to reflect the values and beliefs of society as a whole as is the case with the sociological tradition.

For Berger (1967), although there are many forms of legitimation, the most effective has always been religion. Rousseau, well aware of this, conceived of civil religion as a state's legitimating mechanism. However, it is not only a tool for cultural legitimation. Instead, its ideological/political components may be used in times of social and political unrest in response to crises of legitimation (Cristi 2001). Purdy (1982: 314) agrees and refers to civil religion as a phenomenon that arises in response to "episodic crises of legitimation" rather than a permanent "legitimator of power and authority in the polity". This signifies "loyalty to a sharply defined political structure—indeed, in the extreme case, to a political regime at a particular time" (Wilson 1971: 163).

In the 2014 national elections, for example, the ANC positioned its election manifesto to a large extent as a continuation of the vision and legacy of Mandela. This has occurred and continues to occur in an attempt to counteract "episodic crises of legitimation", be it the arms deal or Nkandla sagas, issues around alleged state capture or corruption allegations President Jacob Zuma. This is in addition to its perceived inability to stem the tide of poor service delivery and unemployment.

Linder (1975) and Regan (1976) suggest that civil religion becomes a necessary political undertaking in times of political instability. As a political tool, it can be described as a "set of ideas or principles intended to reorder collective experience, to regulate political understandings, and to mobilise support and collective action" (Cristi 2001: 120). It was, for example, in the midst of these ongoing political crises that one such component of the Mandela-mythology civil religion, the annual philanthropic Mandela day, was conceived of in 2009.

Whilst I posit that the Mandela-mythology civil religion is being used by the ANC for national grandeur, political and electoral support and to obtain a unified post-1994 citizenry, Pfeffer (1968: 364) also argues that the conscious political usage of the Mandela-mythology civil religion may also result in an "ignoble rather than noble outcome" such as the conscious repression of civil liberties. Critics may argue that we are about to reach such a stage with the impending signing of the Protection of State Information Act which has been attacked for its potential to cover up corruption under the guise of national security.

The democratic or authoritarian capacity of the Mandela-mythology civil religion has its foundations in the "political procedures and uses of civil religion by particular groups at particular times" (Cristi 2001: 154). Wuthnow (1988) suggests that both democratic and undemocratic modern governments utilise public rituals as a compelling way to influence the daily lives of its people.

Cristi (2001) submits that whilst civil religion can never be totally separated from political religion, the latter depends on the degree of political control exercised by leaders. I argue that we are not witnessing an extreme amount of control that would border on totalitarianism in order to secure conformity behind the Mandela-mythology civil religion even though it is imposed upon the people and "demands unquestionable loyalty and unconditional commitment" (Cristi 2001: 232).

Coupled with state manipulation, we are also experiencing a civil religion which South Africans have voluntarily internalised (Anthony and Robbins 1975). It is constantly evolving and may sporadically occur beyond the state's total control but continue to work to its advantage since it entails a continuation of the official narrative. Examples of such non-state controlled evolution include the Limpopo villager who sculptured an uncommissioned Mandela statue, the *46664* and *Long Walk to Freedom* clothing ranges and the *House of Mandela* range of wines. Whilst the latter were undertakings by members of the Mandela family, the government did not object to it presumably because it served to benefit the ends they are striving for.

A Rousseauian civil religion further requires that there be a separation of powers between the lawgiver (the Mandela mythology) and the sovereign. South African constitution propagates the doctrine of separation of powers. The sovereign encroaching upon the lawgiver's powers would push it towards particular matters. In essence, the task of the sovereign in South Africa, which it consciously manipulates and promotes for political ends, is to command over the civil religion's articles which are derived by the lawgiver thus achieving the general will.

In consenting to the social contract, citizens agree rationally to the betterment of all. The Mandela-mythology civil religion does not call for the banishment of those individuals who do not subscribe to it. The constitution of South Africa clearly allows for the freedom of religious belief or disbelief and urges religious tolerance. Rousseau opposed religious intolerance since he aimed to release citizens from the shackles of the clergy and make them obligated to follow the dictates of civil religion (Gourevitch 2001). This is one of the intended outcomes of the Mandela-mythology civil religion.

By founding the Mandela-mythology civil religion on secular articles of faith as opposed to reason, the outcome might entail citizens having to sacrifice rationality and civil freedom that were their initial objectives for entering into the social contract. Nonetheless, I believe that the ultimate ambition of making an individual possess a "religion which makes him love his duties" overrides any potential drawback.

Whilst critics have labelled such a civil religion utopian since factionalism is an innate characteristic of modern states, the Mandela-mythology civil religion does allow for the existence of partisan subsections of a particular society since toleration is one of its key precepts. Such partial societies do not make the existence of a civil religion impossible. Rather, they have the tendency to undermine the unity and social fabric of society. South Africa is beset with factionalism from different political parties to religious denominations and hence, the Mandela-mythology civil religion will most likely achieve a "qualified consensus" as opposed total unity and social cohesion.

Conclusion

This chapter advanced the idea that there is present, alongside South Africa's various religions, a well-defined civil religion along Rousseauian lines. Focusing primarily on the ruling political elites political usages of civil religion, I discovered that the myths of the civil religion aim to serve a unifying function. Even after Mandela's death, most South Africans still have everyday and perhaps unconscious encounter with him through the use of the country's official currency that bears his iconic image. This, however, risks falling into the divisive cash nexus trap, Mandela hoped he laid the foundation for eventual elimination. The notion of the Mandela-mythology civil religion is nonetheless fluid and its future political manifestations will generally be dependent upon South Africa's historical and political contexts. Although the South African state's survival is not in jeopardy nor is ANC rule about to end anytime soon, the Mandela-mythology civil religion will still be continuously utilised as the ruling party's support mechanism.

For Cristi (2001: 230), future manifestations may become "more or less political, more or less nationalistic, more or less orientated towards civil society or the state" and thus has the potential to be utilised as a political religion. Although the biological and physical Mandela is no more, the impact of his symbol and myth will only be enhanced, which I argued, has occurred for the ANC's political gain. This implies a continuation of the conscious manipulation of national myths for political outcomes. Following Mandela's death, the mythology is still vitally important to the ANC and it is not going to surrender its hegemonic usage. It is not simply important in that it can generate Mandela's rainbow nation vision but rather for more strategic reasons—to keep them in power. There is also an unintended consequence, which is that it is something that coheres the country even though the dangerous waters it now finds itself. In the Zuma and now Ramaphosa era, however, I argue that it is now just about strategic intentionality—the use of the mythology for self-interested reasons.

References

Anderson, B. 2006. *Imagined Communities: Reflections on Origins and Spread of Nationalism*. Revised Edition. London: Verso.
Anthony, D., and T. Robbins. 1975. From Symbolic Realism to Structuralism. *Journal for the Scientific Study of Religion* 14 (4): 403–414.
Bellah, R. 1967. Civil Religion in America. *Daedalus* 96 (1): 1–21.
Bennet, L.W. 1979. Imitation, Ambiguity, and Drama in Political Life: Civil Religion and the Dilemmas of Public Morality. *Journal of Politics* 4 (1): 107–133.
Berger, P.L. 1967. *The Sacred Canopy: Elements of a Sociological Theory of Religion*. New York: Double Day Anchor.
Barnard, F.M. 1984. Patriotism and Citizenship in Rousseau: A Dual Theory of Public Willing?. *The Review of Politics* 46 (2):244–265
Barnard, R. 2014. Introduction. In *Cambridge Companion to Nelson Mandela*, ed R. Barnard. Cambridge: Cambridge University Press.

Constitution of the Republic of South Africa. 1996. Available online at www.info.gov.za/documents/constitution/1996/a108-96.pdf.

Cristi, M. 1997. *On the Nature of Civil and Political Religion: A Re-examination of the Civil Religion*, Thesis. University of Waterloo, Canada.

Cristi, M. 2001. *From Civil to Political Religion: The Intersection of Culture, Religion and Politics.* Canada: Wilfrid University Press.

Cobban, A. 1934. *Rousseau and the Modern State*. London: Allen & Unwin.

Dayan, D., and E. Katz. 2009. *Media Events: The Live Broadcasting of History*. Harvard: Harvard University Press.

Dickow, H., M. Harris, and V. Moller. 1999. South Africa"s "Rainbow People", National Pride and Happiness. *Social Indicators Research* 47 (3): 245–280.

Engel, S.T. 2005. Rousseau and Imagined Communities. *The Review of Politics* 67 (3): 515–537.

Evans, M. 2010. Mandela and the Televised Birth of the Rainbow Nation. *National Identities* 12 (3): 309–326.

Evans, M. 2014. *Broadcasting the End of Apartheid: Live Television and the Birth of the New South Africa*. London: I.B. Tauris and Co. Ltd.

Gordimer, N. 1990. Letter from Johannesburg. *African Commentary*, 4–6.

Gourevitch, V. 1997. *The Social Contract and Other Later Political Writings*. Cambridge: Cambridge University Press

Gourevitch, V. 2001. The Religious Thought. In: *Cambridge Companion to Rousseau*, ed. P. Riley, 193–246.

Linder, R.D. 1975. Civil Religion in Historical Perspective: The reality that underlines the concept. *Journal of Church and State.* 399: 399–421.

Lodge, T. 2006. *Mandela: A Critical Life*. Oxford: Oxford University Press.

Mandela, N. 1964 [1994]. The Rivonia Trial: 1963–1964. In *Nelson Mandela: The Struggle is my Life*, ed. B. Feinberg and A. Odendaal, 172–211. Cape Town: David Phillips Publishers.

Mandela, N. 1994 [2003]. Inauguration as President. In *Nelson Mandela: In His Own Words: From Freedom to the Future*, ed. K. Asmal, D. Chidester, and W. James, 68–70. London: Abacus.

Masters, R.D . 1968. *The Political Philosophy of Rousseau*. Princeton, NJ: Princeton University Press.

Mathebe, L. 2012. *Mandela and Mbeki: The Hero and the Outsider*. Pretoria: Unisa Press.

Maylam, P. 2009. Archetypal Hero or Living Saint? The Veneration of Nelson Mandela. *Historia* 54 (2): 21–36.

Meredith, M. 2010. *Mandela: A Biography*. New York: Perseus Book Group.

Modisane, L. 2014. Mandela in Film and Television. In *Cambridge Companion to Nelson Mandela*, ed. R. Barnard, 224–243. Cambridge: Cambridge University Press.

Ndlovu-Gatsheni, S.J. 2014. From a "Terrorist" to Global Icon: A Critical Decolonial Ethical Tribute to Nelson Rolihlahla Mandela of South Africa. *Third World Quarterly* 35 (6): 905–921.

Noone, J.B. 1980. *Rousseau's Social Contract: A Conceptual Analysis*. Athens: University of Georgia Press.

O'Toole, F. 2003. Prometheus Unbound. In *Nelson Mandela: In His Own Words: From Freedom to the Future*, ed. K. Asmal, D. Chidester, and W. James, xl–xlii. London: Abacus.

Pfeffer, L. 1968. Commentary. In *The World Year Book of Religion. The Religious Situation*, ed. D.R. Cutler. Boston: Beacon Press.

Posel, D. 2014. "Madiba Magic": Politics of Enchantment. In *Cambridge Companion to Nelson Mandela*, ed. R. Barnard, 70–91. Cambridge: Cambridge University Press.

Purdy, S.S. 1982. The Civil Religion Thesis as it Applies to a Pluralistic Society: Pancaslia Democracy in Indonesia (1945–1965). *Journal of International Affairs* 36: 307–316.

Regan, D. 1976. Islam, Intellectuals and Civil Religion in Malaysia. *Sociological Analysis* 37 (2): 95–110.

Riley, P. 2001. Rousseau's General Will. In *Cambridge Companion to Rousseau*, ed P. Riley. Cambridge: Cambridge University Press

Rousseau, J.J. 1762 [1997]. The Social Contract. In *Social Contract and Other Later Political Writings*, ed. V. Gourevitch, 41–152. Cambridge: Cambridge University Press.
Rousseau, J.J. 1782 [1997]. Letter to Mirabeau. In *Social Contract and Other Later Political Writings*, ed V. Gourevitch. Cambridge: Cambridge University Press.
Roux, D. 2014. Mandela Writing/Writing Mandela. In *Cambridge Companion to Nelson Mandela*, ed. R. Barnard, 205–223. Cambridge: Cambridge University Press.
Russell, A. 2009. *After Mandela: The Battle for the Soul of South Africa*. London: Hutchinson.
Solani, N. 2000. The Saint of the Struggle: Deconstructing the Mandela Myth. *Kronos* 26: 42–55.
Suttner, R. 2007. (Mis)Understanding Nelson Mandela. *African Historical Review* 39 (2): 107–130.
Swindler, A. 1986. Culture in Action: Symbols and Strategies. *American Sociological Review* 51: 273–286.
Van Heerden, D. 2012. *The Making of the Mandela Myth*. M.A. thesis, unpublished. Department of English Studies, Stellenbosch University.
Van Robbroek, L. 2014. The Visual Mandela: A Pedagogy of Citizenship. In *Cambridge Companion to Nelson Mandela*, ed. R. Barnard, 244–266. Cambridge: Cambridge University Press.
White, H. 2004, June. The Metaphysics of Western Historiography. *Taiwan Journal of East Asian Studies*, 2.
Wilson, J.F. 1971. The Status of "Civil Religion" in America. In *The Religion of the Republic*, ed. E.A. Smith. Philadelphia: Fortress Press.
Wuthnow, R. 1988. *The Restructuring of American Religion*. Princeton, NJ: Princeton University Press.
Zeleza, P.T. 2013. Mandela's Long Walk with African History. *CODESRIA Bulletin* 3–4 (2013): 10–13.

Dr. Ahmed Haroon Jazbhay has a Ph.D. (Political Studies), majoring in Political Theory, from the University of Johannesburg. His Ph.D. thesis was entitled: *Civil Religion in South Africa: Mandela through the lens of Machiavelli and Rousseau*. He is a young developing academic and is currently a Senior Lecturer in Political Sciences at the University of South Africa (UNISA) where he teaches African Political Thought and Political Theory. His research focuses on both mainstream and decolonial political theory and he occasionally delves into issues related to Islamophobia and the Palestinian/Zionist conflict.

Chapter 9
Pharaoh Let My Children Go: Meditations on Blackness Under Democratized Whiteness

Hlulani Mdingi

Abstract South Africa prides herself on what she has "done" by "overcoming" the system of apartheid and the global, diplomatic and democratic face she presents to the rest of the world. However, recent events serve as evidence that cracks are visible in South African democracy—the prophet Daniel (5: 25) captures the traces of the immanent fall at the table of the Babylonian king, Belshazzar, *MENE, MENE, TEKEL, UPHARSIN* (you have been weighed, weighed, divided and have been found wanting). South Africa is listed as one of the most unequal countries in the world, a neoliberal position, which begs the question whether South Africans have in truth crossed the Red Sea to the triumphant entry to Promised Land. The people have crossed over to the Promised Land, ideological, rhetorically and in the urge of nation-building. However, those meant to lead us have chosen to have one foot and hand in the Promised Land and the other hand and foot at the table of former global oppressors such as Pharaoh, Nebuchadnezzar, Belshazzar, Antiochus Epiphanes, Caesar, and the historical gains of white power. The footing of "leaders" in both the Promise Land and the table of the oppressor manifest the ability of how white power maintains a dialectical and perennial continuums of oppression and the servitude of oppressed. The ability of a total liberation of the oppressed impedes the prestige and privileged of the self-appointed and anointed agents of change of power. Capitalism with its tentacles that entails the classification and antagonisms of race and class are adopted as part of the government. In South Africa, leaders maintain the dogma and underlining intents of institutional racism and the total control of the means of production and resources. The core values of freedom and liberation are deferred for international "respectability" and adoration. In short, a good physiological aesthetic is preferred despite the internal failing of the organs of that body. I contend that the Promised Land requires new rulers, new systems and a new humanity that possesses sovereignty and power; in the words of Kwame Nkrumah: "We prefer self-governance in danger than subjugation in tranquility." There are distinct parallels between South Africa and the departure of the Hebrews from Egypt for the Promised Land under

H. Mdingi (✉)
Department of Philosophy Practical and Systematic Theology, University of South Africa, Office 42, 8th Floor Theo van Wijk Building, UNISA Main Campus, Pretoria 0003, South Africa
e-mail: btheology9@gmail.com

new rulers, and South Africa and its black people can look to the freed Hebrews for a model of self-rule.

Keywords Blackness · Black theology · Pharaoh · Liberation · Oppressor · Black church · Colonialism · Racism

Introduction

South Africa prides herself on what she has "done" by "overcoming" the system of apartheid and the global, diplomatic and democratic face she presents to the rest of the world. However, recent events serve as evidence that cracks are visible in the South African democracy. The prophet Daniel (5: 25) captures the traces of the immanent fall at the table of the Babylonian king, Belshazzar, through an inscription on the wall written by the finger of God; *MENE, MENE, TEKEL, UPHARSIN* (you have been weighed, weighed, divided and have been found wanting). South Africa is listed as one of the most unequal countries in the world, a neoliberal position, which begs the question whether South Africans have in truth crossed the Red Sea to the triumphant entry to Promised Land. In this paper, I contend that we, the people, have crossed over to the Promised Land, ideological, rhetorically and in the urge of nation-building. However, those meant to lead us have chosen to have one foot and hand in the Promised Land and the other hand and foot at the table of former global oppressors such as Pharaoh, Nebuchadnezzar, Belshazzar, Antiochus Epiphanes, Caesar, and the historical gains of white power. The footing of "leaders" in both the Promise Land and the table of the oppressor manifest the ability of how white power maintains a dialectical and perennial continuums of oppression and the servitude of oppressed. The ability of a total liberation of the oppressed impedes the prestige and privileged of the self-appointed and anointed agents of change of power. Capitalism with its tentacles that entails the classification and antagonisms of race and class are adopted as part of the government. In South Africa, leaders maintain the dogma and underlining intents of institutional racism and the total control of the means of production and resources. The core values of freedom and liberation are deferred for international "respectability" and adoration. In short, a good physiological aesthetic is preferred despite the internal failing of the organs of that body. I contend that the Promised Land requires new rulers, new systems and a new humanity that possesses sovereignty and power; in the words of Kwame Nkrumah: "We prefer self-governance in danger than subjugation in tranquility." There are distinct parallels between South Africa and the departure of the Hebrews from Egypt for the Promised Land under new rulers, and South Africa and her black people can look to the freed Hebrews for a model of self-rule.

In essence, the biblical stories deal with God, humanity, and the world. However, in these narratives, we also find themes of the oppression, slavery, and bondage of a people, to the extent that *hamartia* (sin), as the source of all that will go wrong in the world and in human life, is expressed in terms of slavery and bondage from which liberation must be sought. In this regard, no story exerts as much influence or offers as much inspiration to believers as the Exodus account.[1] In Exodus, we read of an exit motivated by the revelation of God to a lowly and downtrodden, enslaved, and brutalized people. In the midst of their oppression, identity crisis and pessimistic forgetfulness they are reminded of their God, and seeds of hope and divine existential deliverance are reimagined in the substance of their colonized minds. Although prior to their departure, they endure brutality, whippings, landlessness, and forced labor, they are encouraged to keep the faith and take hope because of the expected deliverance, which eventually was accomplished. It is not in an abundance of food and labor that God reveals Himself as a God of love. The omnibenevolence of God is not predicated on surplus. Out of nothing, God created the world (*creatio ex nihilo*),[2] and all its ontology, metaphysics, and materiality in order to reveal Himself and be known in creation, fitting the theological principle of *creatio continua*.[3] God reveals Himself continually as a God of love, as the God of the oppressed, a God to be known and a God of liberation and the benevolent Creator of humanity, concerned with His handiwork. However, it is in disparity and the absurdity of enslavement that the character, nature and identity of God are revealed to the oppressed and enslaved. The Hebrew and indigenous conceptions of God are not placed within the rigidity of western philosophical and theological abstraction, a metaphysical idol or symbol of the divine. Rather, the God of the oppressed indicates a God of agency, active and a God whose transcendence funnels existentially through the ambience of material existence.

It has been important for God to have, in the Old Testament and in general human history, His "anointed"—an individual of messianic character—who will free the oppressed by His means, will and methods. Wilson Jeremiah Moses, in his book *Black Messiahs and Uncle Toms*, explains:

> The term "messiah" derives from the Hebrew, *mashiah*, meaning anointed. In the traditions of the ancient Hebrews, it signified the belief in a future great deliverer—a priest, king, or prophet—who would come with a special mission from God. Usually this mission was seen as politically revolutionary but culturally reactionary. The belief in a messiah grew out of the Hebrews' experience of oppression at the hands of the great Middle-Eastern empires. It symbolized their hopes for an improvement in the fortunes of their nation and the restoration of their ancient ideals. The messiah would usher in a messianic age. The chosen people would revolt against their political oppressors and revitalize the conservative values advocated by the prophets (Moses 1982, 4).

It is in the Exodus story that such a chosen figure appears and the plan of salvation requires a reversal of roles in that the material deliverer, Moses, comes out of

---

[1] Black theology has found the Exodus account as a point of departure from Egypt, analogous to the black faith geared toward God revelation expressed as deliverance.

[2] *Creatio ex nihilo* is a theological view that substantiates the transcendence of God and a creation without predisposed matter of existing material. It is also a polemic to the creation stories of the Ancient Near East, such as Enuma Elish, a narrative above creation out of the corpse of another deity.

[3] *Creatio continua* the logical and dialectical conclusion of creatio ex nihilo, creatio continua maintains that God has set continual principles of continual creation in the fiber of existence. Although creation continual progress in creation God maintains a relationship with creation and its creatures.

the abundance associated with the house of Pharaoh to deliver the poor, lowly and oppressed Hebrews. He has to forsake this prestige in order to deliver his own, a principle carried down to the messianic age of Yeshua the Messiah. The apostle Paul in Philippians 2:5 emphasizes kenosis, the setting aside of prestige, glory, dominion, and power in order to deliver the wretched, weak, bound and oppressed. Already Moses had out of national pride slain an oppressor of his people. A consideration of our context reveals the persistence of leaders who are unwilling to reject prestige, even at the cost of the poor; Hebrews 11, 24–27 reads:

By faith Moses, when he was come to years, refused to be called the son of Pharaoh's daughter; Choosing rather to suffer affliction with the people of God, than to enjoy the pleasures of sin for a season; Esteeming the reproach of Christ greater riches than the treasures in Egypt: for he had respect unto the recompense of the reward. By faith he forsook Egypt, not fearing the wrath of the king: for he endured, as seeing him who is invisible.

This verse is a confirmation of the Black Theological truth of humanity and the role of the oppressed in God's plan, having God's hand upon them as they struggle. In the words of Biko (1978, 64–65), "I would like to remind the black ministry and indeed all black people that God is not in the habit of coming down from heaven to solve people's problems on earth" (ibid.).

It is clear that God will deliver the oppressed from oppression through human will, struggle, instrument, divine agency, and separation, and not through tolerance, accommodation, assimilation, and tokenism. God's deliverance is not a cocktail of conspiring with former oppressors and their selected tokens of so-called change. However, true God-given deliverance understands the dreams, hopes; groanings, strivings, enslavement, and aspirations of the black bound and oppressed who want to be free. The South African context provides such a situation, where children of God who are supposed to have been free and cut off from the tentacles of Pharaoh are now in bonds, materially and politically. The neocolonial bondage is facilitated through policies and illegitimate laws (that are favorable to and ensure the dominance and privilege of the oppressors); blacks are in bondage through economics and the passive and reactionary spirituality of pacifism at the expense of an authentic human existence. All these atrocities masquerade as integration, transformation, and progress. It is this that Biko and the Black Consciousness Movement speaks of when describing an artificial integration, which will breed only decay and decadence on the part of blacks and is in fact a true reflection of black society today. In this regard, they argue:

> ...an integration based on exploitative values in a society in which the whites have already cut out their position somewhere at the top of the pyramid. It is an integration in which blacks will compete with blacks, using each other as stepping stones up as a ladder leading them to white values. It is an integration in which the black man will have to prove himself in terms of those values before meriting acceptance and ultimate assimilation. It is an integration in which the poor will grow poorer and rich richer in a country where the poor have always been black (Unisa Archives Accession 153 1972, 21).

The democratic South African context is contrary to what Biko and the Black Consciousness Movement (1972, 21) envisions as integration, that is, not assimilated bondage and cultural, political, philosophical, economic, and religious subjugation: "At the heart of true integration is the provision of each man, each group to rise and attain the envisioned self. Each group must be able to attain its style of existence without encroaching on or being thwarted by another. Out of mutual respect for each other and complete freedom of self-determination, there will obviously arise a genuine fusion of lifestyles of the various groups. This is true integration."[4]

The leaders, whether in the political, religious, cultural, or economic arena, are sitting back at the table of Pharaoh and act as a leash on the angry masses. They fear Pharaoh more than the Black God, place their love, and trust in the security of Egypt rather than the new table God is to set for them and the masses who have been oppressed. Unlike Daniel, Meshach, Shadrach, and Abednego, they have eaten and continue to eat the meat offered to idols and have bowed down to the lofty golden image of white supremacy and Western domination. They have collected the coins and the spoils from the Roman soldiers who gamble for money below the bloody and dangling body of the black messiah, the savior of the lowly and oppressed. Theologically, we must assert, as Biko (1978, 61) asserts: "It must also be noted that the Church in South Africa as everywhere else has been spoilt by bureaucracy."

Have We Left Egypt or Carried Over a Bureaucracy?

The bureaucracy is evident in that in the former regime—or rather the same regime that is rather now latent in pronouncement—blackness was of a soteriological nature, as black believers in the church stood up for the persistence of the black voice and the presence of God that required black self-authenticity, black sovereignty and independence in an anti-black world. Cone (1984, 47) rightly claims:

> For blacks in white churches, the white denial of the theological value of black history and culture in the doing of theology meant a denial of black humanity and an establishment of white Christianity as normative for all Christians. Therefore, the fight was not just for the acquisition of economic and political rights, but also for the establishment of the dignity of black humanity as defined in its cultural past and in its current fight for material freedom.[5]

As such, we strove for sovereignty and dignity, understanding blackness as a soteriological insignia, as Biko (1978, 53) notes: "Black Consciousness therefore takes cognizance of the deliberateness of God's plan in creating black people black. It seeks to infuse the black community with a new-found pride in themselves, their efforts, their value systems, their culture, their religion and their outlook to life."[6] What Biko seeks to restore is precisely what was silenced by white supremacy and today continues to be silenced through the ventriloquist logic of synthetic liberation managed by puppet regimes. It is also typical of the Egypt analogy, which reflects

---

[4] Ibid., 21.

[5] James Cone, *For my people: Black theology and the black church (Where we have been and where we are going?)*, 47.

[6] Steve Biko, *I Write what I like*, (London: The Bowerdean Press), 53.

the power relation between slaves and slavemasters and between puppet regimes and the real rulers. Today, in post-apartheid South Africa, whiteness with all its powers has remained and has been legitimized and democratized.

This is done through a sham of a constitution that cannot explain a large number of black incarcerations, does not take cognizance of history and socialization, and is sociologically far from the righteous peak and carrying out of justice. Such an assertion emanates from the fact that white privilege is important socially, economically, theologically, and politically, as it maintains and fuels the running of puppet regimes and wants no rebellion from its subjects in the black colony. Historically, whiteness has been developed by violence, and it is currently maintained by political and ecclesiastical trickery and deceit. Pilger (2006, 177), recording the effects of what one would call the real decolonial project and a crossing over in South Africa to the Promised Land, cites the Soweto Uprising of June 16, 1976. Pilger clearly notes some form of genealogical maintenance of white power after the rebellion in the Soweto colony, manifested as the black confrontation of 1976, and records the aftermath as follows:

> White privilege, which conferred one of the highest standards of living on earth, was at risk, especially as English speaking capitalists decided secretly to get out of bed with the white supremacists, whose rapidly growing status as international pariahs was becoming bad for business. A series of meetings, both clandestine and well-publicised, between white businessmen and ANC leaders in exile would be critical in turning the 'struggle' to the advantage of white business and beckoning the ANC's embrace of the ideology of international capital, neo-liberalism.[7]

Theologically, the children have tried to leave Egypt—as is evident in the Soweto Uprising, one of the many rebellions in the colony—but Pharaoh and his armies, priests, and magicians have passed through and crossed the Red Sea with them. The cross over of both the oppressed and the agents of Pharaoh seeks to point to the fact that neocolonialism and neoliberalism is not imported. However, remains in our midst when aspiring for liberation. The enemy is not an exterior or projection, rather, the enemy is within. In the Promise Land, Pharaoh rules with absolute and sheer stronghold on power, he enslaves, robs, murders, and is unjust, decadent and genocidal toward the oppressed. However, his success is contingent on the agents who are recruited from the oppressed. The recruiting process entails the fallibility of human nature even in the political arena. On the political question, the fickleness of human nature is displayed by the ego that seeks to elevate an individual's proclivities above the existential consensus of freedom and liberation. The leaders have forsaken the task before the sea could close up; to a certain extent, a bridge has been built purely to allow Pharaoh to rule and exploit the Promised Land (Black World) together with the womb of black oppression—Europe and the western world. The biblical text provides an analogy to explain the nexus connexions of oppression as Jacob saw angels ascending and descending upon the ladder connecting heaven and earth (Genesis 28, 12–14), such is the privilege of white power/supremacy throughout the world. Note that it is not Jacob, but the angels who go up and down. Fanon (1963, 175) observes

---

[7] John Pilger, *Freedom Next Time*, 177.

that if there is no separation between oppressor and oppressed, the oppressed will eventually become anchorless, rootless, and ultimately a race of angels. But sadly, only white angels will cross over the bridge in the Red Sea connecting Egypt and the Promised Land, or even ascend and descend the ladder connecting heaven and earth—in short; they bring very little to earth and take a lot to "heaven" because of privilege and structural positionality. South Africa is preoccupied with making us live as humans as if all of us have dehumanized, oppressed, enslaved, raped, and murdered one another. It is not and has never been blacks who were inhumane or dehumanizing. The clutches of political, cultural, intellectual and economic power dating from the 16th century to 21st century have been in the hands of white establishments, institutions and religions. As such, definitions, behaviour and trappings of human definitions solely rest of western civilisation and the human being she has created.

Stokely Carmichael, honorary Prime Minister of Afro-American people in the Black Panther Party, in his Black power speech in 1966, pointed out that the Civil Rights Bill that was passed was not for blacks, but instead for whites, who had to understand that blacks are human and can live wherever they wish; blacks always knew that they were human, whereas it was whites who did not know, and who stopped them from exercising their human rights. The democracy of South Africa is geared toward the preservation of western and white interests and power. Those trusted to usher in an age of justice; peace and equality have chosen rather to side with the rich, elitist, racist and unjust oppressors. In this regard, Gibson makes the following observation in response to Mbeki's view of creating the black bourgeoisie:

> In today's multicultural South Africa, forgetting the fact that 90% of the poor are black simply indicates the assumed logical relationship between poverty and race: that the language of apartheid has been replaced by the colour of money, the language of corporate capitalism and markets. It is not only that exploitation can wear a "black mask", but racism can take many forms that indicates how deeply it is embedded in South Africa's socio-economic structure and, consequently, how deep the uprooting of that structure needs to be.[8]

Saul (2001, 429) says much the same thing:

> A tragedy is being enacted in South Africa, as much a metaphor for our times as Rwanda and Yugoslavia and, even if not so immediately searing of the spirit, it is perhaps a more revealing one. For in the teeth of high expectations arising from the successful struggle against a malignant apartheid state, a very large percentage of the population—among them many of the most desperately poor in the world—are being sacrificed on the altar of the neoliberal logic of global capitalism.[9]

Saul (2001, 429) continues: "One does not know whether to laugh or cry at this kind of realism—'magical market' realism... For there is absolutely no reason to assume that the vast majority of people in South Africa will find their lives improved by the policies that are being adopted in their name by the present African National Congress (ANC) government. Indeed, something quite the reverse is the far more

---

[8] Nigel Gibson, *"The limits of black political empowerment: Fanon, Marx, "the poors" and the "new reality of the nation" in South Africa"*, 96.
[9] John Saul, *"Cry for the Beloved Country: The Post-Apartheid Denouement"*, 429.

likely outcome." Walter Rodney (1973, 90–91) provides insight into the reality and relationship of the Black World and the west, which is existentially perpetual and not a static or historic episode, but rather remains dialectical in black oppression even under democracies:

> Colonialism was not merely a system of exploitation, but one whose essential purpose was to repatriate the profit to the so-called 'mother country'. From an African view-point, that amount to consistent expatriation of surplus produced by African labor out of African resources. It meant the development of Europe as part of the same dialectical process in which Africa was underdeveloped.[10]

It is no secret that South Africa and Africa remain in bondage and that it is blood, sweat, tears, terror, and the exploitation of children in Congo to mine coltan to develop the technology industry that fuels the flamboyance of western arrogance and condescending attitudes toward Africans, Africa and its leadership. Thus, Marikana, service delivery protests, xenophobia and the continual obsession with the threat of chasing away investors through social outcry are an indication of perpetual, accepted and democratized bondage. Thus, if what Rodney and Saul's claim is true, then the world, which is fundamentally western, racist, barbaric, and white, is hypocritical on issues of global progress. The South African context then reflects itself as a puppet regime, mirroring the relationship between Herod (the Edomite king) and the Romans. To elucidate serious and critical concerns of a puppet, regime blacks are being forced to pay the debts incurred by the apartheid regime. On this subject, Palesa Morudu (1997) in the November/December edition of *Mayibuye* puts forward the following view:

> The ANC-led government, faced with the task of transforming South Africa, this year alone paid about R40bn to service debt incurred by the apartheid rulers. There can be no clearer indication, that while the ANC attained political office, the masses of our people have not attained power. This debt is immoral and unjust. It has already been paid many times over through the profits exacted from the labour of black South Africa and the theft of our land.[11]

Further, she rightly calls for the cancelation of this debt:

> The campaign recognizes the international doctrine of "odious debt." The doctrine spells out that lenders who finance totalitarian regimes have no guarantees of protection from international law. It declares that when a government incurs debts to subjugate the population of its territory, these debts are odious to the indigenous population; hence, the incoming government has no moral obligation to honour them. This doctrine matches the circumstances of the apartheid state and rightly informs the campaign for cancellation.[12]

Indeed, if South Africa and its elected government were willing to pay such a debt, then surely politically and economically, we (our rulers) have not left Egypt. This situation is no different from so-called black churches that are satellites to white illegitimate spirituality and theology, the pulpit being the every Sunday device for fueling compromise and maintaining a ventriloquist relationship between oppressors

---

[10] Walter Rodney, *How Europe Underdeveloped Africa*, (90–91).
[11] Palesa Morudu, *Cancel the apartheid debt*, MAYIBUYE November/December 1997 edition.
[12] Ibid., Morudu.

and the oppressed. Instead of preaching and promoting resistance, it takes the form of compromising catharsis, while those who pose as leaders, revolutionaries and armed fighters simply represent a tokenism that should be resisted, rejected and overthrown, a fate destined for the oppressor. Boesak (2004, 19) writes:

> Despite the white Christian interpretation black Christians in South Africa discovered, and believed passionately, that the God of the exodus who brought Israel from slavery and raised Jesus from the dead would help them cross that sea into freedom, would raise them up as they fought for justice. The God of the Bible was the God of justice they prayed to in the silence of their homes, called upon in the midst of their suffering, and relied upon in the heat of confrontation. They understood, despite the mammoth efforts of white Christianity in this country, the liberating and radical call of the gospel in terms of justice and freedom and human dignity.[13]

It is important to note that while the advocates of South African democracy and compromise argue that the negotiations were thought to put civil war at bay, in truth this was a revolution betrayed and postponed. Mabasa (1995) in an article entitled; *"Mr. President, with due Apology, Your African Country is too white!"* states with justification:

> The government's preoccupation with winning the support of white people clearly demonstrates their overall attitude towards Black people and the legitimacy of their grievances. Black people are expected to forget the past and to live as if nothing has happened and to regard their white counterparts as equals. However, the reality on the ground tells a different story. While the new dispensation has rid white people of their guilt about their ill begotten wealth and advantage. Black people still struggle to make ends meet. They are still overcrowded, they are without houses or land, they have no adequate schools, they are still unemployed in their million, they are without adequate medical facilities—their lives remain an unending nightmare.

The children of Israel did not leave Egypt peacefully: God poured out His anger on the oppressor through plagues of flies, lice, leprosy, frogs, and locusts, through turning water into blood and killing their livestock, and finally through the angel of death taking their firstborn. It was an unpeaceful, unpolite, unnegotiable, and unpassive departure. South Africa should not have expected and cannot expect any less when God frees His people from bondage; systems and power must change and the powerless become the powerful. But in the case of South Africa, those who were thought to be overthrown and defeated are victorious behind the veil. In line with what has been mentioned regarding the bureaucracy of the church (Biko 1978, 61), one is reminded of the Old Testament Temple. The Temple served as the spiritual, political, economic, and cultural epicenter of Hebrew life and existence, but it was governed by a few who purposely ignored the needs of the masses and were not open to the notion of equal distribution of wealth. Kolakowski (1981, 55) is correct in pointing out: "As man is endowed with humanity by nature, compulsion to join in the community is not a violation of the individual's freedom but a release from the prison of his own ignorance and passivity."[14]

---

[13] Allen Boesak, *"Truth Crushed to Earth Will Rise Again: Christian Theology in South Africa—Looking back"*, 19.

[14] Kolakowski, *Main currents of Marxism, volume I*, 55.

To push this idea of bureaucracy even further: if the rulers of the temple had been able to expel God from His material abode, they would have done so. However, when the messiah came, challenged authorities and systems and finally bled on the cross, he broke the bureaucratic access to God and wealth by entering behind the veil of the Holy of Holies. Now all could come into the presence of God. But in post-apartheid South Africa, not all are allowed to the epicenter of wealth, resources, land and freedom; this remains the preserve of the few. On Black Consciousness, Black Theology, the Gospel and Jesus, we read as follows in Unisa Archives Accession 153 (1969–1971, 1):

> Accepting the situational character of Jesus, his first interpreters and his 1970 South African followers, the idea of a black theology, ceases to be theological emotionalism. Black theology has to ask 'At what crucial point does the human situation of blacks in South Africa fit in with the human situation of Jesus in Roman occupied Israel? What message of hope did Jesus have for his contemporaries whose situation parallels that of Black South Africans.[15]

Exodus

Black theology as an expression of the Black experience and Diaspora has used the Exodus account of the delivering of the children of Israel from bondage as an analogy of the striving of black spirituality. Also, it has used it as a reminder that the God of Africa, and generally the God of black people, will surely deliver them from oppression, from the sting of the lash and crack of the whip of white supremacy. Boesak (2004, 19) states: "That discovery of the "powerful message of liberation" is precisely the discovery of the biblical story—the story of the God of the exodus, the prophets of social justice and radical conversion, and of Jesus of Nazareth—and the difference that story makes in the human story."[16] Garret (2000, 5) argues:

> When African slaves became Christians and were exposed to the Bible, they naturally gravitated to certain parts of it, such as the liberation of the Israelites from captivity in Egypt, the theme of the Promised Land, and the hoped-for redemption at the end of a period of suffering. From the New Testament they drew sustenance from a doctrine that Unitarians have often regarded as intellectually absurd: namely, the idea that God or God's son Jesus (the distinction was not very important in black Christianity according to Cone) so identified with the suffering people, the victims of injustice, that he became one of them and suffered a terrible death as a result.[17]

Furthermore, the relevance of the Exodus signals a growth in black faith reflected in worship and linked to engagement with the absurdities of physical and spiritual oppression that required black people to labor in plantations, mines, cotton fields,

---

[15] Unisa Archives Accession 153, 1.

[16] Boesak, *"Truth Crushed to Earth Will Rise Again: Christian Theology in South Africa—Looking back"*, 19.

[17] Garret, *Black Christianity and the Prophetic Church, Insights from the Black Theology of James Cone*, 5.

and white homes, and then on Sunday bow down to a God who was not theirs. The analogy is of further significance because of the 400 years of oppression endured by both the Hebrews and Africans. The Exodus account of deliverance holds true in contexts where people have been made to believe and feel that they are of no worth to the society in which they are captive. Also, it is significant to a people who have forgotten themselves, their land, and their God. It is in the Exodus account that God reminds Moses and the Jews of who He is by asserting His name; I AM a name that is linked to lineage and their history; I AM the God of Abraham, I AM the God of Isaac and I AM the God of Jacob. This name, beyond its might, was contextual for a lost people and served as an existential consciousness. Thus, indeed God revealed Himself in the datum of history and existentially to the oppressed. South Africa, too, is a ready litmus paper to be subjected to the test of a God of truth and not deceptive "neutrality". The transcendent God revealed to the Hebrews, *YHWH*, did not display transcendence that is inactive and frozen out of space and time. God was present in the scorching sun in Egypt. God's transcendence demands existentialism, which is a direct cognizance of material conditions. The historical bondage of the Hebrews and oppressed people of the world is the plerotha for God's active revelation, immanence and transcendence. Black theology and the analogy of the Exodus become modern reflections on the interplay of transcendence and the existential solidarity of the transcendent God with the oppressed.

One of the fundamental issues emanating from the story of the bondage, deliverance and liberation of the Hebrews is that God is revealed in oppressive regimes. In such contexts, God is revealed as a liberator and not as a pacifist. Thus, there seems to be a timeless theological truth in the syllogism of a loving and Creator God who must, by His nature and His black handiwork, surely reveal Himself to the oppressed. When one considers black oppression and worship, resistance and the revelation of God, this holds true. Cone (1997, 169) asserts: "The more black people believed that 'God is a God, God don't never change', the more difficult it was for them to reconcile their religious faith with their bondage."[18] Pheko, commenting on the South African context (1982/1995, 78) makes the observation: "If the Bible teaches that the individual is unique of infinite worth before God, colonialism in many respects said the opposite, so that biblical teachings were variance with colonialism, and it became only a matter of time before one ousted the other."[19] Pheko here draws our attention to a threshold in black spirituality in an anti-black world. This point is important in understanding that when God reveals Himself to His people who are oppressed, dispossessed, used, abused and bruised, He does so in their existential conditions that are historic in nature. Their suffering is not an opportunity for God to manifest His power for His own pleasure but is instead a situation, which demands an immediate response from a God who is loving, kind, and just. Cone (1997, 15) asserts: "Our theology must emerge consciously from an investigation of the socioreligious

---

[18]Cone, *God of the oppressed.* Maryknoll, NY: Orbis Books, 169.

[19]Pheko, *The early church in Africa (1–7 century) and today.* (Lusaka: Multimedia Publications) 78.

experience of black people, as that experience is reflected in black stories of God's dealings with black people in the struggle of freedom."[20]

Liberation is confined and confirmed in God's revelation, which does not allow assimilation into an accommodation of existing oppressive regimes, but rather demands a complete separation from such systems. In the words of Biko (1978, 104):

> Let it suffice to say that [Black Theology] seeks to relate God and Christ once more to the black man and his daily problems. It wants to describe Christ as a fighting God, not a passive God who allows a lie to rest unchallenged. It grapples with existential problems and does not claim to be a theology of absolutes. It seeks to bring back God to the black man and to the truth and reality of his situation.[21]

When one considers today what Africa and the people of Africa and colored peoples of the world are subjected to, one is compelled to ask what God is saying if the oppressed are then "silent" or ignored on the subject of the savagery, decadence and barbarism that engulfs their souls, mind, bodies, and lands. Further, this reveals that it is not out of place to suggest that the white world represents all that is evil and that under political diplomacy blacks in the world are owed an immeasurable debt for their planned struggle and oppression. The South African context projects the socialization of historical injustice as justice. On the falsity of truth and reconciliation, Mabasa (1997, 2) expresses the following opinion:

> Our country has experienced a farce in the form of the Truth and Reconciliation Commission which has continued to legitimise the atrocities of apartheid murders, and sought no truth from the aggressors, but the truth from the victims. It provided no room for both truth and reconciliation because the government was not willing to use the implements in their hands to get the truth, but they in turn wanted to depend on the magnanimity and benevolence of criminals to get the truth. The many security officers involved in the atrocities during the apartheid years remain aloof and unwilling to come to the truth commission, including their gang leader, PW Botha. If black tears could wash away the past, we had enough of them to date. The overall weakness of the Truth Commission is that it will forever undermine justice in the interest of expediency.

The expediency mentioned is a reference to the silence of the church, and of the black church in particular, and its failure metaphorically to point out the Egyptian magicians who kept on persuading Pharaoh not to let the Hebrews go because there was reasonable explanation to the plagues. This situation pertains today just as in the past, but today they are aided by those in the ranks of Israel's fold—caught in the middle of land and sea, they neither cross nor want to stay in Egypt—continuing to rationalize injustice, inequality and dispossession as these relate to black people while wanting to represent them. Biko (1978, 55) foresaw this:

> ...while we progressively lose ourselves in a world of colourlessness and amorphous common humanity, whites are deriving pleasure and security in entrenching white racism and further exploit the minds and bodies of the unsuspecting black masses. Their agents are ever present amongst us telling us that it is immoral to withdraw into a cocoon, that dialogue is the answer

---

[20] Cone, *God of the oppressed* (Maryknoll, NY: Orbis Books), 15.

[21] Steve Biko, *I Write what I like* (London: The Bowerdean Press), 104.

to our problem and that it is unfortunate that there is white racism in some quarters but you must understand that things are changing.[22]

While black spirituality has always discerned the truth and been oriented toward the future, its silence suggests the elect who have been deceived themselves. It is fundamental that white "friends", "brothers", "sisters", and believers together with blacks understand that whites in general cannot empathize, sympathize, feel, understand, and record black pain and suffering without manifesting the praxis of reparation and restitution. It is vital to remember that when the Hebrews left Egypt they left with gold, treasures and sheep, a payment due to them for their labor. However, the comments, views, and efforts of whites are futile to blacks because they cannot begin to cover the Black Experience and the Black Diaspora. Food parcels from the west to war-torn African countries is deceit, curtained, and cushioned in our poverty. Historical factors, the building of western modernity reveal that the west is responsible for such atrocities and conditions that exist in the Black Worlds, as Rodney (1973, 90–91) points out. Yet blacks are quick to give praise to a failed democracy, western humanitarianism and false diplomacy. *SNNC Speaks for Itself* speaking on the Basis of Black Power, states:

> …white people coming into the movement cannot relate to the black experience, cannot relate to the word "black," cannot relate to the "nitty gritty," cannot relate to the experience that brought such a word into existence, cannot relate to chitterlings, hog's head cheese, pig feet, hamhocks, and cannot relate to slavery, because these things are not a part of their experience. They also cannot relate to the black religious experience, nor to the black church unless, of course, this church has taken on white manifestations.[23]

Further, it asserts:

> Negroes in this country have never been allowed to organize themselves because of white interference. As a result of this, the stereotype has been reinforced that blacks cannot organize themselves. The white psychology that blacks have to be watched also reinforces this stereotype. Blacks, in fact, feel intimidated by the presence of whites, because of their knowledge of power that whites have over their lives. One white person can come into a meeting of black people and change the complexion of that meeting, whereas one black person would not change the complexion of that meeting until he was an obvious Uncle Tom. People would immediately start talking about "brotherhood," "love," etc.; would not be discussed.[24]

The above is no exaggeration—in fact, it is precisely what has occurred in most African countries that sought liberation and independence from white supremacy. When they found that they could not negotiate with leaders or corrupt them, they then politically and physically assassinated leaders such as Kwame Nkrumah, Patrice Lumumba, Amilcar Cabral, Samora Machel, Malcolm X, and Martin Luther King. Such leaders embody the messianic and Mosaic component of the crossing over to the Promised Land, as they represent black struggle and a possible redemption.

---

[22] Ibid., 55.

[23] "Student Nonviolent Coordinating Committee Position Paper: The Basis of Black Power", accessed 30 August 2016, http://www2.iath.virginia.edu/sixties/HTML_docs/Resources/Primary/Manifestos/SNCC_black_power.html.

[24] Ibid.

The black militancy that exists in the struggle against colonialism, neo-colonialism, slavery, institutional racism, capitalism, and puppet regime typifies and signifies a God of deliverance, not docile, pacifist, and sterile accommodation that turns into mutilation in the name of God's peace and love. In this regard, Stewart (1999, 103) writes:

> Even in examining the more militant black nationalist movements, we discover the presence and influence of the African-American church. Malcolm X's father was a Baptist minister and other more radical leaders have been impacted by the African-American church. Frederick Douglass, Henry Highland Garnet, Henry McNeil Turner, Marcus Garvey, A Philip Randolph, Malcolm X, Martin Luther King, Jr., Huey P. Newton, and even Louis Farrakhan have all been influenced by the black church.[25]

The call then becomes immanent and immediate to the black church that the children must leave Egypt and also their own sorcerers that bewitch and withhold their absolute deliverance and liberation. Black theology and the notion of a black church must vomit, cry, weep, fight, and pray in sackcloth—sackcloth not because of symbolism of the inward metaphysical state but rather sackcloth because these are the actual physical outside clothes worn by the poor who are dressed in rags and on Sundays pray under the old rugged cross. The South African context seems to reflect the ambivalence of motion and praxis in that South Africa is a vehicle that is in motion because of "transcendental" idealism, which is sold to the world. The "transcendental" idealism can be explained as thinking that a vehicle will move because we expect it to move. However, movement requires active participation of mechanisms in place that allows a manifestation of movement, which is physical and optically real. No amount of idealism and speculation can translate to action without serious consideration of what is existentially pertinent. In Christian theology, *Yeshua*, was raised from the dead and it is his resurrection which makes Christians believe in his Second Coming. The event of the *Paraousia* (second coming) is the final destruction and removal of Pharaoh or any other oppressor in human history. I Corinthians 15 indicates that if Christ had not been physically raised from the dead then our faith is in vain. Christianity, more specifically, Black Christianity, cannot have hope in a dead savior. The God of the oppressed in the person of Christ requires a moving and physical savior that proves that God is on the side of the oppressed. This theological outlook then explain why the oppressed, who are dressed in rags, bow before the old rugged cross of the crucified peasant king and God. Furthermore, their worship of the crucified is linked with their participation and crucifixion in the world as they seek liberation. However, the second coming of Christ again in bodily form validates the close intricacies of the blend between the existential and metaphysical presence of God in existence.

---

[25] Stewart, *Black spirituality and Black Consciousness: Soul force, culture and freedom in the African-American experience*, 103.

Conclusion: Hostility, Agitation, and Confrontation

When reading of the oppression of the Hebrews in the Exodus account, one has a sense of a ghetto plagued by poverty, forced labor, and the reality of daily oppression of all inhabitants, from the eldest to the youngest. This outlook is typical of what goes on in South Africa, where the poor continue being poor and the "leaders" wine and dine at the feet of the pagan white supremacist golden image. This act of bowing to the golden image, to the God of the oppressor, upon hearing the sound of the horn in Babylonian captivity, is a symbol of the cowardice in politics, religion, and intellectuality and docility and sterile faith without works on the part of blacks. What is needed is an agitation and hostility in the ghettos and colonies of the oppressed and the immediate revelation of God leading to confrontation, a revolution that overturns temple tables and white racist systems in order that the children may leave oppression and bask in the warmth of black liberation and freedom.

Bibliography

Biko, Steve. 1978. *I Write What I Like*. London: The Bowerdean Press.
Cone, James. 1984. *For My People: Black Theology and the Black Church (Where We Have Been and Where We Are Going?)*. Maryknoll, NY: Orbis Books.
Cone, James. 1997. *God of the Oppressed*. Maryknoll, NY: Orbis Books.
Fanon, Frantz. 1963. *The Wretched of the Earth*. London: Penguin Press.
Kolakowski, Leszek. 1981. *Main Currents of Marxism*, vol. I. New York: Oxford University Press.
Moses, Wilson. J. 1982. *Black Messiahs and Uncle Toms: Social and Literary Manipulations of a Religious Myth*. Pennsylvania State University Press: University Park and London.
Pheko, S.E. Motsoko. 1982/1995. *The Early Church in Africa (1–7 Century) and Today*. Lusaka: Multimedia Publications.
Pilger, John. 2006. *Freedom Next Time*. London: Bantam Press.
Rodney, Walter. 1973. *How Europe Underdeveloped Africa*. London: Bogle-L'Ouverture Publications and Dar-es-Salaam: Tanzanian Publishing House.
Stewart, Carlyle F. 1999. *Black Spirituality and Black Consciousness: Soul Force, Culture and Freedom in the African-American Experience*. Trenton, NY: Africa World Press.

Articles

Boesak, Allan A. 2004. Truth Crushed to Earth Will Rise Again: Christian Theology in South Africa—Looking Back. In *African Christian Theologies in Transformation*, ed. Ernst Conradie, 9–21. Cape Town: EFSA Institute.
Garret, Jan. 2000. *Black Christianity and the Prophetic Church, Insights from the Black Theology of James Cone*, 1–8. Unitarian-Universalist Church of Bowling Green KY.
Gibson, Nigel. 2005. The Limits of Black Political Empowerment: Fanon, Marx, "the poors" and the "New Reality of the Nation" in South Africa. *Theoria* 52 (107): 89–118.
Saul, John S. 2001. Cry for the Beloved Country: The Post-Apartheid Denouement. *Review of African Political Economy* 28 (89): 429–460.

Unpublished Political Articles

Mabasa, Lybon T. 1995. *Mr. President, With Due Apology, Your African Country is too White!*
Mabasa, Lybon T. 1997. *Christmas and New Year Message from BNCR-1997*, 1–3.
Morudu, Palesa. 1997. *Cancel the Apartheid Debt*, MAYIBUYE November/December 1997 edition.

Archive Material

Carmichael, Stokely. 1966. *Black Power Speech*. https://www.youtube.com/watch?v=IMYTN0-2ugI. Accessed on 26 Aug 2016.
Unisa Archives Accession 153, 1969–1971. Steve Biko Foundation.
Unisa Archives Accession 153, 1972. Steve Biko Foundation.

Printed in the United States
By Bookmasters